Praise for

50 Economics Classics

'A fascinating and very timely book.'
Dani Rodrik, Ford Foundation Professor of Political Economy, John F. Kennedy School of Government, Harvard University

'The synopses in this book are fair, balanced, and about as good an introduction to the broad range of modern economic writing, along with a few classics, as one is likely to find.'
Professor James K. Galbraith, University of Texas, author of *Inequality: What Everyone Needs to Know*

'This is not just a book for people who want to save time by reading one book instead of 50. [It] looks into some huge pieces of economic thought which even many important economists have browsed too swiftly. If you are not an economist, this book will teach you a lot. And if you are an economist, it will also teach you a lot.'
Hernan Blejer, economic journalist, analyst for Euromonitor, lecturer University of Buenos Aires, London School of Economics

THE GREATEST BOOKS DISTILLED

by Tom Butler-Bowdon

The *50 Classics* series has sold over 300,000 copies

50 Economics Classics 978-1-85788-673-3

50 Philosophy Classics 978-1-47365-542-3

50 Politics Classics 978-1-47365-543-0

50 Psychology Classics, 2nd ed 978-1-85788-674-0

50 Self-Help Classics, 2nd ed 978-1-47365-828-8

50 Success Classics, 2nd ed 978-1-47365-835-6

50 Spirituality Classics 978-1-47365-838-7

50 Business Classics 978-1-85788-675-7 (coming 2018)

50 Economics Classics

Your shortcut to the most important ideas on capitalism, finance, and the global economy

Tom Butler-Bowdon

London • Boston

First published in 2017 by Nicholas Brealey Publishing
An imprint of John Murray Press

An Hachette UK company

20 19 18 17 1 2 3 4 5

A CIP catalogue record for this title is available from the British Library

ISBN 978 1 857 88673 3
eBook (UK) ISBN 978 1 473 65541 6
eBook (US) ISBN 978 1 473 66042 7

Typeset by Palimpsest Book Production Ltd, Falkirk, Stirlingshire

Printed and bound in the United States of America

John Murray Press policy is to use papers that are natural, renewable and recyclable products and made from wood grown in sustainable forests. The logging and manufacturing processes are expected to conform to the environmental regulations of the country of origin.

Nicholas Brealey Publishing
John Murray Press
Carmelite House
50 Victoria Embankment
London EC4Y 0DZ
Tel: 020 3122 6000

Nicholas Brealey Publishing
Hachette Book Group
Market Place Center, 53 State Street
Boston, MA 02109, USA
Tel: (617) 523 3801

www.nicholasbrealey.com
www.butler-bowdon.com

Contents

Hayek Samuelson McAfee *Hirschman* Rodrik
Brynjolfsson & McAfee Rand *Drucker* Krugman *Sen* Marshall
Sen Polanyi Levitt & Dubner Minsky Piketty
Minsky Schumacher Stiglitz Ferguson
Krugman *Galbraith* Sen George von Mises
Bogle *Keynes* Chang Thaler Schelling
Moyo Veblen Marx
McCloskey Coyle George Coyle *Ricardo* Moyo
Jacobs Friedman Malthus
Rodrik *von Mises*
Stiglitz Schumpeter Friedman
Lewis Ostrom Keynes *Shiller* *Baumol*
Simon Ahamed Ferguson Friedman
Ricardo *Gordon* *Smith* McCloskey
Sen Ferguson *George* Klein Marshall *Becker*
Lewis
de Soto *Bogle* Weber *McCloskey* *Krugman* Gordon Hirschman *Moyo*
Becker Coyle Klein Graham
Schelling *Sen*
Galbraith *Samuelson*
Stiglitz Galbraith
Porter Ahamed Schumacher
Krugman Coase
Ostrom Smith *Simon*

Introduction

"The Age of Chivalry is gone; that of sophisters, economists, and calculators has succeeded."

Edmund Burke

Economics may drive the modern world and shape our lives, but most of us lack knowledge of the key ideas, thinkers and writings in the discipline. Spanning fifty key books, hundreds of ideas, and two centuries in time, *50 Economics Classics* is an intelligent person's guide to capitalism, finance, and the global economy, taking you on a journey from the early days of the Industrial Revolution to the "Second Machine Age" of the internet and artificial intelligence. This is neither a history nor an encyclopedia of economics, but a guide to some of the great reads and seminal ideas – old and new – from Adam Smith's *The Wealth of Nations* to Thomas Piketty's *Capital in the Twenty-First Century*, that help the subject come alive.

Edmund Burke was surely right that economics, money, and finance are at the heart of modern civilization in the way that honor, chivalry, and religion were to the Middle Ages. If, once upon a time, a person's fate was largely settled by the social circumstances of their birth, today each of us is very much an economic being who must produce things of market value if we are to survive and thrive. "All your life," Paul Samuelson said, "from cradle to grave and beyond – you will run up against the brutal truths of economics."

One of the fundamental drives of human beings is for prosperity. If we have money and assets, we can acquire goods and services that provide more personal freedom and power. A political vote gives us freedom and power in theory, but in practice it means little if we can't even sustain ourselves and our families. If many political problems, from increasing inequality to inadequate infrastructure and education, and from inflation or deflation to indebtedness, are in fact economic ones, cracking the code to economic success, for person, firm, and nation, is crucial. This book will go some way towards giving you the knowledge to help you do that.

Beyond the achievement of personal or national security, what is economics ultimately for? John Maynard Keynes, who was a lover and supporter of the arts, thought it was so we could enjoy the good things in life. This was only possible with a stable, growing economy in which damaging cycles of boom and bust were ironed out. Economists, Keynes said, are the "trustees, not of civilization, but of the possibility of civilization."

ECONOMICS AS A SCIENCE

Far from perfect

It is easy to forget that when Adam Smith wrote *The Wealth of Nations* in 1776, the word "economics" wasn't in use. Instead, "political economy" was a branch of philosophy that concerned how governments collected and spent money. Smith's genius was to break away from this, showing how it was the private economy and the industry of individuals, not the state, that created the wealth of nations. In doing so he created the more specialized discipline of economics as we know it today.

However, it is also true that our lives are regulated by laws, political institutions, and social norms as much as they are by the market. We are citizens first, consumers second. In truth, we do not live in "an economy," but in some variant of political economy, whether it be capitalist with welfare provision, socialist, or authoritarian with market elements. Because we cannot analyze economic activity separately from state, society and government, the focus of this book is political economy rather than economics in its narrowest sense.

For a supposedly empirical science, economics has been plagued by ideological divisions, fads and fashions. As Ronald Coase has argued, the biggest problem in economics is that theories and models have been constructed on assumptions which practitioners have not been bothered to examine and admit. He coined the term "blackboard economics," in which everything works perfectly in theory, but not so much in reality. Some of the biggest mistakes in economics came from putting this theoretical cart before the horse. They include:

- The self-balancing market, in which supply and demand, employment and prices, all work in an elegant dance which eliminates the need for government involvement in the economy. Though a powerful paradigm, it only needed one big event, the Great Depression, to demonstrate its flaws. It was articulated in the gold standard, a financial straitjacket which put currencies ahead of employment and people, and today is expressed in the drive for total financial globalization, deregulation, and privatization, irrespective of national priorities.
- The centrally-planned economy, which assumed that it was possible for the state to garner all relevant data to make decisions and allocate resources for the benefit of all. Yet in doing away with normal markets,

> the information provided by prices was lost, and eliminating the chance of personal profit meant innovation ceased and economies went slowly backward. Most importantly, it was seen that such systems required brutal coercion to make all their parts hang together.

In short, economists have been all too willing to believe in "one big thing" when they should be willing to change and fix models according to newly arising facts, and to accept lots of little pieces of data which together make a more accurate picture of reality.

Another serious allegation leveled against economics is that it has ignored the lessons of history. University economics students rarely read books or articles more than 30 years old, and instead have textbooks presenting the current orthodoxy. Yet if there is anything that the financial crisis of 2007–08 told us, it is that economic and financial history matters. Each generation believes that some fundamental change has occurred in the economy such that manias, panics, and crashes won't happen again— and yet they do. At an event at the London School of Economics in the wake of the crisis, Queen Elizabeth II asked the assembled economists, "Why didn't anyone see this coming?" The fact that only about a dozen economists did see it coming (according to Australian economist Steve Keen, who actually counted them) tells us that economics is far from being an objective science that can make reliable predictions—as, for example, meteorologists increasingly do. This is partly because economies today are extremely complex systems involving not just the mechanics of production and the satisfaction of demand, but psychological factors including confidence and expectations about the future. Prediction is also hampered by models which, thanks to ideological bias, are based on wrong assumptions. Deregulation of banking and mortgage lending in the United States, for instance, by increasing the amount of funds available, was expected to lead to an "ownership society." Instead it encouraged a cowboy industry in which lending irresponsibility led to a real estate bubble, financial shenanigans, and a crash that left millions in economic misery.

The economist Hyman Minsky warned that, unless it is well regulated, capitalism will naturally go to extremes and produce instability. When you have banks and corporations lobbying governments for "reform," be sure to check who will benefit. Minsky went as far as saying that, "Only an economics that is critical of capitalism can be a guide to successful policy for capitalism." Until economic policy stops being a tool that can be captured or used for one group's advantage, it will be hard for capitalism to fully realize its potential of increasing well-being for all.

INTRODUCTION

"Political Economy or Economics is a study of mankind in the ordinary business of life . . .Thus it is on the one side a study of wealth; and on the other, and more important side, a part of the study of man."

Alfred Marshall

The "study of man" aspect of the economics discipline has long played second fiddle, but in the last 30 years, behavioural economics has questioned the standard picture of humans as rational beings who always act in their best interest. The belief in our "self-maximizing" nature created a false idea of the efficiency of market economies and the idea that they allocate resources perfectly. In reality, we frequently don't know what is best for us, do irrational things that lessen our chance for happiness, and have cognitive biases which lead us to wrong conclusions. If the whole of economics is based on a theory of rational choice, what you end up with is not human beings, but "consumers with a set of preferences." Marshall, a British economist, saw society in terms of millions of individuals each seeking their highest utility, putting up with the "disutility" of working in order to buy goods and services they wanted. Firms, meanwhile, existed in a state of perfect competition to supply these wants. This neat world (Robert Heilbroner called it a "well-mannered zoo") had apparently nothing to say about war, revolution, or the power of religion. Such areas were excised from economics because they didn't fit the models, or were put down as mere "politics."

Keynes noted that because it involves so much psychology and expectations, and has outcomes that affect lives in a deep and lasting way, economics is a *moral* science. People's decisions can't be reduced to mathematical equations, even if it would be more convenient if they were. French political economist Thomas Piketty criticizes the discipline's attempt to put itself above other social sciences. Its obsession with mathematics, he writes in *Capital in the Twenty-First Century*, "is an easy way of acquiring the appearance of scientificity without having to answer the far more complex questions posed by the world we live in." Ha-Joon Chang, a Cambridge University economist, goes as far as to say that "Good economic policy does not require good economists." The East Asian economic miracle, including the rise of his native South Korea, was implemented mostly by lawyers, politicians and engineers, he notes.

These criticisms aside, there are thousands of economists today who have a healthy scepticism of what their discipline can achieve, who are not ideologues or lost in models, and who study non-economic motives and socially co-operative behaviour. But economists are also clannish, Harvard's Dani Rodrik says, and tend to discount anyone who is not "one of them." The result is groupthink and the inability to see emerging tensions which break out into crises and major events. This is important, because economists are the high-priests of our capitalist culture, followed by politicians as much as the public. Their mistakes of prediction and omission can affect not just today's economy, but whole generations.

However, when economists get it right, through emphasizing simple ideas such as the benefits of markets and trade over defensive self-sufficiency, their ideas can raise the welfare of billions.

THINGS TURNED OUT PRETTY WELL
Separating economic fact from fiction

> *"Here again that last, astonishing fact, discovered by economic historians over the past few decades. It is: in the two centuries after 1800 the trade-tested goods and services available to the average person in Sweden or Taiwan rose by a* factor *of 30 or 100. Not 100 percent, understand – a mere doubling – but in its highest estimate a factor of 100, nearly* 10,000 percent, *and at least a factor of 30, or 2,900 percent. The Great Enrichment of the past two centuries has dwarfed any of the previous and temporary enrichments."*
>
> *Deirdre McCloskey*

As Angus Maddison and other economic historians have noted, the world economy barely grew in the two millennia prior to the Industrial Revolution. Then, it began to grow very fast. Living standards have risen at an astonishing rate during the last two centuries, and explaining this "Great Enrichment," Deirdre McCloskey rightly says, "is the central scientific task of economics and economic history."

If you look back over the writings of economic thinkers during the last two hundred years, you would read a litany of dark warnings about the future, from overpopulation to economic inequality to environmental catastrophe. That these things never happened, or turned out not to be as bad as imagined, is somehow forgotten, while the good news is overlooked.

Yes, a billion people still live in poverty, but thanks to advances in agricultural output famine has become much less common, even as the world's population rises. Just as the risk of dying in a war or natural disaster has diminished, so living standards continue to improve. On present projections, all countries and most of humanity will enjoy today's Western living standards within a century, and yet, economist Julian Simon noted, "many people will continue to *think and say* that the conditions of life are getting *worse.*" If you doubt this, read the chapters on Simon, McCloskey, Diane Coyle and Robert J. Gordon, which provide the empirical basis for the assertion.

But how could it be possible that the world continues to grow, with more people consuming more things, and there not be depletion of the world's resources? What tends to happen is that when any one resource starts to run out, human ingenuity steps in. The discovery of crude oil extraction replaced the need for whale oil, and sustainable technologies such as wind and solar will in time lessen the need for crude. The point is that resources are not fixed, but are the product of *minds* which, history suggests, solve most big problems. In the long run, the direction of travel is clear: the world has got richer and better off on just about every measure, even as there have been more of us.

DOING WHAT WORKS

Creating a discipline beyond ideology

Is the discipline of economics responsible for this Great Enrichment?

Ludwig von Mises argued that it was the classical economists like Adam Smith who were crucial in creating the conditions for modern wealth creation, in that they attacked "age-old laws, customs, and prejudices upon technological improvement and freed the genius of reformers and innovators from the straitjackets of the guilds, government tutelage, and social pressure of various kinds." It was economists, von Mises says, "that reduced the prestige of conquerors and expropriators and demonstrated the social benefits derived from business activity." The laws of economics, in other words, provided a counterweight to the conceit of those in power. The industrial revolution would not have happened without a laissez-faire economy.

In contrast, Karl Polanyi pointed out markets have never existed without the say-so of government and state. That markets, and their wealth-generating quality, have been able to expand and develop, is really on the back of political freedoms that let unprivileged people fulfil their potential by being able to sell some service or good which they had a talent for producing.

Who is right, Polanyi or von Mises? Do we need the state and the political rights it provides to prosper, or does government stand in the way of people and markets? Is the ideal political economy a tightly regulated, planned one, which puts social justice before profits, or a very minimal state which simply provides law and order, defence and the enforcement of contracts, but otherwise gives people total freedom to pursue their own ends?

The correct answer to such questions is "somewhere in between." Economics concerns the trade-off between equality and efficiency. As citizens we have every right to seek certain social outcomes that increase justice, reduce the gap between rich and poor, or provide basic health care and education for all. Yet go too far with these goals, and state finances are bankrupted while personal freedom is eroded, because hard-won wealth gets redistributed.

What is fact is that, in the last half century, people have voted in large numbers for the welfare state, despite its cost, along with regulation of everything from food standards to banking, to the creation of the minimum wage and national parks. In 2009, the year he died, Paul Samuelson penned a frontispiece to the nineteenth edition of *Economics*, his famous textbook, with the heading "A Centrist Proclamation." A centrist approach, he said, celebrates "an economy that combines the tough discipline of the market with fair-minded governmental oversight." The centrist approach looks only to the evidence, and events of the previous 20 years—including the crisis of 2007–08—have clearly shown that neither unregulated capitalism, nor a centrally planned economy, are viable routes to prosperity.

In 1994, celebrated economist John Kenneth Galbraith was asked in an interview where he stood on the political spectrum. He replied:

> *"I react pragmatically. Where the market works, I'm for that. Where the government is necessary, I'm for that. I'm deeply suspicious of somebody who says, 'I'm in favor of privatization,' or, 'I'm deeply in favor of public ownership.' I'm in favor of whatever works in the particular case."*

As a social science, economics must concern only "what works," to go beyond ideology. That said, if we had to make a choice between living under a socialist system, or a capitalist one, the latter, the evidence clearly tells us, is much better at providing the things that we as individuals and societies value.

If that is true, it makes sense to know a bit more capitalism, which is after all the system under which most of the world's population now lives. A significant chunk of *50 Economics Classics* is devoted to that end.

About the list

It could be argued that where economics really moves forward is in academic journal articles and well-known blogs, so why focus on books? Well, a book is one of the best tests of the validity of an idea, because its length requires the author to furnish evidence and examples to back up the theory. The author has something important to say for which no other format will suffice. Many of the books on my list took years to write and are the culmination of a lifetime of research (Gordon's *The Rise and Fall of American Growth*, for example), or set out to be the defining work on the topic (Michael Porter's *The Competitive Advantage of Nations*). Yet the fifty writings are chosen not only because they are important, but because most of them are great to read in their own right. After all, if a major insight is lost in impenetrable scholarly language, its effect on the wider world may be limited. But if the author makes the effort to put it in plain language, it will earn a bigger hearing. Economic issues should not be—as finance types might prefer—some secret alchemy that only a few can really appreciate.

Economists don't have a monopoly on economics, any more than philosophers have a monopoly on philosophy. For this reason, the list includes a range of people in addition to academic economists, including historians, investors, journalists, sociologists, and business professors, who themselves have been influenced by areas of knowledge beyond economics, including psychology, philosophy, and even literature. The writings are selected either because they are undeniably important and must be included in any list of this sort, or intriguing in a way that makes economics come alive. The latter criterion makes some of the choices idiosyncratic, but then no list of key writings in a field can ever be "scientific," and moreover what is considered significant changes over time.

Quite a few of the selections are by "heterodox" (i.e. non-orthodox) economists, but I make no apologies for that. Whatever is thought to be correct at any one time is often later seen as a paradigm based on false assumptions. What is fringe economics today might be mainstream tomorrow, and vice versa, as evidence (or lack of it) surfaces for particular theories.

The hope is that you use *50 Economics Classics* as an entrée to the field that inspires you to read the featured books in full and do further reading and research. To help with that, at the rear you will find a list of "50 More Classics," with short descriptions of each, along with a Chronological List of the works discussed in the main text.

50 Economics Classics is organized alphabetically, but to help you get a feel for the broad ideas running through the book, below are the titles organized by theme.

To start each chapter I have included short quotes from the book in question, chosen because in my view they capture the essence of the work, convey some important idea, or illustrate the author's style of writing. You may also find useful the one-line "nutshell" and "similar vein" features.

The Spirit of Capitalism

Philosophies of the system in which most of us live

Milton Friedman *Capitalism and Freedom*
Friedrich Hayek *The Use of Knowledge in Society*
Deirdre McCloskey *Bourgeois Equality*
Karl Marx *Capital*
Ludwig von Mises *Human Action*
Karl Polanyi *The Great Transformation*
Ayn Rand *Capitalism: The Unknown Ideal*
Joseph Schumpeter *Capitalism, Socialism, and Democracy*
Julian Simon *The Ultimate Resource 2*
Adam Smith *The Wealth of Nations*
Thorstein Veblen *The Theory of the Leisure Class*
Max Weber *The Protestant Ethic and the Spirit of Capitalism*

Growth & Development

Recipes for a more prosperous world

William Baumol *The Microtheory of Innovative Entrepreneurship*
Gary Becker *Human Capital*
Ha-Joon Chang *23 Things They Don't Tell You About Capitalism*
Peter Drucker *Innovation and Entrepreneurship*
Robert J. Gordon *The Rise and Fall of American Growth*
Jane Jacobs *The Economy of Cities*
Thomas Malthus *An Essay on the Principle of Population*
Dambisa Moyo *Dead Aid*
Michael E. Porter *The Competitive Advantage of Nations*
David Ricardo *Principles of Political Economy and Taxation*
E. F. Schumacher *Small Is Beautiful*
Hernando de Soto *The Mystery of Capital*

Adventures in Money & Finance

Booms, busts, and getting rich slowly

Liaquat Ahamed *Lords of Finance*
John Bogle *The Little Book of Common Sense Investing*
Niall Ferguson *The Ascent of Money*
J. K. Galbraith *The Great Crash 1929*
Benjamin Graham *The Intelligent Investor*
Michael Lewis *The Big Short*
Hyman Minsky *Stabilizing An Unstable Economy*
Robert Shiller *Irrational Exuberance*
Joseph Stiglitz *The Euro*

Government, Markets & the Economy

Citizens, not just consumers and producers

Erik Brynjolfsson & Andrew McAfee *The Second Machine Age*
Ronald Coase *The Firm, the Market and the Law*
Diane Coyle *GDP: A Brief But Affectionate History*
Henry George *Progress and Poverty*
John Maynard Keynes *The General Theory of Employment, Interest, and Money*
Naomi Klein *The Shock Doctrine*
Paul Krugman *The Conscience of a Liberal*
Alfred Marshall *Principles of Economics*
Thomas Piketty *Capital in the Twenty-First Century*
Dani Rodrik *The Globalization Paradox*
Paul Samuelson *Economics*
Amartya Sen *Poverty and Famines*

Behavioral Economics

An economics for the real world

Albert O. Hirschman *Exit, Voice, and Loyalty*
Steven Levitt & Stephen J. Dubner *Freakonomics*
Elinor Ostrom *Governing the Commons*
Thomas Schelling *Micromotives and Macrobehavior*
Richard Thaler *Misbehaving: The Making of Behavioral Economics*

50 Economics Classics

2009

Lords of Finance

"More than anything else, more even than the belief in free trade or the ideology of low taxation and small government, the gold standard was the economic totem of the age. Gold was the lifeblood of the financial system. It was the anchor for most currencies, provided the foundation for banks, and in a time of war or panic, served as a store of safety. For the growing middle classes of the world, who provided so much of the savings, the gold standard was more than simply an ingenious system for regulating the issue of currency. It served to reinforce all those Victorian values of economy and prudence . . . Among bankers, whether in London or New York, Paris or Berlin, it was revered with an almost religious fervor, as a gift of providence, a code of behaviour transcending time and place."

In a nutshell

Fixed ideas in economics can have disastrous results. The world hung onto the gold standard long after it had stopped being a means to create stability and growth.

In a similar vein

J. K. Galbraith *The Great Crash 1929*
John Maynard Keynes *The General Theory of Employment, Interest and Money*
Michael Lewis *The Big Short*
Hyman Minsky *Stabilizing an Unstable Economy*
Joseph Stiglitz *The Euro*

CHAPTER 1

Liaquat Ahamed

In 2010, chairman of the US Federal Reserve Bank, Ben Bernanke, was asked by the Financial Crisis Inquiry Commission what books he would recommend to understand the crisis. He mentioned just one, *Lords of Finance*, a new work of economic history which would win a Pulitzer Prize in the same year.

Its investment manager author, Liaquat Ahamed, first had the idea for the book when reading a 1999 *Time* story, "The Committee to Save the World," on the successful efforts of Alan Greenspan, then Federal Reserve chairman, Robert Rubin, President Clinton's Treasury Secretary, and Lawrence Summers, Rubin's deputy, in committing billions of dollars of public funds to head off the Asian financial crisis, which threatened to bring down the global economy.

A similar story, he realized, could be told about the heads of the world's four main central banks in the 1920s: Montagu Norman of the Bank of England, Benjamin Strong of the New York Federal Reserve Bank, Hjalmar Schacht of the German Reichsbank, and Émile Moreau of the Banque de France. A bit like Greenspan in the 1990s and 2000s, the men were considered sages, their every utterance waited on. Yet these "lords of finance," who had been charged with reconstructing the financial world after World War One, ended up contributing to the greatest peacetime collapse of the global economy: the Great Depression. When Greenspan's very loose monetary policies were held responsible by many for contributing to the Great Recession of 2008–2010, Ahamed's book suddenly seemed very relevant.

Ahamed's deeply researched portraits of the main actors in the interwar economic drama and their foibles breathes real fascination into what may otherwise have been a straightforward economic history. It shows how too much faith in individual bankers, and their adherence to outdated ideas (in this case, the "financial prudence" of the gold standard), carried massive risks.

Golden goose or barbarous relic?

Montagu Norman, the most famous of the central bankers between the wars, had a "rigid, almost theological belief" in the gold standard as being fundamental to global order and prosperity. If a nation was on the gold standard, its government could only issue amounts of currency for which there were corresponding amounts of gold in the national vaults, and all paper currency could in theory be redeemed in actual gold. The gold standard was a positive development in the history of finance, since it brought discipline to governments; they could not simply print money to pay for their debts.

When the world economy was in full steam before World War One, the gold standard had seemed to work well, facilitating trade and growth. The war changed everything. Apart from the human tragedy, the belligerents had indebted themselves to the tune of $200 billion, an astonishing 50 percent of their GDPs. The Paris Peace Conference had forced a crippling reparations bill on Germany of around 100 percent of its pre-War domestic output, and its only option to stay afloat seemed to be to print money. This had a cataclysmic result. By 1923, the German Reichsmark had become essentially worthless, and prices were doubling every couple of days. The middle classes found their lifetime savings wiped out; after the political revolution of the overthrow of the Prussian empire, now the social order collapsed.

There was a consensus among horrified central bankers that, to regain the stability and financial prudence of the pre-World War One era, the world must return to the gold standard as quickly as possible. In the way of this was the mountain of paper currency issued by the central banks during the war. There were essentially only two ways to restore the balance between the value of gold reserves and the total money supply: deflation (by contracting the amount of currency in circulation); or devaluation (formally reducing the value of domestic currency in relation to gold).

In Britain, Chancellor of the Exchequer Winston Churchill, against his better judgement, chose deflation, fixing the pound to gold at the same price as the pre-war level. However, lacking large enough reserves of gold and not being able to compete internationally with other countries because its currency was too high, Britain's economy floundered for much of the 1920s, with high interest rates and unemployment. France, on the other hand, which had chosen devaluation and set the franc at a relatively low exchange rate in relation to gold, enjoyed continuous economic growth, with its gold reserves and international exports increasing. Meanwhile, the large amounts of money that America had lent to European powers to finance the war meant that repayments and gold began flowing into its coffers.

Because all nations were connected via the gold standard, the success of one nation (such as France, whose devaluation effectively meant it was exporting unemployment to Britain and Germany) could impact badly on another. Rather than bringing increasing prosperity for all, a return to the gold standard created a zero-sum game in which one country did well at another's expense, increasing hostility. Yet only a few at the time, most notably John Maynard Keynes, were willing to attack the gold standard. Keynes described the standard as a "barbarous relic" and a "fetish" that hamstrung the world economy between the wars. But he failed to persuade the British authorities that a complex modern economy could create credit without gold's backing.

This apparent "umbrella of stability," Ahamed argues, "proved to be a straitjacket." It would take an array of currency crises and a Great Depression for the paradigm to finally change.

Hurtling towards disaster

By the end of 1926, the four central bankers had begun to worry about an overheating US stock market, excessive foreign borrowing by Germany, recession in Britain, and an increasingly dysfunctional gold standard. To alleviate matters, Strong's New York Fed cut interest rates by half a percent to 3.5 percent. Following the cut, gold started flowing back to Europe. But from February 1928, Strong, realizing it might have been a mistake, had the Fed raise its rates to 5 percent. America began attracting the world's gold again, and Britain felt compelled to raise its own interest rates to stop the gold haemorrhage. This rate rise dampened demand, creating even more unemployment. Germany, already in recession, had to raise its rates to 7.5 percent, and other European countries followed.

Meanwhile in America, in a period of 15 months in 1928 and 1929, the stock market almost doubled, far outstripping the underlying value of its component companies. When the crash came in the fall of 1929, close to half of the value of the US stock market evaporated, and it could have gone further were it not for drastic interest rate cuts by the Fed and injections of liquidity by it and a consortium of banks. But the Fed eased its interventions too soon, and so a second downward lurch began in the real economy, which some had hoped might be protected from the market collapse. Meanwhile, the European markets also dropped, but not by as much, as the general public had not bought stocks to the same extent as in America.

Keeping to the gold standard had a perverse effect, Ahamed writes, in that international capital flows increasingly went to those countries which already had plenty of gold (America and France), and less to those with little (Britain and Germany). This winner-takes-all situation was hardly healthy for a world trying to get out of Depression, particularly since European countries had to pay for their US debts in gold, not currency.

Sinking into the mire

In 1931, with increasingly depleted gold reserves, Britain was finally forced off the gold standard. Though the reputation of the Bank of England was diminished, the actual result was a drop in the pound by 30 percent within a couple of months, giving Britain a hope of being competitive in trade again. Many other countries, including Canada, India, and the Scandinavian countries, followed.

1931 was the year, Ahamed says, when a severe recession around the world turned into The Great Depression. The currency problems created by trying to adhere to the gold standard led to runs on the banks, in Europe as well as America, and a vicious cycle of deflationary psychology in consumption and investment set in. In America the following year, investment halved, industrial production dropped by a quarter, prices fell 10 percent, and unemployment hit 20 percent. The stock market's low of 41 points in 1932 was an astonishing 90 percent beneath what it had been at its peak in 1929. When a journalist asked Keynes if there had been anything like this in history he replied, "Yes. It was called the Dark Ages, and it lasted four hundred years."

When Franklin D. Roosevelt replaced Herbert Hoover as US president at the start of 1933, the *New York Times* reported that Washington was like "a beleaguered capital in wartime." Twenty-eight states had shut down their banking systems, and a quarter of all banks had gone under in the previous three years. With precipitous drops in house prices, half of all people with mortgages had defaulted. The steel mills that had not shut down were operating at 12 percent capacity. Car plants had gone from making 20,000 vehicles a day to two thousand. "In the richest nation in the world," Ahamed writes, "34 million men, women and children out of a total population of 120 million had no apparent source of income." It seemed that Marx had been right when he foretold that capitalism would collapse amid increasingly extreme cycles of boom and bust.

Dumping orthodoxy, embracing prosperity

One of Roosevelt's first acts was to proclaim a five-day cross-America bank shutdown, and suspend all exports of gold. His Emergency Banking Act allowed solvent banks to gradually reopen, and provisions were made for the Treasury, via the Fed, to guarantee deposits in those banks. The law also moved the dollar away from being backed by gold; a variety of assets were now redeemable against it.

Roosevelt's package of measures increased confidence overnight. People took the cash from under their mattresses and put it back into banks, and the stock market rebounded. Roosevelt began a Keynesian stimulus program that got some of America working again. Against the advice of economists and bankers, Roosevelt believed that the key to recovery was getting prices rising. To this end, he accepted an amendment to the Agricultural Adjustments Act providing for a "temporary" leaving of the gold standard, with the capacity to issue $3 billion in US dollars without the backing of gold, and the scope to devalue the dollar against gold by up to 50 percent.

"Breaking with the dead hand of the gold standard was the key to economic revival," Ahamed writes. All countries that did so—Britain in 1931, the US in 1933, France in 1935, and eventually Germany, still haunted by the spectre of hyperinflation—got their economies back on track. The Allies virtually gave up on getting reparations out of Germany; these in the end only totalled $4 billion, rather than the $32 billion originally sought, and its economy shot ahead (with significant thanks to rearmament).

But if the gold standard was no good, what could replace it? After World War Two, Keynes worked to create a system based on strong but not rigid rules which would allow countries to shape their own domestic economies by having "pegged [to the US dollar] but adjustable" exchange rates. The purpose, Ahamed says, was "to avoid the need for the sort of straitjacket policies of the twenties and thirties when Germany and Britain had been forced to hike interest rates and create mass unemployment to protect currency values that were in any case unsustainable." The new system was designed to again give countries some control over their own destiny, yet still facilitate international trade.

Final comments

Though it is hard to believe now, at the time no one really questioned the gold standard. Hoover, Churchill, Lenin, and Mussolini all believed in it, and in the 1920s and 1930s it seemed the one thing, perhaps the only thing, linking nations in the world economy. Yet the self-regulating market beloved of classical economists (of which the gold standard was the most powerful symbol), rather than leading to a promised land of prosperity and peace, brought countries to their knees and invited horrifying shifts from extreme liberalism to its antithesis, fascism. One of Ahamed's themes involves the dark effects of enforcing large sovereign debt repayments, as the Allies tried to do with Germany after World War One. Hitler's rise demonstrated the fact that what may seem financially prudent can be politically very dumb.

What is today's "gold standard," that is, the institution that looks good on paper but has in fact caused untold misery? In *The Euro*, Joseph Stiglitz argues that the European currency has been a financial straitjacket that has condemned whole nations to economic failure. As with the gold standard, it became a mark of prestige to join the euro, and a disaster to leave it. Stiglitz believes history will be kinder to nations who insist on keeping their currency independent.

Liaquat Ahamed

Born in Kenya in 1952, Ahamed was sent abroad for his education: private school in England followed by degrees in economics at Cambridge University and then Harvard.

In the 1980s he was an economist at the World Bank, before starting a career in investment banking with Fischer, Francis, Trees & Watts, a New York firm, rising to Chief Executive. He currently advises hedge funds, is a director of an insurance company, and is a trustee of the Brookings Institution, a think tank.

Lords of Finance *won the* Financial Times/*Goldman Sachs Business Book of the Year award and the 2010 Pulitzer Prize for History. Ahamed's other book is* Money and Tough Love: Inside the IMF *(2014).*

2010

The Microtheory of Innovative Entrepreneurship

"The prospects of glory, wealth, and fame hold real value, even if they never materialize. They are, indeed, the stuff of which dreams are made. For the entrepreneur, contemplation of imagined success is only part of the psychic reward. In reading the biographies of the great inventors, one is struck by the fascination, moments of triumph, and even the pleasure of puzzle-solving and experimentation—though punctured by frustration and exhaustion—that accompanied the process of their work."

In a nutshell

Economic growth rests on the development and implementation of new ideas, so it is surprising the extent to which entrepreneurship has been ignored by economics.

In a similar vein

Gary Becker *Human Capital*
Peter Drucker *Innovation and Entrepreneurship*
Robert J. Gordon *The Rise and Fall of Economic Growth*
Deirdre McCloskey *Bourgeois Equality*
Joseph Schumpeter *Capitalism, Socialism and Democracy*

CHAPTER 2

William J. Baumol

"The thing that's wrong with the French," George W. Bush apocryphally said to British Prime Minister Tony Blair, "is that they don't have a word for entrepreneur."

Where did the word come from? Early economic writings in English used the terms "adventurers" or "undertakers" to describe people taking risks to bring some product or service to market. In translating them, French economic thinker Richard Cantillon plumped for "entrepreneur" (literally, someone who undertakes). Jean-Baptiste Say included the word as part of a chain of "producers": the scientists who made discoveries about raw materials and invented things, the entrepreneurs who converted this knowledge into useful purposes, and finally the workers who manufactured the final product. Every successful nation needs all three, Say said, and he recommended government help to finance research, since the benefits of innovation across society outweighed any costs. In Britain, John Stuart Mill and Alfred Marshall also had things to say about entrepreneurs, but it did not constitute a theory of entrepreneurship as such. In the twentieth century, Joseph Schumpeter became the best-known theorist of entrepreneurship, arguing that it was the driving force of capitalism.

Even with Schumpeter's insights, American economist William Baumol felt there was much that had been left unsaid about entrepreneurs, and in a seminal 1968 article ("Entrepreneurship in Economic Theory," *American Economic Review*), complained that mainstream economics, particularly the theory of the firm, had conveniently glossed over the species. One could not explain the huge differences in economic performance between time and place without thinking about the role of the entrepreneur. China had brilliant inventors, but its system of incentives pushed the brightest people to enter the civil service, not industry and commerce. Part of America's great economic success was its celebration of the inventor and the innovator, and its keenness to transform their achievements into wide use via entrepreneurship. Today, of course, China has boomed because, even though it has come up with no recent advances as great as paper or gunpowder, it gives entrepreneurship its due credit as an engine of growth.

Baumol's *The Microtheory of Innovative Entrepreneurship* pulls together the strands of his work on the economics of entrepreneurship over several decades. He is also famous for "Baumol's cost disease" and the theory of contestable markets (see below).

Entrepreneurs are different

Baumol made a distinction between entrepreneurs and managers. The role of a manager is to make existing processes more efficient, and to see the enterprise fulfill its production potential. This often involves significant levels of experience, analysis, and judgement, yet it brings little new into being. It is incremental work.

His second distinction was between two kinds of entrepreneurs. The entrepreneur is commonly defined as anyone who starts a business, even if the business is doing something many others are doing. Baumol refers to this type as a "replicative" entrepreneur. He is more interested in the species that Schumpeter celebrated, the "innovative entrepreneur." This kind must be a leader, irrespective of formal position—it is only an entrepreneur of this type who will be responsible for "revolutionary growth" in an economy. Another way to see innovative entrepreneurs is as *suppliers* of inventions, Baumol says. The inventors invent, but usually have no idea about how their idea or product can become widely used. It takes some time to see the opportunity and get it rolled out to the market. A good example: the McDonald brothers invented a perfect system (small menu, high profit hamburger restaurant with fast service and scrupulous cleanliness), but it took Ray Kroc to see how the system could be endlessly replicated across America.

Traditional theories of the firm imagined a dry decision-making process involving "automaton maximizers" who aim to maximize outputs and profits. Totally left out of the equation, Baumol writes, are the "clever ruses, ingenious schemes, brilliant innovations, charisma, or any of the other stuff of which outstanding entrepreneurship is made."

In economic theory, entrepreneurship is the fourth "factor of production" along with land, labor, and capital. Yet because the activity of entrepreneurs is hard to quantify and measure, it has simply been left out of the economics discipline. Why? Land, labor, and capital each depend to a large extent on other people and external factors. You have to buy or rent land, employ the right kind of labor, and borrow money at interest. In contrast, innovative entrepreneurship is generated by the individual *mind*, so it can't be measured in any normal way.

There is another reason why mainstream economics glossed over the entrepreneur: it tends to favor equilibrium models which minimize or excise the possibility of change, while the entrepreneur's *raison d'etre* is to *upset* equilibrium, by finding holes in existing industries and exploiting them, or bringing into being products which can create new industries. As the very currency of entrepreneurs is change, frequently their activity *precedes* the creation of a firm, so the theory of the firm becomes meaningless.

Entrepreneurship, innovation, and the wealth of nations

Conventional economics focuses on "market failures" that hold back growth, including monopoly, negative externalities (the public cost of private actions e.g. pollution or global warming), poor public infrastructure, and so on. But many studies suggest that such inefficiencies have only a mild effect on economic growth, and that if they were eliminated to create a state of perfect competition, there would be a GDP increase of perhaps 1 percent maximum. Efficiency gains and the fixing of market failures in no way account for the massive growth in income between 1900 and 2000 (583 percent in the US, 1653 percent in Japan, 526 percent in Germany), Baumol argues. It was the productive innovations unleashed by entrepreneurs, which dramatically increased welfare in every part of life (not least, the doubling of life expectancy and the victory over famine and poverty) that surely account for a significant portion of such growth.

Schumpeter believed that the day of the innovating solo entrepreneur was waning, because big business was taking over the function of innovation and making it routine. Baumol disagrees, noting that big companies are not good at the early stages of innovation, when wild creativity, leaps of faith, and irrational amounts of time spent on superficially unpromising ideas are the norm.

Inventions "of enormous significance for our economy," such as the aeroplane, via FM radio, personal computer, helicopter, and pacemaker, were the product of small-scale innovators, Baumol says. The US Small Business Administration concluded in a 2003 study that "A small firm patent is more likely than a large firm patent to be among the top 1 percent" of innovations that make a commercial difference. The reality is that small firms come up with most of the innovations that drive society forward, but they usually don't have the resources to roll them out across society. Big companies buy them out or license their idea, and then are able to properly develop the innovation for public use and distribution.

Government, Baumol says, plays a crucial role in innovation. On the passive side, property rights, enforceability of contracts, patent protection, and laws that do no inhibit the starting of new firms are all needed. On the active side, the financing of basic research is required; this may otherwise not happen if left up to the private sector.

Productive and unproductive entrepreneurship

Schumpeter told us that entrepreneurship extended well beyond technical innovation, and could involve:

- introduction of a new good, or a new quality of a good
- a new method of production of an existing good
- the opening of a new market
- the securing of a new supply of raw materials or half-manufactured goods
- shaking up the organization of an industry, by creating a monopoly or breaking an existing one

In "Entrepreneurship: Productive, Unproductive, and Destructive" (1990, *Journal of Political Economy*), Baumol asked: "What pushes entrepreneurs to focus on a particular combination of these activities, or single one out as the most promising?"

Entrepreneurship is always present in societies, he notes. The more interesting question is what form it takes: whether it is constructive or innovative, or even whether it damages the economy. This in turn depends on the "rules of the game": the system of rewards, incentives and payoffs that society offers to a potential entrepreneur. If entrepreneurs are simply "persons who are ingenious and creative in finding ways that add to their own wealth, power, and prestige," as Baumol puts it, then it follows that not all entrepreneurs will be doing things that add to society. They may be engaged in acts of "unproductive entrepreneurship," such as creatively seizing an opportunity to extract rents before anyone else does, or building an organized crime network. Such allocation of resources will serve themselves, and no one else.

Baumol imagines an activity ('A') that normally would provide both a good payoff for the entrepreneur, and benefit society, but which is thwarted thanks to legislation and/or social stigma. To save their social skin and stay within the law, entrepreneurs will naturally direct their efforts to another activity ('B') which may be less beneficial to society. By its direction of resources towards B, society loses. Moreover, it is not just that the same entrepreneur will change her activity, but a whole generation of prospective entrepreneurs may do so, or simply stop being entrepreneurs.

Such "rules of the game" vary dramatically between time and place, with dramatically different results. Baumol mentions the story of the Roman who took his invention of unbreakable glass to the Emperor Tiberius. Upon demonstrating it, the man's head was cut off on the grounds that the innovation would "reduce the value of gold to mud." If the spread of innovation depends on the whim of a ruler, there will be little incentive to innovate, even if the benefits to society might be great. In medieval China, the system of state examinations to enter the scholar-administrator class meant that the best and brightest became corrupt officials, extracting rents from those they administered. Thus the rewards of society went to those of position, not the innovators in commerce and industry. By 1280, China had invented paper, waterwheels, sophisticated water clocks, and gunpowder. But there was little scope for private enterprise or entrepreneurship, because individuals had no real legal rights compared to those of the state. They could not prevent arbitrary seizure of wealth or inventions by officials, to whom any kind of private sector upstart was anathema. Enterprise was not only frowned upon, but officials clamped down on it if it posed a threat to their existing rent-seeking, or they sought to nationalize innovations for the state's gain.

In the early Middle Ages, Paris had 68 water mills around the Seine, performing all sorts of industrial tasks, from grinding mash for beer to polishing armor. Then, growth slowed in the fourteenth century. Why? Temperatures dropped, there was plague, the Hundred Years War began, but also the Church clamped down on any novel ideas and scientific thinking. As with many times in history, there was now a disincentive to productively innovate. Payoffs again were directed to glory in war.

It was only with the coming of the Industrial Revolution, and the creed of free markets and openness to ideas, that the business person and industrialist were allowed to amass wealth. The fact that this new respect for entrepreneurship coincided with tremendous economic growth, Baumol says, is surely evidence that "the allocation of entrepreneurship does really matter for the vigor and innovativeness of an economy." Innovation and entrepreneurship are easily stifled, and the rules of the game can be quickly changed in favor of power instead of ingenuity. It is no accident, Baumol argues, that the greatest growth surges in history have occurred in free-market economies. This includes modern China, which despite being a one-party state has learned its lessons when it comes to innovation and the profit motive.

Baumol's theory of "contestable markets" seeks to explain why growth in free market economies is always much greater than other kinds of political economy: even if a market is not perfectly competitive (for example, if there is an oligopoly in which a market is tied up by a small number of firms), if the entry and exit barriers are not too high and potential entrants have access to the latest technology, you can have good outcomes in terms of greater productivity and lower prices for consumers. This is because, as Baumol said in an interview, "the oligopoly's main weapon is not price, but invention, in which it is life and death for them. That competition drives them each to try and prevent the others from getting ahead of them in innovation."

Final comments

Partly as a result of Baumol's work, entrepreneurship is now an important part of 'new growth theory', which suggests that economies are driven to new heights through the power of ideas. However, it is also a fact that economic growth creates more consumption, which has knock-on environmental effects. Whereas conventional economics will focus on such failures, Baumol is more interested in the innovations that may transcend it. Just as the use of whale oil was replaced by crude oil as a global energy resource, thanks to the diffusion of engineering innovations, he argues, so the world is likely to get gradually cleaner thanks to entrepreneurs seeking to profit from new energy technologies.

The beginning of the book has a quote from the historian Eric Hobsbawm: "It is often assumed that an economy of private enterprise has an automatic bias towards innovation, but this is not so. It has a bias only towards profit." All innovations eventually become public goods that are enjoyed by all at modest cost or for free, but it is crucial that, in the first place, the entrepreneur can become rich through the power of their ideas.

William J. Baumol

Born in 1922, Baumol grew up in the South Bronx, New York. He attended the College of the City of New York, and after graduating worked at the Department of Agriculture. After a stint serving in the US war effort in France, in 1947 Baumol embarked on a PhD at the London School of Economics. In 1949 he was offered a position at Princeton University, where he taught economics for the next 43 years. Doctoral students included the economist Gary Becker and the finance writer Burton Malkiel. He is currently Professor of Entrepreneurship at New York University and directs the Berkley Center for Entrepreneurship and Innovation in the Stern School of Business.

Other books include The Free Market Innovation Machine: Analyzing the Growth Miracle of Capitalism *(2002),* Good Capitalism, Bad Capitalism, and the Economics of Growth and Prosperity *(with Litan and Schramm, 2007) and* The Cost Disease: Why Computers Get Cheaper and Health Care Doesn't *(2012). "Baumol's cost disease" highlighted the fact that some sectors of the economy, such as manufacturing, are able to enjoy significant increases in productivity over time because they can utilize labor-saving devices, while others, such as hospital care, education, and the arts, barely change because they are people-based—and so keep getting more expensive.*

With Alan Blinder Baumol has written three popular textbooks on macroeconomics and microeconomics. The Baumol Research Centre for Entrepreneurship Studies at Zhejiang Gongshang University is named after him.

1964

Human Capital

"It is clear that all countries which have managed persistent growth in income have also had large increases in the education and training of their labor forces. First, elementary school education becomes universal, then high school education spreads rapidly, and finally children from middle income and poorer families begin going to college. A skeptic might respond that the expansion in education as countries get richer no more implies that education causes growth than does a larger number of dishwashers in richer countries implies that dishwashers are an engine of growth.
However, even economists know the difference between correlation and causation, and have developed rather straightforward methods for determining how much of income growth is caused by a growth in human capital."

In a nutshell

Though it carries some uncertainties, an investment in ourselves pays the greatest dividends.

In a similar vein

Erik Brynjolfsson & Andrew McAfee *The Second Machine Age*
Steven Levitt & Stephen J. Dubner *Freakonomics*
Thorstein Veblen *The Theory of the Leisure Class*

CHAPTER 3

Gary Becker

Gary Becker achieved renown thanks to his willingness to apply economic analysis to all areas of life: What will I get out of marriage? Will my firm falter if I hire only white workers? Should I park illegally and risk the fine? If I invest a lot of time and money in my kids, will they look after me when I am old? Such awkward questions fired his research into the economics of discrimination, marriage, crime, and the family. His insights would win him a Nobel Prize and greatly influence other social sciences, and inspire the authors of *Freakonomics* and pop sociologist Malcolm Gladwell.

But the question that occupied Becker the most concerned education. If you could do a cost-benefit analysis of the benefits going to college, compared to the money and time saved in not going, would it be worth it?

In the 1950s and 1960s, education economics (pioneers included University of Chicago economists Theodore Schultz, Jacob Mincer and Milton Friedman) became popular, even faddish. By the 1993 presidential election campaign, both Bill Clinton and George W. Bush were using the phrase "investing in human capital," and talking up college education and on-the-job training. Having begun as a controversial notion, human capital had entered the public lexicon, and seemed to provide answers to the riddle of economic growth. Consider the success of Asian economies such as Japan and Korea after World War Two, Becker noted. They were lacking in natural resources, and had to import raw materials and energy, but they invested hugely in training, education, and technology, and experienced immense prosperity. In an era of the "knowledge worker," human capital really comes into its own, since much of a company's investment will be in its staff rather than in physical capital.

Theodore Schulz coined the phrase "human capital," but it was Becker's book, which came out relatively early in his career, that popularized it.

What is human capital?

The book begins with a quote from Alfred Marshall in his *Principles of Economics*: "The most valuable of all capital is that invested in human beings."

And yet, Becker notes, the very idea of "human capital" is unsavory to some, because it seems to reduce people to the economic value of their education and skills, as if they are slaves or machines. In the 1950s and 1960s, he said in his Nobel speech, "To approach schooling as an investment rather than a cultural experience was considered unfeeling and extremely narrow." Moreover, if I have more human capital than you (more education, training, social skills and so on), does it mean that I will exploit you in a similar way to how the industrialist exploits the worker? Does human capital create a new class conflict between those who have a lot, and those with not much?

To Becker's relief, most people could see that the term "human capital" simply meant investing in people. It can include schooling, computer training courses, spending on medical care, going to a self-development lecture—basically, anything that raises earnings, improves health, or gives us a greater appreciation of life. Human capital is different to money in the bank, 100 shares in IBM, or a steel plant, in that it forever belongs to the person and cannot be separated from him or her, and with luck naturally grows through a lifetime.

It's worth it: the benefits of going to college

When Becker was writing the first edition of *Human Capital*, it was acknowledged in the economics profession that the growth of physical capital did not really account for the growth in incomes. That is, incomes grew at a faster rate than investments in machinery and land. The most obvious thing to account for this discrepancy was education, which after all should enable people to see problems differently and make better use of resources—indeed, create new resources.

Becker looked at census reports to see what the link was between personal income and education. He found that the rate of financial return (after tuition costs) on a college education for white males was between 11 and 13 percent. Yet white males got more of a benefit than black males, because there were more opportunities for them in the job market. Still, the benefits to black males were clear enough that from the 1950s onwards there was a big increase in college enrolment in that group, and as more opportunities opened up, more went to college. No longer were educated blacks restricted to the clergy or the law; they could enter the mainstream jobs market. After 1940, demand for all educated people ramped up, even though there were more graduates, thanks to spending on research and development (R&D), military technology, and services. As the social mores of society changed, it also became more "worth it" for women to invest in their education, because careers in medicine, the law, and business stopped being as male-dominated.

More people go to college when the benefits are clear, and fewer go when the benefits are unclear, Becker notes. The boom in college education suggests that school leavers know instinctively that they will get ahead more effectively by deferring work and going to college. But why exactly are graduates more valuable to employers? Becker argues that education provides not just knowledge and skills, but "a way of analyzing problems." This is a valuable marketable commodity, and contradicts the idea that the value of education is simply in credentials, and in the time it saves employers in selecting the best people. According to this view, graduates earn more "not because college education raises productivity, but because more productive students go on to college." Yet if it is true that the more productive students go to college in the first place, college only further increases their productivity, knowledge, skills, and judgement—all things that employers want, particularly in an advanced technological economy.

The value of human capital over time

One of Becker's observations is that, unlike with other kinds of capital, returns on investment in human capital often increase over time. The payoff period for a college education, for instance, can be very long, making the initial investment a bargain. Increased longevity means that there is a longer timeframe in which the positive effects of education can manifest themselves.

Yet Becker also asked whether investments in education are superior or inferior to investments in other things. As an investment in a college education involves a fair degree of risk (anything can happen with the economy, with our health, and our skills and knowledge can be made obsolete), and is extremely illiquid (our education can't be separated from ourselves and sold off), it is right to compare it to similar forms of risky and illiquid investment. He refers to research by George Stigler which found that investments in manufacturing capital yield an average return of around 7 percent over time, considerably lower than the 11–13 percent that Becker arrived at for college education. Most inheritances, he notes, are not large enough to be used for buying houses or factories or other forms of capital, so instead they are spent on human capital (education and training). People tend to invest in human capital first anyway, intuiting that it has greater returns than other assets. A good job resulting from a college degree will provide decades of earnings and benefits, including psychic ones, and provides the income to buy one's own house, shares, build a pension, and so on.

However, actual money capital invested in one's education or training is only part of the total investment. The majority is in the opportunity cost of *time* invested in doing so. As the value of a person's time rises as their amount of education rises, the cost of obtaining further education may not make sense in market terms. The major factor in human capital decisions is not money, but whether it is worth the time foregone. Finishing high school and getting a bachelor's degree may be essential to getting a good job, but will spending five years getting a PhD be worth the foregone income you would have got from working? The marginal value and benefits of extra education decrease with every extra unit of education obtained, Becker notes, especially since you have to factor in the shorter working life left after you have completed all this education. People make these calculations all the time, and generally, he says, they make the right call.

Becker was careful to say that the case for a college education was strong, but only because the personal income data and GDP data showed its positive effects. When there was no longer a clear payoff, because college fees rose to ridiculous heights, or on-the-job training became more valuable relative to a college degree, then people should rationally reallocate their investments in human capital. In saying this, he presaged current debates about the soaring cost of college education in the United States and elsewhere.

Human capital and inequality

"The difference between the most dissimilar characters," Adam Smith wrote in *The Wealth of Nations*, "between a philosopher and a common street porter, for example, seems to arise not so much from nature, as from habit, custom, and education." Becker agrees, arguing that everyone has the same potential to benefit from investments in their human capital. He does not try to hide the fact that some people will make more use of the same amount of education than others, and earn more as a result. Yet he also recognizes that differences in environment play a significant role in access to education in the first place, and that these are things that can be changed. Critics of inequality correctly focus on inequality of opportunities rather than inequality of incomes.

In a place where the quality of schooling is unequal (he uses the example of the South of the United States, where education was once split along racial lines), you will end up with very unequal distribution of income, because the payoffs from being in education increase over time. In contrast, in places where nearly everyone goes to the same government schools, which are of a similar standard (Switzerland is a good example), you will get more equality of income.

Final comments

When, in the 1970s, there was a slump in the earnings of people with college educations, there was much talk of "overeducated Americans," but in the 1980s the earnings of college-educated Americans hit new heights. Today, the college premium is even higher, proving Becker's point. In 2014, an analysis of US Labor Department data by Washington's Economic Policy Institute showed that Americans with four-year college degrees were earning *98 percent* more per hour than those with no degree. In the early 1980s, the hourly wage premium had been only 64 percent higher for college graduates. The best investment, it seems, is in yourself.

Gary Becker

Becker was born in 1930 in Pennsylvania, and grew up in Brooklyn, New York. He gained his first degree in economics at Princeton University. His PhD was from the University of Chicago, and his thesis was on the economics of racial discrimination. Mentors included Milton Friedman and George Stigler. After a decade teaching at Columbia University, he returned to Chicago, and in 1967 won the John Bates Clark Medal for the most significant economist under 40.

From 1985 to 2004 Becker wrote a column for Businessweek, *and until his death in 2014 shared a popular blog with Richard Posner, a judge. With Daniel Kahneman and Steven Levitt, he was a founding partner in TGG group, an economic consultancy. Becker won the Nobel Prize in Economic Sciences in 1992, and was awarded the Presidential Medal of Freedom in 2007.*

Significant articles include "A theory of the allocation of time" (1965), "Crime and punishment: an economic approach" (1968), "A theory of marriage," parts I and II (1973, 1974), and "Human capital, effort, and the sexual division of labor" (1985). Books include The Economics of Discrimination *(1957),* A Treatise on the Family *(1981), and with historian wife Guity Nashat,* The Economics of Life *(1995).*

2007

The Little Book of Common Sense Investing

"Successful investing is all about common sense . . . Simple arithmetic suggests, and history confirms, that the winning strategy is to own all of the nation's publicly held businesses at very low cost. By doing so you are guaranteed to capture almost the entire return that they generated in the form of dividends and earning growth."

"[The] stock market is a giant distraction that causes investors to focus on transitory and volatile investment expectations rather than on what is really important—the gradual accumulation of the returns earned by corporate business."

In a nutshell

If you invest in the stock market, put your money in a fund that automatically owns a little bit of every company listed. Over time, it is a sure and almost worry-free way to accumulate wealth.

In a similar vein

Benjamin Graham *The Intelligent Investor*
Robert Shiller *Irrational Exuberance*
Paul Samuelson *Economics*

CHAPTER 4

John C. Bogle

John Bogle is something of a financial maverick. He made his name as the founder, in 1976, of the first ever stock market index fund, the Vanguard 500, and grew Vanguard to be the second largest fund provider in the world, with over $3 trillion under management. In 1999 *Fortune* named him one of four "Giants of the twentieth century" in the investing field, and in 2004, *Time* magazine included him in the "Time 100" list of "the world's 100 most powerful and influential people."

So what is an index fund? Essentially baskets of all the major stocks listed in a certain market, they usually track an established index such as the Standard & Poor's 500 ('S&P 500', established 1926), composing the 500 largest corporations in America, or the Dow Jones Wilshire index, which takes in close to 5,000 stocks.

Traditional index funds don't engage in "trading"—the buying and selling of stocks—as regular managed funds do, but usually buy once and keep. This can make index funds seem very boring. However, the lack of trading excitement is easily made up for by their remarkably good long-term records. Investing is really about common sense, and the basic arithmetic in support of index fund investing, Bogle asserts, is irresistible. They make the apparently complex world of finance simple, and the case for them is "compelling and unarguable," he says. As we would all like as much certainty as possible when investing in shares and stocks, Bogle's book makes intriguing reading.

Who are you making rich?

For the average punter, Bogle says, the stock market is a loser's game. Why? First, we have a misplaced faith in financial experts, who not only do no better, but often worse, than we collectively do ourselves; second, we do not realize the huge eroding effect on our funds of money managers' fees and the tax inefficiency of their way of operating. Those who *always* win are the "financial croupiers"—brokers, investment bankers, money managers and the like—who rake in over $400 *billion* a year. As Bogle puts it, in a casino, "the house always wins".

Returns from the stock market itself vary greatly, much more so than the output of the economy itself, but the *costs* of investing stubbornly remain.

You do not pay lower fees to your fund manager when he has a bad year—or decade. We naturally like to think of the compounding increase in the value of stocks we hold, but we often don't understand the compounding of investment costs (fund joining and operating fees, taxes levied on transactions, and so on). Mutual fund fees range from 0.9 percent of assets to 3 percent, with an average of 2.1 percent. While these do not seem high at the beginning (1.5 percent of $100,000, for instance, does not seem exorbitant), over time these costs can erode a potential fortune.

But how does the actual performance of regular funds versus index funds compare? In the period 1995–2005, index funds returned a compound profit of 194 percent, while managed mutual funds returned only 154 percent. Again, a massive difference.

Stay still and prosper

You may think that your mutual fund is expertly turning over stocks frequently to make the most of your money, but in doing so it is also spending that money, because each transaction has costs both in terms of taxes and management. You can be sure someone is getting paid a lot for calling the buys and sells. To justify their fees, fund managers have to be seen to be 'doing something', but as Warren Buffett has observed, "For investors as a whole, *returns decrease as motion increases*."

Because index funds invest automatically across the board, they do not need layers of analysts or managers. As they do not "trade" but simply buy and hold, they avoid all the usual costs built up by frequent transactions. The longer you hold, the less risk there is, because you have left speculation (with all its costs and fluctuations of fortune) behind.

Invest in capitalism, not the casino

Stock market investors can easily forget that they are investing in the ingenuity, innovation and productive power of *companies*, which in America over the last 100 years have enjoyed a 9.5 percent return on their capital. When this rate of return is compounded over many years, you get astounding results. Over a decade, a dollar invested becomes $2.48, over two decades $6.14, three decades $15.22, four decades $37.72, and over five decades $93.48— from a single dollar. Of course, you have to adjust this for inflation, which significantly reduces the purchasing power of your money in decades hence, but over an investment span of 30 years, for example, an investment of $100,000 in corporate America through an index fund would still become worth over $660,000 in current real (spending power) terms.

Bogle notes that the gains of the stock market, measured over time, almost exactly match the gains made by American business itself. The average return on stocks is 9.6 percent, while return on capital invested directly into businesses averages 9.5 percent. He observes that, "in the long run, stock returns depend almost entirely on the reality of the investment returns earned by our corporations." The stock market may overvalue companies for as long as a decade, then the next decade might undervalue them. But as Benjamin Graham pointed out, there is always "reversion to the mean," with the underlying worth of the companies behind the stocks being revealed.

Bogle asserts that the stock market is a "giant distraction," Shakespeare's proverbial "tale told by an idiot, full of sound and fury, signifying nothing." Driven in the short term by emotions, thanks to this irrationality no one can ever know for sure which way it will turn, and it is a fool's game to try to guess. However, we *can* be surprisingly sure about the long-term productivity of business, and by avoiding the game of "picking winners" and simply investing in the whole stock market, we know we will reap the results of business growth.

Bet on numbers, not people

Bogle's question is, why are people paying *more* money for a way of investing that has *worse* returns?

Unfortunately, most of us do not know any better. Great returns, as Burton Malkiel pointed out in *A Random Walk Down Wall Street*, are often sheer luck. We are stupid enough to invest based on past performance, which is not only no guarantee of future performance, but almost predicts future worse performance.

Fund managers are human, and get excited by the direction markets seem to be taking. Like anyone, they have a tendency to buy stocks at their peak and not buy them when they represent best value. There is none of this risk entailed in having a stake in an index fund that automatically tracks the market overall. In the long term, all gains and losses in the stock market are balanced, so if you invest in the game *overall*, you will win. Bogle expresses it as, "Don't look for the needle—buy the haystack."

Final comments

Bogle describes the shift to put money in index funds as "a revolution," and for many years his strategy made him a lone voice. It was years before other index funds started up copying the Vanguard model, yet now there are hundreds in the United States alone. Some, ironically, are "managed index funds", which mean that they choose stocks in only some industry sectors which pay more dividends or may grow quicker, and therefore try to beat the market. Bogle takes a dim view of them, as they significantly increase costs and risk compared to a traditional index fund. He also predicts that returns on stocks will be subdued in the years ahead, which is another reason to stick with traditional indexers, since managed funds will keep charging the same costs whether they do well or not.

With 18 chapters and over 200 pages, *The Little Book of Common Sense Investing* is not that little, and can seem repetitive— but in a way that affirms rather than annoys. Reading it is like having a fireside chat with one of the masters of investing, except that you may not be able to sleep having listened to his powerful message. His detractors, he notes, have said that the only thing going for him is his ability to state the obvious, but in a financial world of promotion and chicanery, perhaps putting our trust in the "relentless arithmetic" of index investing is the smartest thing we can do.

Some finance academics worry that the increasing role of non-selective tracker or index funds means that the stock market loses its primary function of intelligent allocation of capital; money simply flows to existing companies, no questions asked. This may be true, but sorting out the good from the bad is not the job of the average small investor. Bogle's advice to avoid the complex and instead "profit from the magic of simplicity," remains sound.

John C. Bogle

Born in 1929 in New Jersey, Bogle graduated from Blair Academy before attending Princeton University, where in 1951 he received an economics degree. After graduating he began working at the Wellington Management Company in Pennsylvania. He rose to become chairman of that company, and in 1974 left to start Vanguard.

Other books include Common Sense on Mutual Funds *(1999),* John Bogle on Investing *(2000), and* The Battle for the Soul of Capitalism *(2005), which argues for higher ethical standards in American finance,* Enough: True Measures of Money, Business, and Life *(2010), and* The Clash of Cultures: Investment vs. Speculation (2012). *See also* John Bogle and the Vanguard Experiment: One Man's Quest to Transform the Mutual Fund Industry, *by Robert Slater (1996), and* The Bogleheads' Guide To Investing *(2006) by Larimore, Lindauer and LeBoeuf.* The Little Book of Common Sense Investing *is dedicated to Paul Samuelson, the economist and Bogle's mentor at Princeton.*

2014

The Second Machine Age

"Computers and other digital advances are doing for mental power—the ability to use our brains to understand and shape our environments—what the steam engine and its descendants did for muscle power."

"Not only are the new technologies exponential, digital, and combinatorial, but most of the gains are still ahead of us. In the next twenty-four months, the planet will add more computer power than it did in all previous history. Over the next twenty-four years, the increase will likely be over a thousand-fold."

In a nutshell

As the stock of human knowledge grows, so does our ability to create new wealth, but we can't allow people to be left out of the benefits of technology and innovation.

In a similar vein

Gary Becker *Human Capital*
Peter Drucker *Innovation and Entrepreneurship*
Robert J. Gordon *The Rise and Fall of American Growth*
Thomas Piketty *Capital in the Twenty-First Century*
Joseph Schumpeter *Capitalism, Socialism, and Democracy*
Julian Simon *The Ultimate Resource 2*

CHAPTER 5

Erik Brynjolfsson & Andrew McAfee

Do you ever feel like you are living in the future?

"Every day," the authors write in a new preface to this book, "we come across examples of science fiction becoming reality." It must have felt like this, they say, at the start of the Industrial Revolution. On the other hand, there are still millions of people who have simply stopped looking for work, or who are working in jobs way below their potential. We know rapid technological progress improves living standards, but we also know that many people's skills and education are preventing them from adjusting to, and prospering in, the new environment. What to do?

Brynjolfsson and McAfee, business economists at the Massachusetts Institute of Technology (MIT) are among the "techno-optimists" whom Robert J. Gordon criticizes in his book *The Rise and Fall of American Growth* for overplaying the impact of the internet and information technology on living standards. Yet their bestseller, *The Second Machine Age*, subtitled "Work, Progress, and Prosperity in a Time of Brilliant Technologies," is far from naïve. They admit that advancing technological progress brings losers as well as winners, and see the human desire and need for work as forming one of the big debates of the future. *The Second Machine Age* is contemporary popular economics at its best, inviting us to think about the role of technology in our lives and in the world we are creating.

A new machine age

The early part of the book rests on an analysis by anthropologist Ian Morris (*Why The West Rules—For Now*), who highlighted that for most of human history, technological progress was "achingly slow, almost invisible." If technology is viewed as a line on a graph, we virtually flatlined for thousands of years. Then, 200 years ago, the Industrial Revolution (or what Brynjolfsson and McAfee call the "first machine age") meant that for the first time, technology—not politics, religion, or population—drove human progress.

Humanity's new ability to generate and apply huge amounts of mechanical power changed everything.

Now, the authors say, we are in the second machine age, in which "Computers and other digital advances are doing for mental power . . . what the steam engine and its descendants did for muscle power." Surely, they reason, a huge boost to intellectual and data tools will be as important to humanity's advance as was the harnessing of physical power.

This idea, that we are at a turning point where digital and computer technologies will begin to make massive differences to our lives, remains just a belief, but the authors point to rapid progress in a range of areas. Genuinely useful Artificial Intelligence (AI) and the fact that most of the planet will be connected via a common digital network, will combine to have a more transformative effect on economic growth than the Industrial Revolution, they agree.

The innovation debate

"Innovation," wrote Joseph Schumpeter in 1930, "is the outstanding fact in the economic history of capitalist society." But what *kind* of innovation?

In 1987, Nobel-winning economist Robert Solow famously said, "We see the computer age everywhere, except in the productivity statistics." In fact, Brynjolfsson and McAfee note, there always seems to be a substantial lag between the introduction of a technology and increasing productivity across the economy. For example, despite the introduction of electricity to American factories in the 1890s, there was no labor productivity surge for another twenty years. Initially, factories simply replaced steam engines with electrical plant, and maintained the existing layout and processes. Not surprisingly, there wasn't much increase in productivity. In the 1980s Information and Communications Technology (ICT) was still a small part of the economy, and not until the 1990s were there big productivity improvements thanks to its use. To play out successfully, "general purpose technologies" such as electricity and ICT must be combined with new business processes. ICT, for example, has had the biggest effect when used alongside business process innovation such as lean manufacturing, or management concepts such as Total Quality Management and Six Sigma.

Brynjolfsson and McAfee argue that "innovation is not coming up with something big and new, but instead recombining things that already exist."

Computers allow for the radical combination and recombination of ideas, just as the innovations of printing, the library, and universal education did. The driverless car, for instance, is a combination of the traditional car with cheap sensors, computerized maps and GPS systems. The World Wide Web was a combination of a much older TCP/IP data transmission network, a new programming language (HTML) that governed the display of text and images and allowed hyperlinks, and the browser. Each was an innovation in its own right, but put together the effect was revolutionary.

Technology and inequality

Until 1973, a growing economy was like a tide raising all boats, with wages growing across the board. Since then, incomes in the United States and most developed countries have jumped for 10 to 20 percent of the population with advanced skills and education, and fallen or stagnated for the rest.

Why exactly has income inequality increased? While routine tasks are increasingly automated, leaving more less-skilled people out of a job, work such as big data analytics and rapid product development have only increased the need for people with reasoning, creative, or design skills, who are likely to have more education and training in the first place. The most valuable resource in the twenty-first century is not therefore capital, but highly educated and skilled people who can extract the greatest gains from technology.

It could be argued that such an economic environment is fair, because those who have the most positive impact on society are rewarded. Is it a problem if a few people who create things which bring a lot of benefit get fabulously wealthy, if we all gain from their creation? And does widening inequality matter so much, if there is an increasing bounty of low-cost or free goods and services?

The authors do not buy these arguments, for the simple reason that many people are not just losing out in relative terms, but seeing absolute falls in income at the same time as technology races forward. Housing, healthcare and college tuition are each significantly more costly than they used to be, growing by 50 percent between 1990 and 2008 compared to a 20 percent rise in family income. This might not be so bad if there was a lot of social mobility, but America—the so-called land of opportunity—has lower social mobility than the Scandinavian countries, and is about the same as Britain and Italy, Europe's least socially mobile states.

The authors agree with Daron Acemoglu and James A. Robinson (*Why Nations Fail* – see commentary in *50 Politics Classics*) that economic inequality leads to the richest in society "capturing" government to further their own interests, meaning fewer opportunities for others. Rising inequality leads to stagnation and decline which not even the democratizing power of technology can cancel out.

Job prospects in the second machine age

The usual remedy put forth for "technological unemployment" is to provide a "universal wage," "guaranteed income," or "basic income" (a regular transfer payment from government to all citizens, not means-tested), which will ensure that people still have enough money to be consumers and to keep the economy going even if they're not working.

Brynjolfsson and McAfee are opposed to this idea, however, for the simple reason that work provides many psychological benefits (a sense of purpose, pride, and order) beyond earning a living. Joblessness, rather than poverty on its own, is the cause of many social ills. Instead of a universal wage, the authors look to where humans can retain an edge over machines. Picasso said of computers: "But they are useless. They can only give you answers." Computers don't yet know how to ask better questions or do anything that goes beyond the framework of their programming. "We've never seen a truly creative machine, or an entrepreneurial one, or an innovative one," Brynjolfsson and McAfee write. "We've seen software that could create lines of English text that rhymed, but not that could write a true poem. Programs that can write clean prose are amazing achievements, but we've not seen one yet that can figure out what to write about next." It is the *combination* of human ideation and creativity, and superior computer data-crunching, that offers the most exciting advances in all areas. For clues to the future, it is worth recalling what happened to work in the Industrial Revolution. With the advent of motorized agricultural machinery, millions of farm workers were put out of a job, but new technological industries in the cities absorbed their labor power.

That covers "white-collar" occupations; what about more physical work? Moravec's Paradox (after roboticist Hans Moravec) is the surprising fact that computers can do high-level reasoning without huge effort, but the simplest sensorimotor skills need massive computational power. As things stand, it is extremely hard to give robots the perception and mobility that even toddlers have. For the foreseeable future, cleaners, cooks, electricians, plumbers, and hairdressers are secure in their jobs.

Final comments

In 1930, Keynes imagined a time when the "economic problem" was solved, when prosperity provided for everyone to have a house, transport, and money for education, travel, and entertainment. In this society, people might only work 15 hours a week. Keynes failed to see that human wants are endless, creating unlimited markets for goods and services. As what we demand becomes ever more sophisticated—compare a Ford Model T to a Tesla car—so much more thought, design, analysis, and engineering is required. Coming up with new ideas, communicating complex ideas, and understanding things within a larger context, are where humans still have a distinct advantage. Oxford University researchers Frey and Osborne ("The Future of Employment", 2013) predict that up to 47% of US jobs will be automated in the next 20 years (including many white collar ones) due to machine learning and robotics. They may turn out to be an exaggeration. A 2016 study by the Centre for European Economic Research noted that many jobs involve *bundles* of tasks, only some of which can be automated. If you factor in the variety of tasks most jobs require, and the human interaction aspects, it turns out that 9% of jobs are at risk of automation, not 47%.The second machine age may be more human than we think.

Erik Brynjolfsson & Andrew McAfee

Born in 1962, Brynjolfsson has a Masters degree in applied mathematics and decision sciences from Harvard University, and a PhD in managerial economics from the MIT Sloan School of Management. His doctoral thesis was on the effect of technology on work. He has been the Schussel Family Professor of Management at the Sloan School since 2001.

Born in 1967, McAfee has degrees in engineering and management from MIT, and did his PhD at Harvard Business School. He taught at Harvard Business School from 1999 to 2009, and has since been a research scientist at the Center for Digital Business at MIT, and a fellow at Harvard's Berkman Center for Internet and Society. He is a columnist for the Financial Times *and writes a popular blog.*

Brynjolfsson and McAfee are also the authors of the digital book Race Against The Machine: How the Digital Revolution is Accelerating Innovation, Driving Productivity, and Irreversibly Transforming Business and the Economy *(2011).*

2011

23 Things They Don't Tell You About Capitalism

"Understanding that there is no such thing as an objectively defined "free market" is the first step towards understanding capitalism . . . If some markets look free, it is only because we so totally accept the regulations that are propping them up that they become invisible."

"With only a few exceptions, all of today's rich countries, including Britain and the US—the supposed homes of free trade and free market—have become rich through the combinations of protectionism, subsidies and other policies that today they advise the developing countries not to adopt. Free-market policies have made few countries rich so far and will make few rich in the future."

In a nutshell

The capitalism most widely practiced today is an ideological free market variant; compared to the post-Keynesian capitalism of the 1950s–1970s, it is a failure.

In a similar vein

John Maynard Keynes *General Theory of Employment, Interest and Money*
Naomi Klein *The Shock Doctrine*
Karl Marx *Capital*
Hyman Minsky *Stabilizing an Unstable Economy*
Thomas Piketty *Capitalism in the Twenty-First Century*
Karl Polanyi *The Great Transformation*
Dani Rodrik *The Globalization Paradox*

CHAPTER 6

Ha-Joon Chang

Nothing is more important to the advance of disciplines than the separation of fact from ideology, and economics—perhaps surprisingly for a field supposedly built on numbers—has more ideologues than most.

Writing in the wake of the financial crisis, Cambridge University economist Ha-Joon Chang took aim at two notions that had sustained capitalism for the preceding thirty years: that free markets are efficient (because people and business, left to themselves, will allocate resources in the best way); and that they are just (the more productive you are, the better off you will be).

This outlook had led to privatization of state-owned companies and utilities, deregulation of finance and industry, trade liberalization, and lower income taxes and welfare payments. Although these policies would result in "adjustment" for some parties, overall, we were told, everyone would benefit. In fact, Chang says, the opposite happened. Most rich countries that have adopted these measures have seen increased inequality, slower growth, and economic and political instability. In developing countries, the effects have been worse. The truth is, many countries put themselves on the road to economic independence through what free market economists such as Milton Friedman would call socialism: protecting industry, limiting foreign direct investment, running state-owned enterprises, and so on.

Markets aren't "free" or "natural"

There is no such thing as a "free" market, Chang says. All markets are created and have rules and conditions. What constitutes a market is always a *political* definition. Moreover, people lobbying against government involvement nearly always have some private motive to get the market skewed in their favor.

When, in 1819, Britain's Cotton Factory Regulation Act stopped children nine and under from working in the factories, and restricted older children to twelve hours work a day, there was huge opposition. The legislation, many said, went against freedom of contract and freedom of labor. Now, of course, such protections are taken for granted, part of the landscape of markets.

Chang's point is that, over time, it is we as citizens who decide what constitutes a "free" market. The idea that there is natural, free market aside from society or government is a myth. Markets are full of rules which have become almost invisible over time. Stock exchanges are highly regulated, and many countries have extensive legislation on conditions of trade, including product liability, product labeling, and zoning laws which determine where you can set up shop. Wages are usually thought to be up to the free market, when in fact they are often politically determined, because it is government that decides on levels of immigration, and immigration affects the demand for labor. In classical economics, interest rates rise and fall according to market demand for money. In reality, it is central banks, which are political creations, that determine interest rates. If wages, interest rates, and by extension, prices, are all shaped by political factors, the idea that we live in a free-market economy is therefore a fiction.

Free market policies don't make poor countries rich

Britain's first real industry, wool manufacturing, was a classic "infant industry" that involved the copying of technology from the Low Countries, and it was only tariff protection on imports, plus government subsidies, that allowed it to get going in the eighteenth century. This industry paved the way for Britain's nineteenth century industrial revolution, but during its industrial rise, from the 1720s to the 1850s, Britain was one of the most protectionist nations of the era. In was only in the 1860s, when its industry dominated the world, that Britain adopted a free trade stance. Nineteenth century America was also highly protectionist, with import tariffs running at 40-55 percent. It was this high industry protection, Chang says, that transformed "a second-rate agrarian economy dependent on slave labor into the world's greatest industrial power."

Contemporary China has become an economic superpower even though it was highly protectionist for decades; there are still significant restrictions on foreign investment and cross-border flows of capital, and many giant corporations are state-owned. It took forty years of protection and subsidies, Chang notes, for Japan to grow an automobile industry.

Economic orthodoxy says these steps were a mistake, and only their replacement by free market policies could have allowed countries to grow. This is clearly not true for the rise of Britain, America, China, or Japan, so why should it be so for today's developing countries? Chang supplies the surprising fact that their performance has been better (with stable growth and employment) in periods with state-led development compared to periods of market-oriented reform and liberalization. Sub-Saharan Africa had a growth rate of 0.2 percent between 1980 and 2009, when many countries were subject to neoliberal "structural adjustment" programs. In the 1960s and 1970s, in contrast, the cumulative growth rate was 1.6 percent per capita. Latin America grew 3.1 percent in the 1960s and 1970s. Between 1980 and 2009 growth was 1.1 percent.

Protecting young industries makes sense because in a country's early stages of development, weak infrastructure and a small market would otherwise hold them back. In addition, the absence of strong private sector companies often requires the government to kick-start industries and provide the money for large capital projects. Yet aid and loans to developing countries, administered by rich nations, are usually given on the condition that such policies are abandoned. It's a case of "Do as I say, not as I did".

The myth of the "post-industrial" age

In our knowledge-based society, so current thinking goes, manufacturing doesn't matter as much as it did. If they want to do well, developing countries should leapfrog manufacturing and go straight to a service-based economy. India, for instance, should forget manufacturing and become the "office of the world" in the way China has become the factory of the world.

Yet Chang points out that it is difficult to develop a deep service economy without having created a manufacturing one first. Moreover, the consumers of services are usually in the same place where they are created (you don't go overseas to get your hair done), so the scope for exports is limited. And without export income you can't buy technologies from abroad. The other great benefit of manufacturers over services is that making things provides a lot more scope for productivity growth compared to services.

Yet many still believe that deindustrialization is actually a good thing, a sign that actual manufacturing (which can be done more cheaply by countries like China) is being replaced by more high-end activity such as finance, consulting, R&D, design, and computing services. However, in Britain the trade surplus from such services amounts to less than 4 percent of its GDP. In America, service exports account for only 1 percent of GDP. In both cases, services don't make up for a 4 percent deficit in the trade in industrial goods.

With the rare exception of places like the Seychelles which depend on tourism, "no country has so far achieved even a decent (not to speak of high) living standard by relying on services and none will do so in the future", states Chang.

Governments often know better than business

The free-market view is that governments are incompetent when it comes to sponsoring the development of new industries. In fact, Chang says, governments have often picked winners, sometimes in spectacular fashion. True, there have been many "white elephant" highways, steel mills, and vanity projects in poor countries, but there have been plenty of other projects that achieved their purpose of building a national industrial economy.

From the 1970s to the 1990s the Korean government pushed private sector firms into new industries, with the incentive of high tariffs or subsidies, or threats to withdraw loans from state-owned banks. The LG group wanted to enter the textiles business, but the government forced it to make electric cables instead; this intervention laid the foundation of a global electronics business. General Park Chung-Hee, Korea's dictator, threatened the Hyundai company with bankruptcy if it did not enter the shipbuilding industry. It is now one of the biggest shipbuilders globally. According to free-market theory, none of this should have happened, because businesses (being close to their markets) make the best decisions on where to invest, whereas the government is at a remove.

Though governments in most capitalist countries are shy of being seen as "planners" of their economy, they still play a big role in certain areas. Governments fund directly or indirectly 20 to 50 percent of R&D in rich countries, and though free marketeers hate to admit it, most of the areas where the US has a technological lead have been assisted by generous state R&D and military funding. Successful Singapore's state-owned enterprises make up 20 percent of its economy, and the French government retains big stakes in 'strategic' industries that employ a lot of people and need periodic injections of money to buy or develop technology.

Chang does not deny the many failures of government picking winners, but these do not invalidate the fact that government has often picked winners, or that private firms frequently make colossal mistakes. His point is that free market ideology, with its insistence that "government is bad, business is good," can cut off a nation from many options for achieving economic development.

Regulation protects us from ourselves

Herbert Simon, one of the twentieth century's great thinkers on organization, reminded us that the rationality of individuals is limited. Faced with uncertainty and complexity, instead of acting like a computer to crunch the data and spit out the best solution, we actually shrink back and voluntarily restrict our options. This is smart, and provides a model for government's role in regulating finance.

In the wake of the 2008 financial crisis, Federal Reserve chairman Alan Greenspan admitted to a Congressional hearing that it was a mistake to "presume that the self-interest of organizations, specifically banks, is such that they were best capable of protecting . . . shareholders and their equity in the firms." If the smart people did not understand what they were doing, why should we presume that self-interest will result in optimal outcomes? Regulation works, Chang says, not because the government pretends it knows more, but because in a Simonian sense it reduces the "unknown unknowns," catastrophic economic events which arise from individuals or firms pursuing their self-interest without being aware of the consequences.

Stiff regulation or banning of financial instruments might seem extreme, Chang says, but isn't this what governments do all the time with drugs, car safety, aviation safety, and electrical products? The short-term profit-seeking of today's financial system is at odds with the patient investment in firms and infrastructure that countries actually need if they are to prosper.

Education isn't the answer

Richer countries have more educated people, but does that mean their wealth is *because* of their higher levels of education? There is surprisingly little evidence of the link, even in today's "knowledge economy."

Education was *not* the key to the East Asian economic miracle, Chang says. Taiwan developed much faster than the Philippines, for instance, while having lower rates of literacy. And rich Switzerland has the lowest rate among rich countries of school leavers going on to university.

The reality is that lots of education has no "use" in the real world, and even apparently practical subjects such as physics and math are not used that much when people are in the workplace. On-the-job training counts for more, yet if there are few existing companies, laws and institutions to support this, an economy will find it hard to grow. Rather it is "command over technical, organizational, and institutional knowledge," Chang observes, that makes a country rich and developed, and whether its people are organized into "highly productive enterprises"—whether giant ones like Boeing in America or Volkswagen in Germany, or the smaller exporting businesses of Switzerland and Italy.

Final comments

Chang claims his book is not an "anti-capitalist manifesto." He is a believer in the power of the profit motive and sees markets as an "exceptionally effective" machine in achieving social and economic goals. Yet ideological free-market capitalism is just one form of capitalism, and the evidence from the last 30 years is that it hinders growth, increases inequality, and produces more frequent financial crashes. To correct the damage that free-market orthodoxy has done, one of Chang's startling conclusions is that "Government needs to become bigger and more active." He mentions the Scandinavian states who manage to combine larger government and big welfare provision with economic growth.

When you consider the most successful countries, governments, and firms, Chang says, you find that their view of capitalism is nuanced and pragmatic rather than ideological. Any economic theory that sees people and firms as being driven only by self-interest, misses the fact that trust, co-operation, honesty and solidarity are highly valued, and make for more successful societies over the long term. The question running through the book is: Do we want to live in "market states," or be citizens of states that have markets?

Ha-Joon Chang

Born in Seoul, South Korea in 1963, Chang studied economics at Seoul National University. In 1991 he completed his PhD on industrial policy at the University of Cambridge, and has taught economics, political economy, and development studies there ever since.

Chang has been a consultant to several UN organizations, the World Bank, the Asian Investment Bank, and national government agencies in the UK, Canada, South Africa, Ecuador, Venezuela, Mexico, Indonesia, and Singapore. His ideas influenced Rafael Correa, the Ecuadorian President whose administration saw both economic growth and increased social welfare provision. Chang is a senior research associate at the Center for Economic and Policy Research, a Washington DC think tank.

Chang's other books include Economics: A User's Guide *(2014),* Bad Samaritans: The Myth of Free Trade and the Secret History of Capitalism *(2007), and* Kicking Away The Ladder: Development Strategy in Historical Perspective *(2002).*

1988

The Firm, the Market, and the Law

"Markets are institutions that exist to facilitate exchange, that is, they exist in order to reduce the cost of carrying out exchange transactions."

"In my youth it was said that what was too silly to be said may be sung. In modern economics it may be put into mathematics."

In a nutshell

To understand economics, you must understand the role that transaction costs play in shaping firms, markets, and institutions.

In a similar vein

Milton Friedman *Capitalism and Freedom*
Albert O. Hirschman *Exit, Voice, and Loyalty*
Elinor Ostrom *Governing the Commons*
Michael E. Porter *The Competitive Advantage of Nations*

CHAPTER 7

Ronald Coase

If you have ever wondered whether economics offered a long-term career path, consider Ronald Coase. He wrote two of the most cited and influential papers in economics, the first, "The Nature of the Firm" (1937), published when he was only 26, and the second, "The Problem of Social Cost" (1960) when he was 50. Coase won a Nobel Prize when he was 80, and at 102 co-wrote a book on Chinese capitalism.

Coase was that rare economist ready to question every assumption in his discipline. Economics had been strangely remiss in looking in detail at the nature of firms and of markets. Coase looked at both under a microscope. He was also wary of economics trying to make itself into a mathematical science. "In my youth it was said that what was too silly to be said may be sung," he writes, "In modern economics it may be put into mathematics." Each of his papers is short, contains no math, and can be understood by the layperson.

The famous Coase Theorem recognized that in a market system property rights are all-important, and it is the market that should ultimately determine to what use property is put. Generally, it makes the right call. Coase's "'institutional" approach to economics emphasized that individuals and firms thrive or are thwarted by the legal and political environment in which they exist. Regulations and court judgements were for Coase "transaction costs." The only way we could understand an economy and its potential was to account for these costs. Although Coase's thinking transcended left and right, and he was certainly no ideologue, such insights inspired the deregulation revolution of the 1980s, and continue to affect a range of areas including environmental policy. Coase is an example of an economist whose effects on the real world could hardly have been greater.

The Firm, the Market, and the Law contains Coase's most important writings, his own reflections on his work, and rejoinders to his critics.

What is the purpose of markets?

Markets are created not only to facilitate exchange, Coase pointed out, but "to reduce the cost of carrying out exchange transactions."

In Britain, markets and fairs were originally set up by individuals who had obtained permission from the king. Part of the deal was that they would organize security for the event. Nowadays, security for markets is generally provided by the law itself, but the cost of being able to trade in safety is a transaction cost which organized markets reduce.

A perfect market (or something approaching it) and perfect competition, Coase says, requires tight and careful rules and regulations. Economists normally think that a lot of rules lead to imperfect competition, but in fact most rules are designed to *reduce* transaction costs. That is the real purpose of a market. Adam Smith said that sellers have an interest in restricting competition ("narrowing the market"), but they also have an interest in rules that *widen* the market too.

Why do firms exist?

If well-run markets bring together people who want to exchange things, and the mechanism of prices ensures that everything is instantly sellable or buyable at the right price, why do people build islands, "small planned societies'" with their own internal rules, which are protected *from* the market? For Coase, this question of why firms exist was perhaps the most fundamental question of economics.

In orthodox economic theory, a firm was simply "an organization which transforms inputs into outputs," and used the price mechanism of the market to determine what and how much it could produce. Within the firm, though, the price mechanism doesn't apply. Indeed, Coase says, "the distinguishing mark of the firm is the supersession of the price mechanism."

Why would a firm want to insulate itself to some extent from the market and the constant activity of price discovery and price-making? Well, every transaction made on the open market has costs. In theory, production could occur via individuals or entrepreneurs making contracts with each other in a decentralized way. In reality, organizations (firms) will emerge so that the costs of these transactions will become less than making them on the open market. Companies exist, Coase realized, primarily to lower the cost of doing business. Indeed, he ventured that you could easily work out how large a company would grow (in terms of number of employees) by identifying the cost of its transactions. When that firm reached a point where it saved no more money and time by keeping operations "in-house," it would let the open market do the work.

One of the fascinating aspects of today's large technology companies is the small number of employees they have compared to their huge market value and their numbers of users and customers. Even their most important products or decisions can be determined by vast amounts of user data and feedback. The twenty-first century will bring Coase's question about the *raison d'être* of firms even more into focus. What do they do which absolutely cannot be done by an atomized open market in which, thanks to technology, there are low or zero transaction costs?

What is a social cost and what is a social benefit?

Coase's work on social cost, or what British economist Arthur Cecil Pigou called "externalities," is fascinating. He defines the problem of social cost as "those actions of business firms which have harmful effects on others," such as a factory belching smoke over a neighboring suburb. The conventional view in economics is that the firm's owner should be held responsible for the damage to people's health caused by the smoke, or be subject to a tax on the factory's emissions which can indirectly pay for the damage it causes to the health of society. The law can also ensure that factories of this type are not allowed to be built next to where people live.

For Coase, none of these ways of dealing with social costs are satisfactory, because of a wrong assumption that the factory is *inflicting* harm on the local community. Could it also be said that the residential area around the factory is inflicting harm on the factory's owner, and by extension, society itself? After all, if no factories are allowed to be built where they are needed, won't there be a social cost that is at least as harmful as the smoke? We must accept that it is a consequence of living in a society that the goods and services we all use must be created somewhere, and also that people have a right to enjoy their asset or property. "Nothing could be more 'anti-social,'" Coase writes, "than to oppose any action which causes harm to anyone." A person living near a train station should expect some noise, soot and vibration as a normal part of its operation, and someone buying a house near an airport should not complain of noise.

An example Coase gives is the noise and vibrations from a sweets factory that is affecting the work of a doctor next door. Should the confectioner be shut down? Perhaps, but who is to say whose product should have precedence, the doctor's ability to see patients or the confectioner's ability to make sweets? Society demands both.

Coase criticizes Arthur Pigou, who assumed that when anything went wrong in the economy, it was up to government to intervene. Many government enterprises, laws and institutions themselves create social costs, but of course government itself tends to see them as having a favorable social benefit. In general, Coase argues, the costs of regulation and court decisions on the productive capacity of nation are too high, and courts usually don't understand the economic consequence of their decisions, which often amount to a sledgehammer to crack a peanut. Taking matters to court is a high transaction cost that drags down the productive power of an economy, when firms, individuals and organizations could be making voluntary bargains which lead to resources being valued properly. But if courts *are* the final arbiter, it is the responsibility of government to make property rights very clear in the first place.

Strike a bargain, hold an auction

Social costs are not just the possible harmful by-products of production, but the costs of unemployment and lower wages. It is hard to imagine a taxation system being so perfect, or a judge so wise, that it can decide exactly where these costs and benefits lie. It is more likely that an individual enterprise, and the people or communities affected by its production, are clear on the costs and benefits to each, and can therefore can come to some agreement (outside of government or the law) in which all can benefit, and which leaves a community or a country richer overall.

In 1959, Coase published a now-famous paper in the *Journal of Law and Economics*, "The Federal Communications Commission," on the Commission's practice of awarding frequencies to firms or organizations whom the government considered met "public interest" criteria. Coase made the radical suggestion that the process best be left to the market, with frequencies sold to the highest bidder. His idea was opposed or ridiculed by experts, the broadcasting industry, and lawmakers, and even Milton Friedman took issue with part of his argument. Such vested interests were only overcome in the 1990s, and today auctioning frequencies is considered the best means of allocating the resource. Coase once quipped that an economist who is able, through an idea or observation, to postpone by a week a government program which wastes $100 million a year, has through that idea earned his salary for the rest of his life.

Final comments

In the succinct nature of his style and his powerful reasoning, Coase's writings are more akin to those of a philosopher who happens to be focusing on economic life, than the scribbling of a regular economist. What links his work over a long life is one phrase: transaction costs.

Most economic models barely took account of such costs, yet they were very much part of operating in the real world. In reality, Coase argued, the optimal allocation of resources in a society is not down to some complex formula of taxation or subsidies, and neither should it be dependent on the wisdom of politicians or judges. Rather, such optimality can come from bargains made between firms and between individuals. Indeed, the Coase Theorem (actually coined by George Stigler, not Coase himself), that "when there are zero transaction costs, negotiations will lead to an agreement which maximizes wealth," assumed that government is not required to be part of the wealth-creating equation. A good example of a Coasian bargain is one struck between miners and aboriginal communities in Northern Australia: in return for access to minerals, the native owners of the land get royalties, jobs, training, and infrastructure. In other places, fracking has been outlawed before stakeholders have been given the chance to come to some bargain which may benefit both. Coase's larger point was that we still think government knows best, when usually it is people who do.

Ronald Coase

Born in 1910, Coase grew up in London. His father was a telegraphist. As a boy he was made to wear leg irons and was enrolled at a local school for "defectives", but his natural intelligence won him a place in a good grammar school. At the London School of Economics (LSE) he was awarded a traveling scholarship and chose to go to the United States, where he visited firms and factories to find out how and why they were organized. Through his twenties Coase held teaching positions in Scotland, Liverpool, and London, and when war broke out was assigned to do statistical work for the British government. Afterwards, he returned to the LSE, teaching and doing research on public utilities including the Post Office, and on broadcasting regulation.

At 40, Coase moved to the United States and the University of Virginia, and when not teaching studied the Federal Communications Commission. In 1964 he took up a position at the University of Chicago, and in 1991 was awarded a Nobel Prize in Economics. In 2012, Coase published, with co-author Wang Ning, How China Became Capitalist. *He died in 2013.*

2014

GDP: A Brief But Affectionate History

"Economic growth is essential. It is one of the key contributors to our well-being, although clearly not the only one. It is for this reason politically vital. Without economic growth, there would not be enough jobs to keep the unemployment rate down to a tolerable level. It is not possible to redistribute incomes unless the economic pie is growing. Democracy itself is more fragile when growth halts. 'No growth,' desired by some, is for the rich. There is, for now, no alternative to using GDP to measure economic growth."

In a nutshell

Economic growth is not everything, but it supports the existence of many highly-valued social goods, and so it is crucial that we measure it.

In a similar vein

Erik Brynjolfsson & Andrew McAfee *The Second Machine Age*
Robert J. Gordon *The Rise and Fall of American Growth*
John Maynard Keynes *The General Theory of Employment, Interest, and Money*
E. F. Schumacher *Small Is Beautiful*
Julian Simon *The Ultimate Resource 2*

CHAPTER 8

Diane Coyle

For decades, Gross Domestic Product, or GDP, has been the standard measure of national prosperity. The US Department of Commerce described the measure as "One of the great inventions of the twentieth century."

Diane Coyle's book is the story of how GDP came to be so central to national economic life. Coyle, a UK economist with a research focus on technology, notes in the preface to a new edition that she didn't expect the topic would interest so many people. That it does tells us that, despite the many criticisms, GDP is still a potent symbol of economic power. While significant chunks of the book are devoted to the limitations of GDP, the subtitle, "A brief *but affectionate* history" gives away her final assessment that the measure was a big advance in economics, that it can be refined, and that the economic growth that GDP does its best to measure is still what funds so many of the social goods we hold dear.

The rise of a statistic

GDP was a product of World War Two, Coyle notes, but its roots go back further. In the 1660s William Petty, an English official and early economist, was asked to make an assessment of the nation's income, expenditure, population, land, and assets. The purpose was to test England's ability to finance the next war from taxes. His assessment was the start of a system of national statistics (the words statistics and state have the same origin), giving Britain over a century's head start on France.

Writing in *The Wealth of Nations* in 1776, Adam Smith saw the national income as simply being all physical assets minus national debt. Smith made the distinction between productive labor (which went towards the making of physical things of value, and so could be counted as an investment), and unproductive labor (such as the work of domestic servants, which were a cost which did nothing but keep a lord from working). A century later, Alfred Marshall was not so pernickety, arguing that all kinds of services should be included as wealth.

In the 1920s and 1930, national accounting reached new sophistication in Britain, with quarterly statements of income and expenditure and the state of the government's finances. The Great Depression only increased the demand for such detailed statistics, as governments wanted to know how best to respond to changing circumstances.

In the United States, Simon Kuznets spearheaded a similar statistical revolution with the National Bureau of Economic Research. President Roosevelt wanted a detailed picture of economic output during the Depression, and Kuznets' first report, covering 1929 to 1932, showed the economy had shrunk by a half. Surprisingly, the report was a bestseller, and enabled Roosevelt to justify big policy measures to get the country out of its economic hole.

When the young economist John Maynard Keynes was asked to help prepare Britain for war, he set about improving the data available with a new statistics agency. It is no exaggeration to say, Coyle writes, that Britain's national statistics helped ready it for, and win, the war. After World War Two, the United Nations developed international standards (the "System of National Accounts") for measuring national accounts, which were used in assessing the need for aid to European countries under the Marshall Plan.

The post-war predominance of Keynesian economics, which involved greater intervention of the government in the economy, was a perfect fit for the increasingly sophisticated science of national accounting. After all, governments would only be able to regulate demand in the economy in an intelligent way if they knew what was actually happening in it. Advanced econometric modelling allowed policy-makers to see what effect an increase or decrease in spending would have on the economy—whether, say, extra money from a tax cut would be spent or saved and therefore whether it was worth doing. British economist Bill Phillips even built a machine—not software, a physical machine—in which colored liquids simulated the flows of income and wealth in an economy.

Measuring GDP is not simple, not even in its basics. For instance, it is an arbitrary judgment whether an item constitutes a cost, is income, or can be framed as an investment; and GDP can be measured in no less than three ways: national income, national expenditure, and national output. The interesting fact about GDP is how it describes the *circular* nature of economic activity. As Coyle explains it, "One consumer's spending is a business's sales revenue—when added up for the whole economy, those corresponding flows have to balance." In other words, the sum of all income has to come to the same amount as all spending.

Changes made to the way a country weights the component elements of a representative basket of goods can dramatically change its real (i.e. adjusted for inflation) GDP figures. For example, Kenya revised its GDP figure up

25 percent overnight, simply by taking more account of the role of its fast-growing mobile technology sector, compared to other sectors in the economy. Such revision can make a big difference to the perception of a country, even if it changes nothing about the underlying economy. When Ghana did a similar revision in 2010, its GDP jumped 60 percent, turning it from a "low-income country" to a "low-middle-income" country at a stroke.

Not the measure of all things

Coyle's point is that GDP is not simply an objective tool but carries political and social baggage, saying something about the what governments and people value most. The following is hardly an exhaustive summary of its perceived failings, but gives a taste:

- GDP doesn't measure environmental values such as clean rivers and lakes, unpolluted air, forests, good soil, or even non-rising sea levels and stable temperatures. If it doesn't measure such natural resource wealth, how will policy be made to preserve and enhance that wealth?
- GDP doesn't measure innovation very well, such as the progression from unsafe tallow candles or kerosene lanterns to the powerful, safe, and cheap electric light bulb, or the shift in computing over a few short decades from expensive mainframe computers to powerful and inexpensive laptops and smartphones for all. GDP measures changes in the prices of goods over time, but not the increase in their quality and variety, and the fantastic degree of customization available today on many products, which reduces waste.
- As GDP measures only activity that happens in markets that have prices, it can't tell us much about well-being or social welfare. For example, growing my own vegetables is surely a gain for me, but national accounts will see it only as a loss to vegetable growers and supermarkets. And how do you measure the value of owning your own home instead of renting?
- GDP is good for measuring "the mass production of things," but doesn't measure a service economy very well. For instance, GDP statistics take little account of the "sharing economy" and the rise of services like Uber car-sharing and Airbnb room rental.
- GDP doesn't measure unpaid activity that contributes to the economy, such as housework. As economists like to put it, "A widower who marries his former housekeeper is reducing GDP since he is no longer paying her a wage." Nor does GDP measure the having and rearing of a child, even though that child will become a contributor to the economy.
- GDP doesn't measure how sustainable an economy is, for instance whether

it is in bubble territory and may soon implode. It assumes that all financial services are contributing to the economy, when in fact—as came out in 2007–08—many financial products were undermining real growth and making the economy more unstable.

- GDP only measures the provision of goods and services and their use, omitting the reasons for their use. A terrible natural disaster like Hurricane Katrina somehow becomes a plus in terms of consumption because thousands of homes have to be rebuilt and expensive new flood defences erected.
- GDP doesn't tell us much about the distribution of growth among different people or groups in society, and so doesn't tell us whether inequality is increasing or decreasing.
- Informal, cash-based, or illegal activities can be a big part of a country's GDP, but even if a country wants to make detailed statistics of the sex and drugs trades, they can be hard to measure.
- Human capital (the depth of education and training) and social capital (the quality of political and other institutions such as legal frameworks) are crucial to the future growth of economies, but are not easy to measure in terms of GDP.

For critics such as Amartya Sen (*Development As Freedom*), a nation's GDP numbers matter less than factors including citizens' *access to resources* including food, health care and education, the existence of infrastructure such as roads and electricity, and the presence of political freedoms like women's rights and democracy.

Mahbub Ul Haq, a Pakistani development economist, developed the UN's Human Development Index (HDI), which measures poverty and welfare. When you compare the list of countries by GDP to the HDI there is broad similarity, Coyle notes, but they are not the same—and perhaps for good reason, for surely what is most important in a poor country is not its rate of GDP growth, but whether it is successful in housing, feeding, and educating its people. Interestingly, although the gap between the world's richer countries and the poorer in terms of income has widened, measures such as life expectancy and infant mortality have narrowed. This should tell us that GDP figures are not everything.

What's the alternative?

Many have argued that countries should be measuring, instead of GDP, "Gross National Happiness" (as Bhutan famously does). For Coyle, such ideas are a bit of a red herring, because while GDP growth can increase without limit, happiness tends to go up and down within a surprisingly narrow band. What's more important, surely, is that we can be made miserable if we lose our job thanks to an economic downturn. By the same token, if the economy does well for many years, enabling us to earn good wages and buy a house, we will be happier. Seen this way, GDP *is* more important than many critics give it credit for, as a measure of well-being, even if its official purpose is to measure production.

In terms of alternatives to GDP, what makes sense to Coyle is the "dashboard" approach, in which a country publishes a range of measures and indicators on well-being and prosperity.

Final comments

There is no sign, Coyle notes, that such alternatives are replacing the "one big number" of GDP that makes it so reportable in the news as an apparent measure of national status and well-being. This is surely because, although GDP may not be the best measure for a range of things, including innovation, quality, intangible services, or productivity growth, it is still the best one we have of change in the economy: in other words, whether things are moving forward, stagnating, or declining. And it is economic growth which is crucial for the provision of a range of social goods and the maintenance of political institutions. As we know from countries who fall into economic stagnation, such goods easily become vulnerable.

Diane Coyle

Coyle was born in 1961 and grew up in Lancashire, England. Following grammar school she studied politics, philosophy, and economics at Oxford University, then completed an MA and PhD in economics at Harvard University. She worked as an economist in the UK Treasury from 1985 to 1986, and in the 1990s was an editor for Investor's Chronicle, *and economics editor of* The Independent.

Coyle is a professor of economics at the University of Manchester, is a Fellow of the Office for National Statistics, and runs a consultancy, Enlightenment Economics. She was a member of Britain's Competition Commission, and since 2011 has been vice-chair of the BBC Trust, the governing body of the British Broadcasting Corporation. In 2009 she received an OBE from the Queen for services to economics.

Other books include The Economics of Enough *(2011),* The Soulful Science *(2007), and* Sex, Drugs and Economics *(2002).*

1985

Innovation and Entrepreneurship

"Entrepreneurship rests on a theory of economy and society. The theory sees change as normal and indeed as healthy. And it sees the major task in society—and especially in the economy—as doing something different rather than doing better what is already being done. That is basically what Say, two hundred years ago, meant when he coined the term entrepreneur. It was intended as a manifesto and as a declaration of dissent: the entrepreneur upsets and disorganizes."

In a nutshell

Management of entrepreneurship and innovation is as important to economics as traditional factors such as technology, capital, labor, and land.

In a similar vein

William J. Baumol *The Microtheory of Innovative Entrepreneurship*
Joseph Schumpeter *Capitalism, Socialism, and Democracy*

CHAPTER 9

Peter Drucker

Peter Drucker's book starts with a mystery: why, in the American economy from 1965 to 1985, despite inflation and oil shocks, recessions and major job losses in certain industries and government, there had been huge jobs growth? The jobs—40 million of them—had not been created by large corporations or government, but mostly in small and medium-sized businesses. Most people explained the growth in one expression: 'high-tech'.

In fact, only 5 or 6 million of the new positions came from the technology field. The key "technology" driving jobs growth, according to Drucker, was not widgets and gadgets, but entrepreneurial *management*. Management, or how things can be done better, is best appreciated as a "social technology," as much as a discipline like engineering or medicine.

Over 30 years on from its publication, *Innovation and Entrepreneurship* is still the landmark work on a subject that, before Drucker, had had little real analysis. In his field, Drucker always seemed to be years, if not decades, ahead of anyone, and the book was, perhaps remarkably, the first to treat the subject in a systematic, non-sensational way. Drucker began teaching innovation and entrepreneurship in the mid-1950s, so it represents three decades' testing of his ideas. He was unusual among business gurus for working with people in all types of organizations including unions, girl scout bodies, science labs, churches, universities, and relief agencies. His message was: wherever you work, there is huge scope for changing how you do things that can make a massive difference.

At the beginning, there was the entrepreneur

"The entrepreneur," Frenchman J. B. Say said in 1800, is one who simply "shifts economic resources out of an area of lower and into an area of higher productivity and greater yield."

This was the original definition—and the best, Drucker maintains. Entrepreneurship is not a "personality trait"; it is a feature to be observed in the actions of people or institutions. Entrepreneurs in health, education, or business work basically the same way. Essentially, they do not just do something better, but do it *differently*.

Classical economics says that economies tend towards equilibrium—they "optimize", which results in incremental growth over time. But the nature of the entrepreneur is to "upset and disorganize". He or she is a wild card generating wealth through the process economist Joseph Schumpeter described as "creative destruction." This involves dealing with uncertainty and with the unknown, and having the ability to exploit or respond intelligently to change. It is a misconception, Drucker says, to think that everyone who starts a new business is being entrepreneurial. People do take a risk in opening a shop or a franchise, but they are not really creating anything new, not creating a new type of value for the customer.

The risk myth

Drucker asks why entrepreneurship has the reputation of being very risky, when its purpose is simply to shift resources from where they yield less, to where they yield more? In fact, it is less risky than just "doing the same thing better"; in following this course it is easy to totally miss out on new opportunities and run an enterprise into the shoals without noticing. Embracing change and assiduously trying out different things is actually the best way to invest resources. He points to the amazingly successful record of constantly innovating high-tech companies—Bell Lab, IBM, 3M (today, you would say Apple)—to see that this is true. Entrepreneurship is only risky, he observes, when so-called entrepreneurs "violate elementary and well-known rules." Entrepreneurship is not risky when it is systematic, managed, and purposeful.

Entrepreneurship can exist in large organizations, and in fact Drucker says such organizations must become entrepreneurial if they are to have long-term futures. General Electric in America and the retailer Marks and Spencer in the UK are both big companies which have strong records of creating new value.

How to be an innovator

According to Drucker, innovation is ". . . whatever changes the wealth-producing potential of already existing resources."

The best innovations can be alarmingly simple, and often have little to do with technology or inventions. For example, there was nothing technically remarkable about creating a metal container that could be easily offloaded from a truck onto a ship, but the advent of container shipping as a standardized *system* of moving things around the globe was an innovation that quadrupled world trade.

Many of the greatest innovations are some kind of social value creation, such as insurance, the modern hospital, buying by installment, or the textbook. Drucker suggests that science and technology are actually the least promising of all the sources of innovation, generally taking the most time to realize any benefits, and costing the most. In reality, anything that takes advantage of an unexpected change in society or a market is actually quicker, easier, or more likely to result in success. The entrepreneur is on the lookout for:

- "The unexpected": an unexpected success, failure, or event (see below).
- Incongruities: between things as they ought or are said to be—and how they actually are.
- Problems with an existing process for which no one has provided a solution.
- Changes in how an industry or market operates that takes everyone by surprise.
- Demographic (population) changes.
- Changes in "perception, mood or meaning".

The unexpected success

Drucker includes several fascinating examples of the "unexpected success", and the extent to which those involved were able to take advantage:

- Macy's, the New York department store, did poorly for several years because it considered itself primarily a fashion store, and was downplaying the growing effect of appliance sales on its bottom line. To the company's directors, these sales were an "embarrassing success". Only later, after it had accepted the place of appliance sales as a bona fide part of its image and range, did the store again prosper.
- IBM and Univac initially made computers aimed at the scientific market. Both were surprised by the interest from business users. IBM steamed ahead, though, when it "lowered itself" to sell to the business market.
- The big American steel companies, used to gargantuan steel-making complexes requiring huge investment, did not invest in the new type of "mini mill", even though they were throwing away cash and profits, because it was not "how things were done".

Changing your whole direction to take account of an unexpected success requires humility. If you are a company that has staked its reputation on a particular quality product, but a cheaper, less grand product has booming sales, it is difficult not to view it as a threat, because, as Drucker puts it, "The unexpected success is a challenge to management's judgment."

Presaging Clayton Christensen's work on disruptive innovation, Drucker notes that industries change because "newcomers", "outsiders" and "second raters" are willing to create new products or change old ones that segment the market. They see niches in which the existing players either are not interested, or in which they do not see the market potential.

The customer is everything

Most people associate innovation with the "bright idea", like the clothes zip or the ballpoint pen. But Drucker notes that barely one in five hundred such "bright ideas" ever cover the costs of their development. It is only when innovation meets the market through the catalyst of entrepreneurial management that you start to create things of great value.

For example, De Havilland, the British company, produced the first passenger jet plane, but Boeing and Douglas took the industry lead because they created ways for airlines to finance such expensive purchases. DuPont did not just invent Nylon. It created new markets for its product in women's hosiery and underwear, and automobile tires. The innovator must figure out the market and system of delivery for their product, or the markets will be taken away from them.

In openness to new innovations, conventional wisdom is often wrong. The King of Prussia predicted failure for railroads, because, he asserted, "no one will pay good money to get from Berlin to Potsdam in one hour when he can ride his horse in one day for free." You can't do market research on people's reactions to things which don't yet exist. In this sense, innovation will always be a risk, but becomes less risky when you remain open about how, and by whom, your innovation will be used.

Good innovations are very focused, Drucker observes, not trying to do many things, but just one thing extremely well. They are not too clever, and can be used by ordinary people. They attract the comment, "Why wasn't this done before?" David Ricardo once said, "Profits are not made by differential cleverness, but by differential stupidity." Successful products or services are those which allow their users not to have to think, saving effort, money, and time. A good example is the disposable razor developed by King Gillette. Prior to it, shaving was a time-consuming and difficult business best left to barbers—if you could afford them. People do not buy products, they buy what the product can do for them.

Final comments

Innovation and Entrepreneurship concludes with Drucker's noting that the welfare state had been with us for over a century, but that the burden it had put on wealth producers meant it would not be around for long. He then wonders: Is it being replaced by the Entrepreneurial Society? In most countries today, entrepreneurialism is more than a fad; there are university programs, foundations, and policies focused on creating a new generation of wealth creators, and managerial economics is a field in its own right. Drucker died in 2005, but he saw the future clearly, putting flesh on Joseph Schumpeter's insight about the essentially creative–destructive nature of capitalism, which unlike other forms of political economy puts the management of innovation and entrepreneurship at its center.

Peter Drucker

Drucker was born in Vienna in 1909. His father was a civil servant in the Austro-Hungarian empire. After leaving school he went to study in Germany, obtaining a doctorate in public and international law at Frankfurt University. He worked as a journalist in London before moving to the United States in 1937, and became an American citizen in 1943.

From 1950 to 1971 Drucker was a business professor at New York University, and in 1971 was appointed Clarke Professor of Social Science and Management at Claremont Graduate University in California, a position he kept until his death. In 2002, in his 90s, Drucker was awarded the Presidential Medal of Freedom by George W. Bush.

He wrote 39 books and was also a columnist for the Wall Street Journal *from 1975 to 1995. His 1946 book* Concept of the Corporation, *based on a study of the inner workings of the General Motors Corporation, made him well known. Other titles include* The Practice of Management *(1954),* The Effective Executive *(1966), and* Post-Capitalist Society *(1993).*

2008

The Ascent of Money

"Poverty is not the result of rapacious financiers exploiting the poor. It has much more to do with the lack of financial institutions, with the absence of banks, not their presence."

"Far from being a 'monster that must be put back in its place' . . . financial markets are like the mirror of mankind, revealing every hour of every working day the way we value ourselves and the resources of the world around us. It is not the fault of the mirror if it reflects our blemishes as clearly as our beauty."

In a nutshell

Finance has been the crucial ladder in the making of the modern world. All ladders are precarious, but without them it is hard to build anything.

In a similar vein

J. K. Galbraith *The Great Crash 1929*
Benjamin Graham *The Intelligent Investor*
Michael Lewis *The Big Short*
Robert Shiller *Irrational Exuberance*
Joseph Stiglitz *The Euro*

CHAPTER 10

Niall Ferguson

In 2007, Lloyd Blankfein, the head of Goldman Sachs, took home $68 million in salary, bonus and stock awards. In the same year, the income of the average American was $34,000. Goldman's revenues of $46 billion were greater than the GDPs of over a hundred countries.

Such facts, says Harvard historian Niall Ferguson, tell us that "planet finance" is several times larger than the real economy of planet Earth, and at least as important as the production of goods and services. Throughout history, people have despised financiers on the basis that they seem like parasites on the "real" economy of agriculture and manufacturing. And because financial crises have happened so often, the financial world seems to be the cause of poverty, not a contributor to prosperity.

It is easy to have been led to the conclusion that finance is the enemy of humankind, Ferguson writes in *The Ascent of Money*, but this would be wrong. The book's title is a play on Jacob Bronowski's *The Ascent of Man*, a history of scientific progress that became a popular television series (as would Ferguson's book). Bronowski observed that civilization would not have been possible without the rise of money and financial innovation, including debt and credit. The Italian Renaissance was facilitated by advanced banking and a bond market, while corporate finance powered the Dutch and British Empires. The United States grew and grew in the twentieth century thanks in no small part to insurance, mortgage, finance, and consumer credit. "Behind each great historical phenomenon," Ferguson writes, "there lies a financial secret."

Built by bonds

One of the great innovations of early medieval Italy was the bond, used to finance wars among the Italian states. "After the creation of credit by banks," Ferguson writes, "the birth of the bond was the second great revolution in the ascent of money."

A bond is simply a way for governments to borrow money from citizens, paying them back some interest in return. The funds can be used for productive things, like investments in roads, schools, and hospitals, or to create armies and prosecute military campaigns. The nineteenth century's biggest bank, the house of Rothschild, rose on the back of the bond market and its success in financing war. The rise of the Rothschilds saw a transition from wealth being based on land and aristocracy to a newer, higher-yielding and more liquid form of wealth centered around bonds. This paper wealth allowed the owners of securities to live where they liked, and increased the importance of cities as the place where the rich wanted to be. The new wealth based on money and paper undermined old elites and created a new social order.

Bond markets are powerful because they are the judges of a country's creditworthiness, determining the interest rates it will have to pay investors and the cost of its credit. When governments debase currencies by simply printing more money (as the German state did in the Weimar Republic to pay its debts), they render government bonds pretty much worthless because interest payments lose their value. Thus a whole bond-owning class (such as wealthier Germans in the 1920s) could see their incomes and fortunes dry up. Bondholders can also lose their money through governments defaulting on their sovereign debt to external lenders and bondholders, as Russia did in 1998, and Argentina in 2001.

Despite such calamities, bonds are as popular as ever. Big pension funds have to put their funds somewhere, and bonds seem more stable than company stocks. Bonds are one of the great financial innovations because everyone wins (most of the time): governments can finance nation-building efforts and the expenses of the state (through a combination of borrowing and taxes), and citizens get a fixed income in an uncertain world.

A piece of the action

After the invention of banking and the rise of the bond market, the modern, limited-liability "joint-stock" company was another crucial step in the ascent of money. It allowed many people to take a stake in big, risky ventures (such as financing a fleet of ships sailing to the Dutch East Indies to acquire spices), yet it limited the downside. If things went belly-up, you lost only your stake, not personal wealth like your house.

The rise of stock markets allowed people to take arms-length stakes in a number of companies, thus reducing the risk that their wealth would be swept away by one errant boss or ill-judged venture. Stock markets allow individuals to get a piece of the growth in new industries, and be part of the wider dynamism of their national economy. The difference between investing in stocks and bonds is well-justified, since by buying a stock you have a stake in a profit-making enterprise, whereas a bond depends on a government remaining financially solvent and inflation staying low. Of course there are risks in investing in stocks (for which there is an "equity risk premium" built into stock prices), but they provide a lot more potential upside than bonds.

That is, of course, over the long run, taking into account the failures of individual companies and stock bubbles and busts. Ferguson includes long sections on the Mississippi land bubble of the eighteenth century, the 1929 stock market crash, the tech bubble of the 1990s and the financial crisis of 2007.

Are you insured?

Insurance is among the great financial innovations, and Ferguson tells its fascinating story.

Early forms of insurance were little more than gambling, but a science of risk evolved, including probability theory and actuarial mathematics. The first modern insurance fund was created by two Church of Scotland ministers, Robert Wallace and Alexander Webster, and a mathematician, Colin Maclaurin, who were motivated by the penury of wives and children left behind when a minister died prematurely. Their "Scottish Ministers' Widows' Fund" would take in premiums and invest them, and the widows and orphans would be paid out in annuities from the fund's returns. What became Scottish Widows (still running today as a life insurance provider managing over £100 billion) became the model for all funds insuring against premature death. Within a couple of decades, similar funds were set up around Britain and America, and by 1815 it was even possible for soldiers to insure their lives so that wives and children would not be left destitute by war. Being insured became a mark of middle-class stability.

However, as only the better off could afford insurance, and as the voting rights extended to more and more of the population, pressure grew on governments to offer lower-cost schemes to protect against illness and unemployment. The first social insurance legislation was passed in Germany in the 1880s by Otto von Bismarck, providing an old-age state pension. Britain copied it in 1908 with its own means-tested pension for those over 70, followed by the 1911 National Health Insurance Act. The Beveridge Report of 1942 called for the establishment of national compulsory schemes for social insurance so that ill-health and unemployment would no long carry terror and stigma. The rationale for the state's role was that private insurers were not willing to carry many risks, compulsory schemes saved lots of money on advertising and sales campaigns, and the huge numbers of people signed up meant that economies of scale could be exploited. Yet as time passed the welfare state became a right citizens expected, whatever the cost. Today, many countries are beset with a combination of rapidly aging populations and unfunded pension and medical liabilities. Yet thanks to insurance (private and state) in difficult times we no longer face the terrible choices of our Victorian ancestors, such as the workhouse or the debtor's prison.

'Safe as Houses'

The modern house mortgage is actually quite a new innovation. In 1920s America, for instance, homes mortgages were much less common, and if you could get one they lasted only four or five years. You paid only the interest each month, then one balloon payment of the whole capital outstanding when the mortgage ended. When the Great Depression hit, many banks simply withdrew their loans, and foreclosures happened at a rate of a thousand a day.

Franklin D. Roosevelt's New Deal wisely included measures for greater housing affordability to head off the electoral gains being made by socialists. He set up the Home Owners' Loan Corporation for the refinancing of mortgages and lengthening the terms of mortgages up to 15 years. His encouragement of Savings and Loans mutual associations helped people get on the property ladder, and he established federal deposit insurance to protect people's savings.

All this government underwriting of the American mortgage market meant that, particularly after World War Two, home ownership and house-building soared—but not for everyone: areas of American cities identified as "black" by lenders were considered uncreditworthy, and African Americans, if they could get a mortgage, sometimes had to pay 8 percent more than whites in the same city. In 1968 further federal corporations ("Ginnie Mae" and "Freddie Mac") were set up to end such injustices, and also helped poor white people and veterans to become homeowners. For the most part they succeeded.

Ferguson argues that the English-speaking world has a particular passion for property, which has made countries including the UK, US, Australia, and Canada into genuine property-owning democracies. However, things change. When Ferguson was writing, in 2008, the US home ownership rate was 68 percent. In 2016 it had dropped to 63 percent. In the UK in 2008, home ownership was 73 percent of the population. Today it is 64 percent.

These falls notwithstanding, it is worth recalling that for most of human history the ownership of property was something reserved for the aristocratic elite. The fact that, with a combination of a job, savings and family help, most people will end up as homeowners is a real advance. We have much to thank modern mortgage financing for.

Final comments

Ferguson wrote the final lines of the book in April 2008, and so the strength of the financial crisis and likely recession tempered somewhat the book's theme of the civilizing power of finance. Yet even big financial catastrophes, in his mind, don't contradict the good that financial innovation has done. In places like the East End of Glasgow (the city where he grew up), many people lack access to proper banking and credit, and so are forced into the grip of loan sharks (and, increasingly, online payday loan firms that charge exorbitant rates of interest). His point is that poverty is most usually to be found where there is an *absence* of financial institutions and services, not because they're present.

Niall Ferguson

Born in 1964 in Glasgow, Ferguson attended the Glasgow Academy, a private school, before winning a scholarship to Magdalen College, Oxford. He obtained a degree in History in 1985, followed by a DPhil in 1989.

Ferguson is currently the Laurence A. Tisch Professor of History at Harvard University and a Senior Fellow of the Hoover Institution, Stanford University. His fourteen books include The House of Rothschild *(1998),* The Cash Nexus: Money and Power in the Modern World, 1700–2000 *(2001),* Empire: How Britain Made the Modern World *(2003),* Civilization: The West and the Rest *(2011),* The Great Degeneration: How Institutions Decay and Economies Die *(2013), and* Kissinger: 1923–1968: The Idealist *(2016). Ferguson is married to Ayan Hirsi Ali, the Somali-born activist, writer, and former Netherlands politician.*

1962

Capitalism and Freedom

"The great advances of civilization . . . have never come from centralized government . . . Newton and Leibnitz; Einstein and Bohr; Shakespeare, Milton, and Pasternak; Whitney, McCormick, Edison, and Ford; Jane Addams, Florence Nightingale, and Albert Schweitzer; no one of these opened new frontiers in human knowledge and understanding, in literature, in technical possibilities, or in the relief of human misery in response to governmental directives. Their achievements were the product of individual genius, or strongly held minority views, of a social climate permitting variety and diversity."

In a nutshell

The free market, not government, ensures protection of individual rights and standards of quality, and delivers extraordinary prosperity.

In a similar vein

Ronald Coase *The Firm, the Market, and the Law*
Friedrich Hayek *The Use of Knowledge in Society*
Naomi Klein *The Shock Doctrine*
Ludwig von Mises *Human Action*
Ayn Rand *Capitalism: The Unknown Ideal*
Adam Smith *The Wealth of Nations*

CHAPTER 11

Milton Friedman

Capitalism and Freedom, a major work of twentieth century economics and political philosophy, opens controversially.

Milton Friedman asserts that John F. Kennedy's famous statement in his inaugural address as US president—"Ask not what your country can do for you—ask what you can do for your country," was not worthy of the role of an individual in a free society.

Government, he writes, should neither be the patron of an individual, nor should that person consider themselves a servant of the government. In a real democracy, the nation exists only for the will of the people; governments are a means towards an end, and nothing more.

Capitalism and Freedom is a reiteration of what Scottish economist Adam Smith had said less than two centuries before—that, left to their own devices and free of excessive government control, people prosper and create civilized communities. Yet in the twentieth century, in the face of various socialist experiments and growing state intervention in Western countries, Friedman's reminder became an urgent one. Making a clear connection between economic freedom and political freedom, he showed that free markets were not a luxury but the very basis of personal and political liberty.

How the free market protects

Historically, political freedom has followed the emergence of free markets and capitalist institutions. This is because, Friedman notes, a healthy private economy naturally provides a check on the power of the state.

Where monopolies and trading restrictions are rife, so is special treatment of one social, racial, or religious group over another; the ability to "keep people in their place" remains. In a genuinely free market, economic efficiency is separated from irrelevant characteristics such as skin color or faith. "[The] purchaser of bread" Friedman remarks, "does not know whether it was made from wheat grown by a white man or a Negro, by a Christian or a Jew." Further, a businessman who favors one group over another will be at a market disadvantage against a businessman who does not, and one who is blind to differences among his suppliers will have more choice of from whom to buy and hence lower costs.

During the period of "blacklisting" of Hollywood actors and screenwriters as the result of Senator McCarthy's anti-communist witch-hunts, many writers continued to work anyway, often under assumed names. Without an impersonal market which created a demand for their services, they would have lost their livelihood. In a communist society, Friedman notes, such a thing is impossible since all of the jobs are controlled by the state.

Friedman's message: government often seeks to protect citizens from all sorts of things, failing to see that the "invisible hand" operating in free and open markets—for goods, labor and information—somehow manages to offer much greater protection of personal liberty.

That free markets do this was the exact opposite of what intellectuals had been saying through most of the twentieth century. The individual was seen to be vulnerable in the face of corporate power, and to need governmental protection. This view evolved out of the horrors of the Great Depression, which was considered to be a terrible failure of the markets.

Meddling in the market

Both "full employment" and "economic growth" have been put forward as reasons why governments should have more control over the economy. The Great Depression, people invariably say, is surely evidence of the inherent instability of markets left to their own devices.

In fact, Friedman says, the Depression was caused by government mismanagement. He and Anna Schwartz argued at length in *A Monetary History of the United States, 1867-1960* that the US government's Federal Reserve System, through clumsy use of the levers of the monetary system—specifically, not increasing the money supply in the wake of bank collapses—turned what would have been a contraction lasting a year or two into a catastrophe. The "mistakes of a few men" caused untold misery to millions. Though Friedman accepts that it is the role of government to create a stable monetary system, he asserts that the responsibility is a grave one, and should be severely limited.

In his chapter on fiscal policy, Friedman observes that Keynesian government spending to kick-start stagnant or depressed markets is simply "economic mythology" not proven by empirical studies. For every $100 spent there may be a $100 effect, but the real consequence is a growth in government spending, which, however well-intentioned, is mostly inefficiently allocated.

Progress via people, not governments

There is never any shortage of "good reasons" why government should get involved in curing market or social ills. Sometimes, the good intentions are matched with impressive achievements. Friedman applauds, for example, the creation of a US national freeway system, the building of major dams, its public school system, and some public health measures.

However, most of the advances in the American people's standard of living, he contends, have arisen from their ingenuity, and have nothing to do with government. Prosperity has come despite all the laws and "projects", not because of them. Generally, excess regulations "force people to act against their immediate interests in order to promote a supposedly general interest." Many policies sound good and necessary in theory, but in truth they often have the reverse effects to those that were intended. For instance, the minimum wage was partly aimed at alleviating poverty amongst African-Americans; what actually happened was that the unemployment rate amongst teenage blacks shot up. Public housing was designed to alleviate poverty; instead, it concentrated poverty in pockets. "Social security" policies were intended to provide a safety net for those unable to work, but instead created dependants who might otherwise have contributed to the economy. Friedman's damning conclusion: "Concentrated power is not rendered harmless by the good intentions of those who create it." There are really only two ways a society can organize economic activity, Friedman writes: through centralization and coercion, or through facilitating a marketplace for the trade of goods and services.

Friedman accepts that after World War Two the United States had to centralize and enlarge its military spending in order to defeat the USSR, but dealing with this danger created a back door for a large increase in government's share of national spending and control. A bigger threat than Russia was the erosion of freedoms and free institutions at the expense of the growing power of "the nation."

Freedom first, equality second

Friedman argues that inequality is always less in capitalist countries. Many will disagree with this, pointing to the vast gaps between say, a corporate executive earning $10,000 a day, and a retail assistant earning $20,000 a year. Yet even low-paid people in a capitalist economy, he points out, are better off than the privileged classes were a century ago. Even if an individual does not seem to do well out of capitalism, he or she still benefits in many ways. In contrast, with stratified social systems and socialism, the "goodies" always seem to go only to those at the top.

The heart of liberal philosophy, Friedman writes, is people having equal rights and equality of opportunity. It does *not* mean there should be equality of wealth. If all people grow richer in a capitalist system, this is a welcome by-product of freedom, but it is not its purpose. The purpose of a free, capitalist system is the freedom of the individual.

Final comments

Capitalism and Freedom may shift your beliefs about economic morality. You may have assumed that the government which intervenes to "help" people the most is morally superior, but Friedman showed us how free economic and political systems ensure the dignity of the individual in a myriad of often unforeseen ways.

Countries fashioned according to the views of Adam Smith and Friedman should in theory be monsters of selfish consumerism. But as Friedman pointed out, people wish to be free not just so they can get rich, but so they can live according to deeply held values. Prosperity is not just about making money, but about the freedom to live the way you want.

The Economist described Friedman as "the most influential economist of the second half of the twentieth century . . . possibly all of it." His influence was not just in what he said, but in the fact that he was able to say it to non-economists. When Friedman died in 2006, tributes from the mainstream media (which had chosen to ignore *Capitalism and Freedom* when it was published) flowed, but he has also been demonized by the left, who see him as a dangerous ideologue who believed that the markets are always good, and government always bad, leaving a legacy of inequality, weaker regulation in areas where the state has a clear role, and slower growth compared to the post-war decades. Paul Krugman has given credit to Friedman for having the courage to promote markets and capitalism during the Great Depression, when many thought socialism was America's future. Yet in Krugman's mind Friedman became an absolutist who couldn't admit that a successful country combined the best elements of market and state.

Milton Friedman

Born in 1912 in Brooklyn, New York, Friedman was the youngest child of Jewish immigrants from Ukraine. They moved to New Jersey when he was still a baby and ran a garment factory (Friedman called it a "sweatshop"). After graduating from school at 15, he won a scholarship to Rutgers University before doing a Masters degree in economics at the University of Chicago. At Chicago he met his future wife and collaborator, Rose Director, and studied under distinguished economists Jacob Viner and Frank Knight.

Unable to find an academic job during the Depression, Friedman worked as an economist in the Roosevelt administration. During World War Two he worked at the Division of War Research at Columbia University, receiving his PhD in 1946. In the same year he accepted a teaching position at the University of Chicago, where for the next 30 years he formed the center of the "Chicago School" of free market economics. His own intellectual guide was Friedrich Hayek, who taught at Chicago in the 1950s.

In 1964 Friedman was an adviser to Barry Goldwater in his campaign for the US Presidency, and later to President Nixon. His ideas were influential in the acceptance of fluctuating exchange rates and the floating of the dollar. In 1966 he began a regular column for Newsweek, *which continued until 1984, and became a household name through his* Free To Choose *television series promoting capitalism. Friedman won the Nobel Prize for Economics in 1976, and was given the Presidential Medal of Freedom by Ronald Reagan in 1988.*

Other works include his magnum opus, A Monetary History of the United States, 1867-1960 *(with Anna Schwartz, 1963) and* Free To Choose: A Personal Statement *(with Rose Friedman, 1980).*

1955

The Great Crash 1929

"The signal feature of the mass escape from reality that occurred in 1929 and before—and which has characterized every previous speculative outburst from the South Sea Bubble to the Florida land boom—was that it carried Authority with it. Governments were either bemused as were the speculators or they deemed it unwise to be sane at a time when sanity exposed one to ridicule, condemnation for spoiling the game, or the threat of severe political retribution."

"The government preventatives and controls are ready. In the hands of a determined government their efficacy cannot be doubted. There are, however, a hundred reasons why a government will determine not to use them."

In a nutshell

Rather than championing financial markets, government must make sure that speculative frenzies do not warp or ruin the real economy.

In a similar vein

Liaquat Ahamed *Lords Of Finance*
Michael Lewis *The Big Short*
Hyman Minsky *Stabilizing an Unstable Economy*
Robert Shiller *Irrational Exuberance*

CHAPTER 12

J. K. Galbraith

In the wake of the 2008 financial crisis a truckload of books were published. Whatever their merits, one wonders if many will be read in ten or twenty years' time. John Kenneth Galbraith's *The Great Crash 1929*, in contrast, seems to provide insights into each new financial disaster.

When Galbraith was writing the book in the summer and autumn of 1954, the American stock market was in a mini-boom, reminding him of what was common to all booms: people's belief, "that they were predestined by luck, an unbeatable system, divine favor, access to inside information, or exceptional financial acumen to become rich without work." Greed is the fuel of every bubble, but it is government's duty (through regulation and monetary policy) to prevent the fizzy elixir of markets poisoning the economy at large. Indeed, it is what governments *don't* do, Galbraith argues, that usually allows the brew to boil over—with such terrible consequences to lives and livelihoods.

Delusional optimism

In the 1920s there were viable reasons why the stock market should be rising. Corporate earnings were growing and stock prices seemed reasonable compared to their yields. Production and employment were high and going up, consumer prices were stable, and manufacturing was seeing a dramatic increase in output. Stock prices began rising steadily from 1927, reflecting good corporate earnings, but from early 1928 the market began to be de-anchored from underlying values and saw "a mass escape into make-believe," Galbraith writes.

The conventional explanation was that low interest rates were to blame for the frothy market. The US monetary authorities felt an obligation to keep rates low as America's European partners were seeing a flood of gold leave their shores to earn higher rates in the US. These low rates, in turn, meant people could borrow cheaply to buy stocks on margin and earn fantastic returns. Galbraith does not accept this explanation, noting that "There were times before and there have been long periods since when credit was plentiful and cheap—far cheaper than in 1927–9—and when speculation was negligible." Far more important was a mentality that had developed among ordinary people that, seeing so many millionaires being minted, they were meant to be rich too. Blind trust was put in banks and institutions who were giving constant reassurance that stock values were reasonable and would keep rising. The frenzy was also fueled by brokers' loans to private individuals, which by 1929 were increasing at a rate of $400 million a month.

In the summer of 1928, many big stocks like Westinghouse and General Electric jumped 30–40 percent in value, and not only the New York exchange but smaller exchanges around the country were booming. As 1929 began there were a few contrarian voices—banker Paul Warburg predicted a drastic fall in the market—but as it kept rising they were dismissed as "un-American" and anti-prosperity. Not everyone was putting money into stocks (between one and two million people had trading accounts, out of a population of 120 million), but the frenzy captured the public's imagination. Scores of women bought stocks for the first time, and the market dominated conversation in cultural and artistic circles, which in other times might have disdained money talk. Many people were making considerably more from holding stock than they were earning in wages.

In a time when insider trading laws were virtually non-existent, manipulation of the market and rigging of stock prices was a part of the scene. With such easy money to be made, the market, Galbraith says, "came to be considered less and less a long-run register of corporate prospects and more and more a product of manipulative artifice."

Adding to this was the "most notable piece of speculative architecture of the late twenties," the investment trust, whose number had increased elevenfold since the beginning of 1927. Trusts, the forerunner of today's mutual funds, offered an easy way for people to get into the market without having to think too much about individual stocks, but the absence of regulation meant they were dangerously leveraged and often more like pyramid schemes than real investment vehicles.

The crash and its aftermath

The crash itself, when it finally came, was not a one-day event but rolled out over a couple of weeks. The great 1920s bull market came to an end on September 3, but broker's loans continued to increase, and even amid falling prices people believed they were snapping up bargains. The morning of Monday 21 October saw a steep fall, but by the afternoon prices had stabilized. The Thursday of that week ('Black Thursday') was the start of the real crash in psychological terms, with the morning session seeing "a wild, mad scramble to sell." Yet fear turned to joy when on the same day a group of eminent bankers met to stabilize the market; some stocks even ended the day higher than they began. This optimism seemed to continue the next day and over the weekend.

The following Monday, however, "the real disaster began," and over two days massive selling shocked America. Bizarrely, stocks rose again on the Wednesday and Thursday, perhaps helped by a statement by John D. Rockefeller that he had been buying. "Business is sound," chimed in General Motors' head Alfred Sloan, and Ford lowered prices on its cars. Perhaps the market was entering a new equilibrium. But over a three-day period in which the New York exchange had closed itself to calm nerves, sell orders were mounting. The biggest casualties were the trusts, now exposed as little more than Ponzi schemes. Realizing that their trust stock was close to worthless, people sold their quality securities, which further depressed the market. Meanwhile, trust owners tried to buttress themselves by buying their own stock. "If one has been a financial genius," Galbraith observes "faith in one's genius does not dissolve at once."

The hope was that the storm would quickly blow over and not affect the rest of the economy, but rather than rebounding the market continued to slide over the next two years. Its rise had been the most spectacular event in finance since the South Sea Bubble, yet "The ruthlessness of its liquidation," Galbraith writes, "was, in its own way, equally remarkable."

President Herbert Hoover made various announcements that the economy had turned a corner, and each time it only got worse. GDP in 1932 was a third less than it had been in 1929, and it would be years before it approached 1929 levels. The Great Depression that followed the Great Crash lasted more or less a decade.

Cause and consequence

We don't really know why the stock market underwent such a mania in 1928 and 1929, Galbraith admits, and neither can we really say why the Great Depression was so long and so deep. He does point, however, to systemic weaknesses in the American economy which made the crash, when it came, more devastating.

Extreme inequality of income, he argues, was important. In 1929 the highest earning five percent of Americans received approximately one-third of all personal income. This meant that the health of the economy depended on high levels of investment and consumer spending from the rich which, after the stock market crash, suddenly plummeted. He also points to the bad banking structure. When one bank failed, the assets of others were frozen, leading people to make a run on their own bank. A better system could not have been designed to ensure panic and the withdrawal of funds needed to run the economy. The subsequent law which brought in a Federal guarantee of bank deposits was crucial for the nation's financial stability. Another factor was "the poor state of economic intelligence." The commitment to a balanced budget might have made sense in normal times, but it prevented extra government spending to reduce unemployment and general misery. People feared inflation, but this should have been their last worry. There was also America's foreign balance. After World War One, America's trade surplus and Europe's war debts to America were large. Europe was paying for both of these with gold, which was increasingly disappearing from Europe. America responded by increasing its imports, but the fall in exports contributed to the Depression and hurt farmers. Finally, poor corporate structures had allowed a shady new landscape of investment trusts and holding companies to flourish. Highly leveraged, their focus was on the payment of dividends to keep up appearances, rather than investment. Any shock to their prices meant collapse or a sudden curtailment of expenditure, adding to any deflationary spiral.

"The regulation of economic activity," Galbraith writes, "is without doubt the most inelegant and unrewarding of public endeavors," and yet each of these factors involved some element of government failure. In a capitalist system, those pulling the levers of government do not want to seem party poopers who curtail a boom, or they have direct conflicts of interest in their positions. Secretary to the Treasury under President Coolidge, Andrew Mellon, for instance, had a huge financial interest in the 1920s boom continuing and so was a "passionate advocate of inaction". Indeed, the Coolidge and Hoover administrations did not even try to cover over their tight links with the big financial players and institutions of the day. Have times changed? There is more regulation of finance today, although it is often reversed or watered down in the face of lobbying.

Galbraith concludes with the warning that government inaction in the financial field is as big a threat to capitalism as the much more popular bogeyman (in his time) of communism.

Final comments

What makes Galbraith's study timeless is his observation of the weakness of historical memory. Crashes and depressions can bring huge psychological shock, the effects of which can last for a long time . . . until they are forgotten. For instance, the Securities Exchange Act of 1934 was designed to prevent the banking and finance frauds that had led to the Great Crash, but it was only the horrible *memories* of the Crash that prevented it happening again, Galbraith argues. "As a protection against financial illusion or insanity, memory is far better than law," he writes. Yet from the early 1960s onwards, many bad practices had returned, and there were glamor stocks that people fawned over as signs of a "New Era", as if the rules of economics no longer applied.

In a Foreword to the 2009 edition of *The Great Crash*, Galbraith's son James, a noted economist, draws important parallels between 1929 and 2007. In both years, "the American government knew what it should do. Both times, it declined to do it." In 1929, a sharp rise in interest rates, a prosecution of shady practices on Wall Street, or a clampdown on margin lending for stock speculation might have headed off the crash and saved the real economy from tanking. In 2007, a hands-off "Greenspan doctrine" in relation to financial markets, combined with the Bush administration's demolition of the array of regulations covering housing and mortgages (which had kept the system stable for decades), allowed a real estate bubble to inflate.

One of the outcomes of the 2007 crisis was, rightly, a call to rethink the teaching of economics itself, and the inclusion of economic history units in curricula. Galbraith Snr knew that the best teacher is surely not theory, but experience.

J. K. Galbraith

Galbraith was born in Canada in 1908, and grew up on a farm. He studied animal husbandry at Ontario Agricultural College before focusing on agricultural economics. A scholarship led him to the University of California, Berkeley, when he gained a Masters degree and PhD.

In the 1930s he worked at the US Department of Agriculture, and during World War Two was deputy director of the Office of Price Administration, helping to prevent price-gouging and inflation in the private sector. He was hired by media proprietor Henry Luce to write for Fortune, *giving him a platform to promote the new ideas of John Maynard Keynes. In 1947, with Eleanor Roosevelt, Reinhold Niebuhr and others, he established Americans for Democratic Action, a think tank to promote progressive policy.*

In 1961 President Kennedy made Galbraith, now a full professor at Harvard, US Ambassador to India. He advised Kennedy against America going into Vietnam. Galbraith also worked for the campaign of George McGovern in his contest against Nixon for the 1972 presidency.

The Affluent Society *(1958), Galbraith's other classic, suggested that America's focus on private wealth came at the expense of proper investment in public amenity and infrastructure.* The New Industrial State *(1967) argued that American business was not as competitive as orthodox economics held, and that consumption and prices were shaped by big corporations. In 2000 Galbraith became one of the few people to be awarded a second Presidential Medal of Freedom; the first was given by Truman in 1946.*

Galbraith died in 2006, aged 97.

1879

Progress and Poverty

"Where the conditions to which material progress everywhere tends are the most fully realized—that is to say, where population is densest, wealth greatest, and the machinery of production and exchange most highly developed—we find the deepest poverty, the sharpest struggle for existence, and the most of enforced idleness."

"What is necessary for the use of land is not its private ownership, but the security of improvements. It is not necessary to say to a man, 'this land is yours,' in order to induce him to cultivate or improve it. It is only necessary to say to him, 'whatever your labor or capital produces on this land shall be yours'."

In a nutshell

When land, rather than people and production, is taxed, prosperity increases and inequality decreases.

In a similar vein

Jane Jacobs *The Economy of Cities*
Thomas Malthus *Essay on the Principle of Population*
Karl Marx *Capital*
Elinor Ostrom *Governing the Commons*
Thomas Piketty *Capital in the Twenty-First Century*

CHAPTER 13

Henry George

Henry George swayed the minds of millions, helped shape American politics, and was lauded by the likes of Leo Tolstoy and George Bernard Shaw. Despite never having gone to university, he was the most famous economic thinker of his day, spawning movements devoted to his ideas in the United States, Britain, Europe, Australia, and elsewhere.

He had read his Adam Smith, Malthus, and John Stuart Mill, so had some grounding in economic theory, but it was one of Ricardo's ideas, that land belongs to all of humanity, and so should not be monopolized as private property, that really inspired George. In 1871 he published a pamphlet, *Our Land and Land Policy*. It made no waves, so he decided to expand his thinking in a book, *Progress and Poverty*. In an era when it was difficult to shift works on political economy, it was an instant success, serialized in newspapers, outselling the popular novels of the day, and was translated into several languages.

A rising tide doesn't raise all boats

In his twenties, George was working as a journalist and editor for a variety of newspapers. He watched as his adopted hometown of San Francisco developed into a city. However, on a trip to New York he was struck by its greater extremes of rich and poor. Why was it that its poor seemed so much worse off here than in San Francisco?

In his Introduction, George marvels at the advances in technology that had happened in his time, many of which were labor-saving and heralded a new golden age of greater wealth and less work. What happened, instead, was recession, factories going idle, unemployment and increasing inequality. There were large underclasses fed by charity, and amid great new buildings, churches and museums, "beggars wait for passers-by." The fact that a rising economy did not alleviate poverty, but indeed seemed to increase it, suggested that there was something about the process of capitalist development, or "progress," that was to blame. If not all boats were lifted with the rising economic tide, something must be wrong.

George's shocking conclusion was that "material progress does not merely fail to relieve poverty—it actually produces it." As a village turns into a town, and then into a city, poverty increases along with the wealth. This link between poverty and progress was the "enigma of our times," George writes, because so long as it existed, "progress is not real and cannot be permanent." It created a society ripe for revolution, since there is a big disconnect between a political system in which people are theoretically equal, but have little opportunity to be so in fact. It makes society vulnerable to "the leadership of charlatans and demagogues." Yet political economy, George believed, could provide a solution.

Land before everything

George did not agree with the Malthusian contention that population would outstrip food supply. However, he did observe that as population increases, so the land becomes more valuable, not because it is more productive, but because location allows people to be close to other goods and services which can be bought in exchange for what they themselves have created. They are close to industries, to markets, and to jobs. Density of population, he notes, transforms a piece of land so that its productive power is "equivalent to multiplying its original fertility a thousandfold." Rent, a measurement of the difference between this added productivity and that of the least productive land in use, increases accordingly. All innovations and inventions that save on labor, from the tractor to the telegraph to the sewing machine, make the land on which they are used more valuable, because from it can be generated more wealth than is possible with the old forms of production. The problem is that most of the proceeds of this increased productivity go to the landowner, in the form of "unearned" rent (their land happens to be in the right place at the right time), and less to employees and capital, which actually creates the wealth. This, George says, accounts for the "perplexing fact that labor-saving machinery everywhere fails to benefit laborers." The increasingly productive nation does not require that wages rise in step with its prosperity, or interest rates. But an increase in rents is certain.

When you put land at the center of political economy, George said, it explained why newer cities such as San Francisco had more income equality than older cities such as New York, and why newer countries such as the United States had more income equality than Europe. For newer places tended to have cheaper land, and if the proportion of wealth going to landowners was less, there was more going to workers and capital.

While Adam Smith celebrated the division of labor as the driving force of the wealth of nations, George had a more skeptical view. The division of labor does create wealth, but it turns the individual worker into "a mere link in an enormous chain of producers and consumers, helpless to separate himself, and helpless to move, except as they move."

A remedy

History is really the monopolization of land by one group to exploit another, George says, and the rise of institutions designed to protect that monopoly at the expense of labor. The obvious example is slavery, but other evils included the Highland clearances and the enclosure of common land by the English aristocracy. Most societies had begun with a common right to use of the soil, and only force and greed had seen the rise of private property.

Yet what of the commonly-voiced notion that private property ensures the best use of land, and that if all property were made common, it would see a reversion to social and economic anarchy?

George's response is that the issue is not one of whether land is private or public, but whether the land is being improved. For after all, it is not ownership alone which motivates a person to cultivate or improve land, more whether or not the results of their labor will belong to them at the end of the day. If there is security of gain of the benefits of improvement, private property becomes superfluous. Keep land private, and a lot of land will lie undeveloped and unimproved, because labor will not have access to it.

To go with this logic, George came up with an elegant solution: tax land, not the produce of it. Get rid of all other taxes, and just have a location or land tax which recognizes that the land really belongs to everyone, and so everyone will benefit from taxation of it. This would free up labor and capital to be more productive, since they will no longer be taxed. The beauty of his system, George says, is that it would not require any change in ownership or redistribution of land. Because land is being taxed, it reverts to belonging to everyone. Taxes on business, capital and labor naturally reduce output, and taking these taxes away (to be replaced by a single land tax), would provide a huge fillip to economies, and at the same time workers (without having to pay income or value added taxes) would see a significant rise in their prosperity. There is another great benefit to taxing land: ease of collection. "For land cannot be hidden or carried off," George writes, "its value can be readily ascertained, and the assessment once made, nothing but a receiver is required for collection." In contrast, other taxes are hard to collect, arbitrary and open to corruption.

You didn't build that

One of George's key points is that individuals benefit and profit from private property ownership only because of public investment (this is known as the Henry George Theorem). As the community is the source of government authority, so the community at large should benefit from any increase in the value of private property. For instance, if a government builds or funds a railway that increases the value of private properties near it, surely everyone should benefit from its rise in value, not just the property owner? A tax on land would mean that everyone benefits from a country's infrastructure development, not just the developers and speculators. Without speculation the price of land would fall, and the monopolization of land would no longer pay.

Perhaps the most crucial benefit of George's plan is the reduction in inequality, because it would end "the natural monopoly which is given by the possession of land." As time goes on, most societies tended to get more unequal, with resources monopolized by a few. A land tax would reverse this, by giving each new generation a clean economic slate. Less of society's income would come from rent and ownership, and more from actual production and work. Inequality, George notes, entrenched by narrow ownership of land and property, often checks and cancels out advances and progress in society.

Final comments

Why is George is much less famous today than he was in his own time? George himself hinted at the answer in *Progress and Poverty*, by noting that land tax systems had rarely been implemented because of the influence of landowning classes on government. Neoclassical economics, which became the dominant paradigm, thus came to reflect the interests not of the people, but of a plutocracy.

With many arguing that America is fast becoming a plutocratic state, far from the ideals of its founders, George's ideas are perhaps due for a resurgence. Although his Single Tax (on land, and nothing else) has never really been tried, "location value taxation" has been implemented in many countries. Today, the OECD is in favor, and some economists believe it is key to reducing inequality. But if it is such a great idea, why has it not taken the world by storm? The main obstacle is that a single tax on land would have to be high (if it were to abolish the need for all other taxes), which would infuriate those who enjoy rents on land previously purchased out of earned, taxed income. There would also be an outcry from homeowners whose property is valuable but who are unable to pay a high annual tax.

That said, as cities increasingly become the engines of growth, location matters more and more. With income inequality pushed to the top of the political agenda, we could well see in the future greater taxation of valuable property, and less of wages and businesses profits—just as George wanted.

Henry George

Born in Philadelphia in 1839, George was brought up a strict Episcopalian. He left school at 14 and got a job on a ship sailing to Australia and India. A couple of years later he was back in America, working in San Francisco as a typesetter. After marrying, George began working as a journalist, and by his late twenties was managing editor of the San Francisco Times. *Between 1871 and 1875 he ran his own newspaper, the* San Francisco Daily Evening Post, *and was active in Democratic politics.*

After the success of Progress and Poverty, *George based his family in New York and became a popular speaker and public intellectual. He ran unsuccessfully to be mayor of the city, but his policy platform was influential. It included: a basic income for all citizens, derived from land rents; more public investment in transport; giving women the vote; cleaning up political corruption; and limiting intellectual property protection, which he saw as a form of rent. He was also a vocal supporter of free trade, and his book* Protection or Free Trade *was widely read.*

George died in 1897. One of his followers, Lizzie Phillips, invented a board game, "The Landlord's Game," designed to show the unfairness of the landlord-tenant relationship. Ironically, the game only became a success when it evolved into one celebrating property ownership: "Monopoly."

2016

The Rise and Fall of American Growth

"The economic revolution of 1870 to 1970 was unique in human history, unrepeatable because so much of its achievements could happen only once."

"Electricity, motor vehicles, public transit, and public sanitation infrastructure changed American life, particularly in the cities, virtually overnight between 1890 and 1929. The telephone and the phonograph were part of this epochal set of changes. Telephone lines linked at least half of total households and most of those in urban areas, adding further connections to the "networked" house already hooked up to the outside world with electric, gas, water, and sewer lines."

In a nutshell

The last 150 years have seen a cavalcade of progress unlike any in human history, but most of the big gains in living standards have already happened.

In a similar vein

William J. Baumol *The Microtheory of Innovative Entrepreneurship*
Erik Brynjolfsson & Andrew McAfee *The Second Machine Age*
Diane Coyle *GDP: A Brief But Affectionate History*
Peter Drucker *Innovation and Entrepreneurship*
Thomas Piketty *Capital in the Twenty-First Century*

CHAPTER 14

Robert J. Gordon

In *The Rise and Fall of American Growth*, venerable American economic historian Robert Gordon argues that, compared to the technological advances in the period 1870–1970, which saw electricity, the telegraph, indoor plumbing, modern medicine, and mass transportation, the advances of the post-1970 era have not been as great. Most of the innovations have been in communications, information processing, and entertainment, not in areas which materially improve our lives. The book's argument is perhaps best summed up by venture capitalist Peter Thiel's now-famous remark, "We wanted flying cars, and instead we got 140 characters." As wonderful as smartphones and the internet are, they are no match for mains water and sewerage or the mass-produced automobile in dramatically raising living standards. As a result, the growth rate of the last 45 years has been less than half that enjoyed between 1920 and 1970.

Gordon's thesis is that "some inventions are more important than others," and that the fast-growth century after the American Civil War was made possible by a unique clustering of these "Great Inventions", most of them having their strongest effect after 1920. "The economic revolution of 1870 to 1970 was unique in human history," he writes, "unrepeatable because so much of its achievements could happen only once."

The Rise and Fall of American Growth is a big book and the culmination of a life's work unravelling the causes of economic growth. The hardback edition, with William Gropper's 1938 mural, "Construction of a Dam" adorning the cover, is a thing of beauty. The sheer length and detail of the work makes it one to savor at bedtime over a few weeks or months. You will learn about the transition from small general stores to the supermarket age, the importance of the Sears catalog (the Amazon.com of its day, allowing people outside cities access to a cornucopia of goods), the thriving world of radio in the 1920s and 1930s, how air conditioning made possible Miami, Las Vegas, Los Angeles, and Houston, the big productivity increase from a national highway system from 1950 to 1970, the rapidly increasing quality and decreasing cost of appliances including televisions, washing machines, and dishwashers, the incredible fall in cost, and stratospheric increase in power, of computers over the last 50 years, and the convenience and efficiencies unleashed by photocopiers, ATMs, and electronic ticketing.

Despite its title, much of the book is a celebration of industrial progress. It was partly inspired by Gordon's chance finding, in a Michigan bed and breakfast, of Otto Bettmann's *The Bad Old Days: They Were Really Terrible* (1974), a look at everyday life in nineteenth-century America which provides a reality check for romantic views of the past, reminding us just how much the standard of living was transformed in the space of a few decades.

Rising living standards: life getting better fast

It was the innovating entrepreneur, Gordon argues, more than mere efficiency gains, that drove the big changes and advances in our economies. Part One of the book, spanning 1870 to 1940 and 300 pages, covers in detail how the great inventions changed everyday life.

Gordon describes it as "a flashback to another age when life and work were risky, dull, tedious, dangerous . . . A newborn child in 1820 entered a world that was almost medieval: a dim world lit by candlelight, in which folk remedies treated health problems and in which travel was no faster than that possible by foot or sail." Most importantly, life expectancy improved at a rate "twice as fast in the first half of the twentieth century as in the last half." The rapid decline in infant mortality Gordon describes as "one of the most important single facts in the history of American economic growth." The millions of babies who went on to live full, productive lives helped transform the US into an economic juggernaut.

"What made the century so unique," Gordon writes, "is not only the magnitude of its transitions, but also the speed with which they were completed." Life not only became significantly longer, safer, healthier, and less risky, but most of the gains happened within the space of a few decades.

Mid-century magic: a special 50 years

Having painted a broad picture of this "special century" (1870 to 1970), Gordon shows how the mid-century period of 1920 to 1970 was even more remarkable. Total Factor Productivity growth was triple what it was 1870–1920, and triple what it has been since 1970. Why? There was "one big wave" of fast innovation and technological change that has not been seen before or since. From 1920 to 1950 electricity transformed manufacturing, long after it first began to be used in the 1880s. The internal combustion engine had similar effects. Despite the Great Depression, the 1930s was a decade of innovation, seeing the rise of the plastics industry and the establishment of a National Bureau of Standards which had an unsung positive effect on industrial efficiency. Advances included:

- Antibiotics, X-rays, and modern cancer treatments, which saved millions of lives. The death rate for pneumonia, rheumatic fever, and rheumatic heart disease fell 90 percent between 1940 and 1960, and by the late 1960s the use of polio vaccines meant the virus had been wiped out in America.
- Big improvements in city air quality, and large declines in the number of people smoking.
- Big reductions in the number of fatal car crashes; catching a plane became safer than crossing the road.
- Radio, which brought live, free, constant entertainment and news into living rooms where before there had only been the family piano or phonograph. (In his autobiography, comedian George Burns said, "It's impossible to explain the impact that radio had on the world to anyone who didn't live through that time.")
- A universal postal service, connecting even remote areas of the United States to the rest of the country and world on a daily basis.
- The telephone, whose increasing ubiquity saved lives because it was suddenly possible to summon help quickly, and brought people together socially and commercially.
- The talking movie, which created a sizeable industry. Between 1930 and 1950, 60 to 70 percent of Americans were attending a movie theater on a weekly basis, watching such classics as *Gone With The Wind* (1939), *The Wizard of Oz* (1939), *Citizen Kane* (1941), and *Casablanca* (1942). Television, first showcased at the 1939–40 New York World's Fair, also established itself.

The productivity of the era was spurred on by unexpected, seismic political events: the Great Depression and World War Two. The misery of the Depression prompted the New Deal, which promoted unionization, which in turn made workers more productive. Working hours were reduced, so capital had to get smarter at getting more out of people. The war effort put pressure on manufacturing to become more efficient, while the federal government financed whole new sections of industry that might otherwise not have come into being. Between 1940 and 1945, the number of machine tools in the United States doubled. The war, Gordon contends, "saved the US economy from secular stagnation" by deepening the stock of capital to such a great extent that everything was in place for the economy to keep expanding into the 1950s and beyond, helped by big productivity increases from things such as the creation of a national highway system.

A revolution awaiting us? Today's innovations in perspective

The almost-decade 1996 to 2004 saw a spike in productivity thanks to the diffusion of computers, but unlike the productivity increase caused by electricity, which lasted decades, the one involving computers lasted eight years. Today, Gordon says, most of the benefits of digitalization have already worked through the economy. The period 2000–2014 brought the slowest growth in productivity in any decade in American history. It was a time of "continuity rather than change" in offices, stores, hospitals, schools, universities, and the financial sector. "In short, the changes created by the internet revolution were sweeping but were largely completed by 2005," Gordon writes.

Could supercomputing, artificial intelligence, and robotics create a similar wave of growth as that occurred 1920 to 1970? Gordon includes Erik Brynjolfsson and Andrew McAfee (see commentary on *The Second Machine Age*) among the "techno-optimists," who predict a big lift-off in productivity over the next decade or two from a startling array of new technologies coming to the fore, including medical advances, small robots, 3D printing, big data, and driverless vehicles.

Gordon's responses are as follows:

- Medical advances will continue, but at only an incremental rate, held back by over-regulation.
- If machinery, including small robots, really does supplant human labor, Gordon asks, why is the unemployment rate today not 25 or 50 percent, instead of 5 percent? Machines do not just substitute for labor, but complement it. In today's cutting-edge Amazon warehouses, the robots make the stock more accessible, but it is still humans that pick up the product and pack it in boxes.
- 3D printing will certainly help designers of new products and entrepreneurs to create new things at low cost, but is unlikely to have a big impact on mass production and how everyday goods are made.
- So far, advances in big data and artificial intelligence have not brought a productivity boom. The algorithm is no match for the mass production assembly line or even the self-service supermarket in terms of jumps in productivity or customer well-being.
- Gordon argues that the benefits of driverless cars will be minor "compared to the invention of the car itself or the improvements in safety that have created a tenfold improvement in fatalities per vehicle mile since 1950." The benefit of being able to sit in a car while going shopping or commuting, but not actually drive it, is relatively minor.

We think that our time is full of great innovations, but can they compare to the "networked house" covering water supply, sewerage, electricity, gas, and telephone which was a reality by 1940? When you look at a house today, the only real advance is wiring for cable TV and Wi-Fi for the internet, but these are not necessities in the same way that piped water, light, and central heating are. Ticket prices for plane trips have gone down substantially, but "In the nearly six decades since the first jet flight," Gordon notes, "there have been no improvements at all in the speed and comfort of jet travel." In fact, the experience has got worse.

Gordon's colleague Joel Mokyr, an economic historian, argues that "History is always a bad guide to the future and economic historians should avoid making predictions." For all the array of new technologies coming out, from DNA sequencing to supercomputers, nanochemistry, and genetic engineering, we don't know how life will be radically improved until these technologies play themselves out. Yet Gordon sees all of these as incremental rather than revolutionary. As a result, the future is more likely to resemble the incremental growth of 2000–2014 than the period 1994–2004.

The four headwinds

Gordon calculates that if productivity growth between 1970 and 2014 had been as strong as it was between 1920 and 1970, real GDP per person in America would be almost $100,000, not the $50,000 it currently it is. There are four demographic and political factors—"four headwinds"—which he thinks make it unlikely that the United States will suddenly get back onto a higher growth track:

- Inequality: since the late 1970s there has been a steady increase in the proportion of US national income going to the top 1 percent of earners, which means less to divide up amongst the other 99 percent.
- Education: a rising number of more educated people is not resulting in a productivity payoff for society at large.
- Demography: the labor force participation rate of working age people aged 25–54 has declined since 2000. Fewer people working means that the nation as a whole becomes less productive.
- Fiscal: if current social security and tax entitlements stay the same, there will be an increasing ratio of US federal debt relative to GDP during the period 2015–35. This is likely to mean that taxes increase or benefits are reduced, but if either happens there will be a fall in disposable income, which will damage the economy.

These headwinds lead Gordon to a prediction that disposable income will barely grow for most people in the next two decades. Any measures to ramp up growth will be either "difficult" or "controversial" or both. At a talk Gordon gave at the London School of Economics in 2016, I asked him: why is economic growth so important? Shouldn't we be happy to grow at one or two percent instead of four percent? His answer was that without solid economic growth, societies do not generate enough money to provide for welfare services, public infrastructure, and the like. These things, in turn, keep the whole of society moving forward, for the many and not for just the few. A successful society is therefore, almost by definition, one that is growing healthily.

Final comments

In the postscript, Gordon writes that the title of the book would seem to suggest a story of success followed by failure, but this is not his meaning at all. The theme is not that the United States has lost out (indeed, it has been the productivity leader among rich countries for over a 100 years, and still is), but that it is remarkable how fast America's growth rate was over a certain period (1920–1970). This superfast growth slowed "not because inventors had lost their spark or were devoid of new ideas, but because the basic elements of a modern standard of living had by then already been achieved along so many dimensions." Rich countries can't expect to keep growing at the rate of 1920–1970, any more than today's China or India can expect to maintain growth rates of 8–10 per cent.

Despite the "headwinds" argument, the fact is that even if growth is much slower over the next few decades, the diffusion and lower cost of technology will surely mean that living standards will rise anyway. Indeed, one of Gordon's main points is that official measures of real GDP "fail to capture many aspects of the revolutionary changes that have occurred since 1870" in everyday standards of living. Growth may be slower today, but we have access to medical advances that the kings and queens of history never had, to forms of information and entertainment that are like magic to older generations, and to standards of transportation safety that are truly remarkable. It is telling that, when I asked Gordon to sign my copy of his book, he did not scrawl a dark warning about the future, but instead wrote: "Enjoy the cavalcade of historical progress. R. J. Gordon".

Robert J. Gordon

Gordon was born in 1940 in Boston and grew up in Berkeley, California, where both his parents were economics professors at the University of California. He studied economics at Harvard before completing further degrees at Oxford on a Marshall Scholarship. He obtained his PhD in economics from the Massachusetts Institute of Technology (MIT) in 1967.

Gordon taught at Harvard and the University of Chicago in 1973 before becoming a professor of economics at Northwestern University in Chicago, where he has remained since. He has been an adviser to the US government, serving on the Boskin Commission on the accuracy of the US Consumer Price Index. He is a Distinguished Fellow of the American Economic Association and of the American Academy of Arts and Sciences.

Other books include Macroeconomics, *a textbook first published in 1978 and now in its twelfth edition,* The Measurement of Durable Goods Prices *(1990), and* Inflation, Unemployment, and Productivity Growth *(2004).*

1949

The Intelligent Investor

"[Though] business conditions may change, corporations and securities may change, and financial institutions and regulations may change, human nature remains essentially the same. Thus the important and difficult part of sound investment, which hinges upon the investor's own temperament and attitude, is not much affected by the passing years."

"Intelligent investment is more a matter of mental approach than it is of technique."

"Too many clever and experienced people are engaged simultaneously in trying to outwit one another in the market. The result, we believe, is that all their skill and efforts tend to be self-neutralizing, or to 'cancel out', so that most expert and highly informed conclusions end up being no more dependable than the toss of a coin."

In a nutshell

In stock investing, consider yourself part owner of a company, not a trader.

In a similar vein

John C. Bogle *The Little Book of Common Sense Investing*
Niall Ferguson *The Ascent of Money*
Robert Shiller *Irrational Exuberance*

CHAPTER 15

Benjamin Graham

When Benjamin Graham first started working on Wall Street in 1914, most investing took the form of railroad bonds. Stocks and shares in companies as we know them today were aimed at insiders rather than the general public, and were seen as highly risky investments compared to bonds. This impression was only boosted by the Great Crash of 1929 and the ensuing Depression.

However, Graham's focus on the value of companies, as opposed to the speculation on stocks (he has been variously called the "Dean of Wall Street" and the "Father of Value Investing") showed it was possible for regular people to invest wisely without getting swept up in market hysteria. In the last 40 years, Graham's profile has been boosted by billionaire investor Warren Buffett, who was tutored by Graham at Columbia University and then worked at his Graham-Newman brokerage business. Buffett has described *The Intelligent Investor* as "By far the best book on investing ever written."

Writing against a background of various post-war political upheavals, Graham considered it vitally important to highlight investing principles that worked irrespective of changes in society or government or great swings in the market. The book is essentially about the difference between investment and speculation, between quoted stock prices and the underlying or real value of the companies behind them. This "value" investing approach requires a long-term horizon, the ability to tune out market noise in the interim, and having enough confidence in your investing choices that you won't be rattled by a correction, crash or recession.

An investor, not a speculator

Graham notes that the "intelligence" the title of the book celebrates is not of the "smart" or "'shrewd" type but relates more to the character of the investor: that is, not someone looking for a quick profit, but with a long-term view minded to conserve their capital, who can be firm about their investing principles in the face of an emotion-driven market.

He sticks with the distinction between investing and speculation given in his earlier book *Security Analysis* (itself a classic): "An investment operation is one in which, upon thorough analysis, promises safety of principal and a satisfactory return. Operations not meeting these requirements are speculative." With speculation or "trading", he notes, you are either right or you are wrong, the latter often disastrously so. An investor, in contrast, considers themselves a part owner in a large enterprise, looking mainly to its results and the quality of its management. Such a thing as intelligent speculation does exist, Graham says, but it is dangerous when people who think they are investing are actually speculating. Any stock purchase that you do quickly, when you don't want to "lose out on a great opportunity" is probably speculation driven by the emotions of the market.

The only time an investor should take account of the ups and downs in the market is when they choose to buy a stock they had their eye on anyway, and can pick it up at a low price if market sentiment is bearish. If an investor starts "swimming with the speculative tide" (particularly during a bull market when it seems easy to make money), they will lose sight of the companies they are investing in and focus only on the price of stocks.

How to find value

Graham reflects that the long-term prospects of a company can only ever be an educated guess. If those prospects are clear enough, then they will already be reflected in the company's stock price. This is why "growth" stocks are often expensive, and why there is rarely good value to be found in the "sexy" companies that everybody likes.

Better, Graham believed, to invest in companies without dramatic predictions attached to them, "boring" companies that are overlooked and undervalued. He noted that when a company loses ground against the overall market, speculators will cast a pall of gloom over its stock and write it off as hopeless. The intelligent investor, however, will see that this is an overreaction. Surely the company is still selling things, has some market share, and may turn around?

Graham observes that the real money to be made in the stock market is not in the buying or selling, but in having the discipline to hold and own, earning dividends and waiting for perceptions of the value of a company to align with reality. To do this obviously requires a degree of psychological strength, and indeed Graham observes that "Intelligent investment is more a matter of mental approach than it is of technique."

Margin of safety

The secret of investing success, Graham says, could be summed up in the term, "Margin of Safety." In technical terms, this means evidence of a company's earnings above what is required to service its interest on debt, particularly in the event of a significant sales or market decline. The intelligent investor always looks for this buffer because it means they do not need to have accurate estimates of a company's future. A speculator does not usually consider the margin of safety important, but for the investor it is their touchstone.

There are two ways to invest, Graham notes: the predictive approach, or how well you think a company will do within its market given its management, products and so on; and the protective approach, which involves looking only at the statistics of a company, such as the relationship between selling price and earnings, assets, and dividend payments. Value investors favor the second because it is based "not on optimism but on arithmetic."

Two types of investor

Within the Graham framework of value and safety, there is room to be either a defensive or an aggressive investor.

Graham's guiding rule for the conservative investor is to keep a split of roughly 50 percent of their funds in high-grade bonds (or savings accounts with an equivalent interest rate), and 50 percent in large, prominent, financially conservative companies which have a history of continuous dividend payments and whose price is not more than 25 times annual earnings (this generally excludes all growth stocks). When the market looks dangerously high, you can reduce your exposure to common stocks to less than 50 percent—or, in a down market, go over 50 percent to pick up low-priced but good stocks. This formula stops the investor from getting swayed by the hysteria of the market, but at the same time gives exposure to higher potential returns. When the market goes down, Graham notes, he will feel good compared to his bolder friends who have gone into stocks in a big way.

The conventional wisdom is that if you are prepared to take higher risks you will get higher returns. Graham rejects this, saying that high returns are not necessarily related to risk, but to putting more time and effort into your investing. For the more aggressive or enterprising investor who decides to make their own stock picks but still require the margin of safety, Graham's pointers include:

- Look for companies that have a regular dividend payment record going back 25 years or so.
- Do not invest in companies with price to earnings ratios of more than 10.
- When looking at a company's annual report, separate out non-recurrent or "one off" profits and losses from the normal operating results.

- Don't invest in an "industry", invest in companies. For example, a lot of money went into air transport stocks in the post-War period and into the 1950s, but various factors meant that the industry as a whole had poor financial results.

If you do ask others to manage your funds, Graham counsels, either limit the investing activity contracted out to very conservative investments, or make sure you have "an unusually intimate and favorable knowledge of the person" who is going to direct your funds.

Never go with the advice of people who promise spectacular returns. Be careful also of getting advice from friends or relatives: "much bad advice is given for free."

Final comments

On the penultimate page, Graham writes, "Investment is most intelligent when it is most *businesslike*". This, Warren Buffett thought, was the wisest sentence ever penned on investing. Graham meant that people in the financial world too easily forget the basic fact of investing: that it is about *companies*, and buying a stock means part ownership of a "specific business enterprise". Trying to make money beyond earnings related to a firm's performance was fraught with danger.

Reflecting on whether there were any rules of investment that had stood the test of time, he noted that most of the rules relating to particular types of securities (e.g. "A bond is a safer investment than a stock") were no longer valid, while the ones relating to human nature did not date, such as "Buy when most people (including experts) are pessimistic, and sell when they are actively optimistic." Everything changes, including companies, regulations and the economy, but people do not, and people are what drive markets.

Benjamin Graham

Graham was born in 1894 in London. His parents emigrated to the United States while he was still a baby. He did well in school and won a place at Columbia University in New York.

Graham started working on Wall Street in 1914 when he was 20, and later founded the famous Graham-Newman Partnership brokerage business. He also taught at Columbia's Graduate School of Business from 1928 to 1957.

His other key books are Security Analysis, *with Graham Dodd, Sidney Cottle and Charles Tatham (1934) and* The Interpretation of Financial Statements *(1964). Graham died in 1976.*

1945

The Use of Knowledge in Society

"What is the problem we wish to solve when we try to construct a rational economic order? On certain familiar assumptions the answer is simple enough. If we possess all the relevant information, if we can start out from a given system of preferences, and if we command complete knowledge of available means, the problem which remains is purely one of logic . . . This, however, is emphatically not the economic problem which society faces . . . The reason for this is that the 'data' from which the economic calculus starts are never for the whole society 'given' to a single mind which could work out the implications and can never be so given."

In a nutshell

Centralization of knowledge is good in theory, but in practice economies are most efficient when millions of people act independently using the information available to them through prices.

In a similar vein

Milton Friedman *Capitalism and Freedom*
Ludwig von Mises *Human Action*
Ayn Rand *Capitalism: The Unknown Ideal*

CHAPTER 16

Friedrich Hayek

Some economists are remembered for short journal articles as much as for big tomes that took years to write. Friedrich Hayek made his name with significant works such as *Monetary Theory and the Trade Cycle* and *The Pure Theory of Capital*. Later, *The Road To Serfdom* (see *50 Politics Classics*), would bring him fame. It argued that an economy planned or directed by the government not only means that resources are allocated inefficiently, but that the life choices of individuals are progressively narrowed according to state-defined goals. Therefore, a true democracy must be based on a free-market economy.

Yet in the year following *The Road to Serfdom*, Hayek wrote a 5,000-word piece for *American Economic Review* that also became influential, and which showed that he was not simply a free-market ideologue but a social scientist. "The Use of Knowledge in Society" proceeds from a deceptively simple question: how do you create a rational economic order?

Any economic system has to rest on access to information, Hayek notes, which allows for judgements about how best to allocate resources. The problem is that no one person ever has access to all the necessary information that leads to good solutions and decisions. This knowledge is dispersed throughout society, in an unorganized way, in thousands of sources and in the minds of millions of individuals. There can never be one best solution that fits all, but *millions* of solutions.

Hayek's thinking seemed radical at the time. After all, hadn't the socialist states grown quickly thanks to the efficiency of central planning boards and five-year plans, in contrast to the randomness of capitalism? His Austrian School mentor Ludwig von Mises had written an influential article in 1920, "Economic Calculation in the Socialist State," which argued that only a system of market prices and total freedom to pursue profits could work, because prices are the indispensable hand guiding non-wasteful investment. In the "socialist calculation debate" that ensued, economists Oskar Lange and Abba Lerner advocated "market socialism," in which hundreds of state-owned firms would be left to pursue profits, but with the state still setting prices to guarantee certain social outcomes.

The idea seemed promising, but history would prove von Mises and Hayek correct. State ownership and pricing in Soviet Russia led to shortages or to overproduction of goods, because the state could never get complete enough information to make correct planning decisions. Innovation was held back because there was no place for the risk-taking entrepreneur and his chance to get rich from a new idea or product.

The beauty of unorganized knowledge

All societies and the individuals within them are involved in planning their futures, but the question is *who* does the planning. Is it more effective when done by one central planning body, or should there be system of competition in which the best ideas, products and services come to the fore? The system that works the best, Hayek says, should be determined by which one is able to deploy existing information and knowledge to its fullest extent. Should we trust the experts, which seems logical, or trust the decisions of the general public? In reality, Hayek writes, only some knowledge is scientific and objective, and therefore able to be centralized. A lot of knowledge is personal and local, yet no less socially useful for this. As Hayek puts it:

> *"the shipper who earns his living from using otherwise empty or half-filled journeys of tramp-steamers, or the estate agent whose whole knowledge is almost exclusively one of temporary opportunities, or the arbitrageur who gains from local differences of commodity prices, are all performing eminently useful functions based on special knowledge of circumstances of the fleeting moment not known to others."*

This kind of unorganized knowledge is not given much respect compared to theoretical, technical, or scientific knowledge, but if society is to achieve optimal use of resources, it is just as necessary. The problem of long-term central planning is that it assumes that things will not change much over time. But of course they do, and the big advantage of decentralized and personal decision-making is that it responds to change, minute by minute, precisely because changes are right in front of us. In business and industry, for instance, the big variable in producing anything is cost, and it is only the manager on the floor who has a constant eye on keeping costs down who can ensure profits.

The information such managers are receiving is often qualitative rather than quantitative, cannot be translated into statistics, and therefore can't be given to a central body in statistical form. Because "the economic problem of society is mainly one of rapid adaptation to changes in the particular circumstances of time and place," Hayek observes, it makes sense that the people closest to these circumstances are best placed to deal with the adaptations using the resources at their disposal. If all relevant information was first sent to some central planning body, by the time it got back opportunities would have been lost, even assuming they made correct decisions.

It may be asked: won't the "'person on the spot'" be lacking the wider picture of what is happening in the larger production process and indeed the wider economy? In fact, Hayek says, the manager or operative doesn't actually need to know *why* some raw material is in short supply or why the price of another input has risen. He just needs to know how the factory can get its hands on what it needs, and whether changes in the market mean that what he is producing is more or less wanted. Through awareness of market prices alone, "he can appropriately rearrange his dispositions without having to solve the whole puzzle *ab initio* or without needing at any stage to survey it at once in all its ramifications." In such a way, the price system coordinates resource use in society without any central body or individual needing to know everything that is going on.

The marvel of prices

Hayek describes the price mechanism as a "marvel," the most salient fact of which is "the economy of knowledge with which it operates, or how little the individual participants need to know in order to be able to take the right action."

He likens market prices to symbols of real changes happening in the economy. Like all symbols, they work elegantly and powerfully in providing information. The obvious conclusion is that if prices are "set" by some central body, or if they become rigid for some reason, all this vital information on resources is lost or miscommunicated. The result is their poor allocation, and an economy operating far from optimality.

If the price mechanism had been designed by a person, Hayek says, it would be considered one of the great triumphs of the human mind. That it was not, and evolved organically as a self-managing system, unfortunately prompts many to think that "conscious direction" might do better. Yet no government or central body will be as good as prices, he argues, in making "individuals do the desirable things without anyone having to tell them what to do."

This is not just a matter for economics, Hayek says, but for society generally. He recalls Alfred North Whitehead's insight, "Civilization advances by extending the number of important operations which we can perform without thinking about them." Real progress is not having to think about causes, but just following signs, pointers, and rules of thumb which move us all in the right direction.

This assertion (first voiced by von Mises), Hayek notes, was met with "howls of derision" by the political left, yet has become accepted as the basis of running a complex society while preserving the freedom to choose one's work and path in life. That it has transcended politics shows that it is something approaching a universal truth. Even Trotsky, he notes, said, "economic accounting is unthinkable without market relations." It is a waste of time imagining a central body or person obtaining all the relevant information to make the best decisions. Rather, we should begin by assuming that each person's knowledge is far from perfect, and therefore recognize "the consequent need for a process by which knowledge is constantly communicated and acquired"—that is, markets and prices.

Final comments

Finding the best allocation of resources that the price system can bring would appear to be a matter of economics, but with this essay Hayek also wanted to take account of the *social* nature of knowledge. That is, how knowledge itself can advance simply by millions of people taking what they believe are optimal decisions for them, and how the result can be greater than the sum of its parts.

In the 1980s, a young American college student, Jimmy Wales, read Hayek's article, and was fascinated by the contrast between limited individual knowledge, and the possibilities of pooled wisdom. The open source software movement had already demonstrated the power of mass collaboration, and in the 1990s new 'wiki' open-editing tools led him and a partner to launch an experimental website, Wikipedia, which would allow anyone to contribute and edit encyclopedia articles. Hayek thus provided an intellectual rationale for today's distributed knowledge platforms and community finance enterprises (from Wikipedia to Kickstarter), which demonstrate the "wisdom of crowds."

This messy, bottom-up way of providing solutions could not have been more counterintuitive when Hayek's article was published—after all, the Allies' war effort had been based on central planning, and the *uber*-centralized USSR was emerging as a superpower—but in hindsight the notion that "government knows best" now seems terribly naïve.

Friedrich Hayek

Born in 1899 in Vienna, Hayek was just old enough to enlist in the Austro-Hungarian army in World War One, and spent time on the Italian front. He studied a range of subjects at the University of Vienna, and was influenced by the "Austrian school" economists Carl Menger and Friedrich von Weiser. After graduating, Hayek worked under Ludwig von Mises in his work for the Austrian government.

In 1927 Hayek and von Mises founded what is today the Austrian Institute of Economic Research; their primary interest was in business cycles and prices. In 1931 Hayek was lured to the London School of Economics by Lionel Robbins, who was keen to provide a counterview to Keynes. In 1947, together with Karl Popper, Milton Friedman, and von Mises, he set up the Mont Pelerin Society to promote open free-market societies. In 1950 Hayek took up a professorship at the University of Chicago, giving lectures in the philosophy of science and the history of ideas in addition to economics and political philosophy. From 1962 to 1969 he was at the University of Freiburg. Hayek shared a Nobel Prize in economics with Swedish economist Gunnar Myrdal in 1974. In 1984 he was made a member of the Order of the Companions of Honour by Queen Elizabeth, on the recommendation of his friend Margaret Thatcher, and in 1991 was awarded the Presidential Medal of Freedom by George H. W. Bush. He died in 1992.

Other books include The Constitution of Liberty *(1960), the three-volume* Law, Legislation, and Liberty *(1973–79), and* The Fatal Conceit: The Errors of Socialism *(1988).*

1970

Exit, Voice, and Loyalty

"In Nigeria, then, I had encountered a situation where the combination of exit and voice was particularly noxious for any recovery: exit did not have its usual attention focusing effect because the loss of revenue was not a matter of the utmost gravity for management, while voice did not work as long as the most aroused and therefore the potentially most vocal customers were the first ones to abandon the railroads for the trucks."

"Exit is unsettling to those who stay behind as there can be no talking back to those who have exited. By exiting one renders his arguments unanswerable. The remarkable influence wielded by martyrs throughout history can be understood in those terms, for the martyr's death is exit at its most irreversible and argument at its most irrefutable."

In a nutshell

"Exit" (moving to a competitor) has traditionally been the domain of economics, and "voice" (protest) the domain of politics. To stay healthy and relevant, firms, institutions, and states must allow for and learn from both strategies.

In a similar vein

Gary Becker *Human Capital*
Steven Levitt & Stephen Dubner *Freakonomics*
Thomas Schelling *Micromotives and Macrobehavior*
Richard Thaler *Misbehaving: The Making of Behavioral Economics*

CHAPTER 17

Albert O. Hirschman

Orthodox economics assumes that firms, faced with competition, shifting consumer preferences, and changing supply and demand, will rationally alter their plans to keep on track. A firm's failure is usually well-justified; it did not allocate resources efficiently, and so another firm will simply take up where it left off, redeploying the same resources in a better way. This is the efficiency of market capitalism.

This rosy view makes sense, Albert Hirschman noted, until you remember that most capitalist countries contain monopolies and oligarchies where such optimal reallocation fails to happen, leaving "more or less permanent pockets of inefficiency and neglect". Modern capitalism is less a process of Schumpetarian "creative destruction," than muddling through in the light of human irrationality and very imperfect information. Instead of the perfect competition that classical economics imagined, Hirschman pointed to other mechanisms that limited the social losses from declining firms, organizations and states. He called these mechanisms "exit," "voice," and "loyalty."

The polymath Hirschman is sometimes described as "the best economist who never won a Nobel Prize." *Exit, Voice, and Loyalty*, in challenging the assumption that individuals, firms, and states act rationally, was a forerunner of behavioral economics.

The myth of the naturally optimal economy

Hirschman imagines a firm making products, or an organization providing some kind of service or public good, whose output deteriorates. There are two ways that dissatisfaction with the quality of the existing offering becomes apparent:

- Exit: people stop buying a firm's products, or the influence or membership of an organization declines.
- Voice: the same customers or members, instead of deserting, voice their disapproval of the current offering, and demand change.

In both cases, standard economic theory is that management will take on board the feedback and seek to change the offering by changing or improving it. Economies are like taut machines, constantly allocating resources in an efficient way. Hirschman, however, argued that organizations are not continually optimizing to attain higher profits, rather most firms do only what is necessary to maintain their position.

In short, economies are characterized more by microeconomic slack than they are by tautness. Irrespective of external conditions, Hirschman noted, firms often make mistakes in judgement ("repairable lapses"), or even just "lose their mojo," and if there is not a lot of competition in a market, or people can't be bothered to complain, the economy will continue at suboptimality. Indeed, one of the features of human history, Hirschman says, is the "latitude for deterioration," that is, the apparent willingness for people to put up with social systems in which an elite generate a surplus that is either not shared with the majority, or which results in mediocre living standards for all. The only thing stopping further decline and slackness is that eventually counterforces come into play that restore health and create new vitality. But this dynamic is hardly the "optimal allocation of resources through competition" that orthodox economics says drives economies forward.

Exit can bring decline as well as improvement

Economists much prefer exit to voice as a way of explaining how consumers and markets work. If a person stops buying a product because it is not up to scratch, sales go down and a reappraisal of the product is likely by the company.

In the 1960s, Hirschman had a chance to question this conventional wisdom. Doing field research as a development economist in Nigeria, he noticed something strange about the country's government-owned rail network. It should have been moving the bulk of the country's freight and people, but instead goods were moving by road and people were taking buses. Why were the railways performing so poorly against road transport, when on the face of it rail would have been a much more logical way to move commodities and people? In the face of competition by road transport, why did the railways fail to respond? Why was competition not enough?

It was precisely because the Nigerian railway system was state-run, but *not* a monopoly, Hirschman argues, that it had been allowed to deteriorate. If it had been a monopoly, businesses and patrons would likely have risen up and demanded improvements (exercising "voice"), but the fact was that there had always been the option of using trucks and buses, and road transport was reasonably efficient, meant that people didn't bother complaining about rail travel; they just stopped using it.

The railway, for its part, kept on operating because it could confidently assume that the national treasury would keep funding it at a loss. In this situation, neither "exit" nor "voice" worked to prevent the decline or end of an institution.

The perennial power of voice

The conventional wisdom held that a democracy only works when large portions of citizenry are actively engaged in political life. Studies of voter behavior and engagement, Hirschman notes, showed that apathy is more the norm. The decision to stay and put up a fight against decline requires time and energy, and indeed, one of Hirschman's points is that "The presence of the exit alternative can . . . *atrophy the development of the art of voice*." While exit is the simple decision of a consumer, exercising voice is a creative act by a *citizen*, signaling that one is not simply choosing for one's self, but caring what happens to the polity at large. Indeed, significant power lies with the person who for whatever reason is *unable* to exit, and so turns to voice to highlight the iniquity. Such a motivated person may be a lot more dangerous to the firm or organization that is their target, than a person who quietly withdraws their custom or loyalty. For example, a Republican may be very dissatisfied with the direction his party has moved in, but voting for the Democrats is unthinkable. Therefore, he will become a "party rebel", loudly agitating for the positions he wants adopted. In doing so, he (and others seeing things the same way) will be heard much more than if he just left the party. When exit is not possible, voice becomes potentially very powerful.

Hirschman admits there is a natural connection between economic life and "exit", and between political life and "voice", yet the power of each mechanism increases when it is used against the norm. For example, the consumer revolution sparked by Ralph Nader was more than about unsafe cars; it increased the profile of "voice" as a way of righting wrongs in the economic sphere, as opposed to the natural American default of exit.

Hirschman's conclusion is that to fight decline, organizations need a dose of voice (if their normal feedback is through exit), or if their normal "reaction mode" for keeping on course is exit, they must change their structure so that it becomes easier for people to speak their minds.

Loyalty and its role in preventing or aiding deterioration

Loyalty to an organization usually prevents a member leaving, and prompts her to voice her preferences for the way it should be moving. Indeed, the member does not want the organization to decline to such an extent that her loyalty may be tested. Loyalty, Hirschman says, "far from being irrational, can serve the socially useful purpose of preventing deterioration," giving the organization some breathing space to reform or improve.

Voice is creative, and requires effort, and loyalty may push a person to make this effort. This is exactly why divorce is quite a complicated process, Hirschman observes; it serves to make people think twice about the loyalty they are giving up before taking final action. Loyalty serves other social purposes. Loyalty and patriotism are like a glue that binds together a society, in a way that a simple aggregation of self-seeking consumers could never achieve.

We see exit, voice, and loyalty play themselves out in nations all the time. If you let your citizens voice dissent, they will be motivated to stay and change things. If there is no free speech, they may simply give up and live elsewhere, which does nothing to help a country's problems. In the Soviet Union of the 1970s and 1980s, people were not allowed to leave, so those wanting political change had to stay put and hope that it would come. In today's Russia, people are free to come and go, but "exit" has clearly had a big impact, with a "brain drain" of people who can no longer find career and intellectual fulfillment at home. In countries vulnerable to brain drain, Hirschman observed, loyalty or patriotism is often the only thing that can make people stay or draw them back.

Final comments

Examples abound of Hirschman's theme that both exit *and* voice need to be present to stop decline. In commerce, the smart company knows that if people can easily voice complaints or raise issues, particularly at an early stage, they are much more likely to stay loyal, since they feel valued. Negative feedback is vital to any supplier of a product or service, and should be prized rather than scorned. It is the people who silently stop buying your product who are the killers of a business, not the ones who call out flaws and problems. Hirschman's ideas resonate in an age in which people may not simply stop buying a product if they deem it no longer good, but take to social media and start campaigns to have a company revert to the original. When "voice" is so easily articulated in the commercial sphere, it becomes as important as "exit" as a means of valuable feedback.

In politics, by contrast, "voice" is often rejected in favor of the stronger message of "exit." The United States, Hirschman writes, "owes its very existence and growth to millions of decisions favoring exit over voice." Most came to escape persecution or poverty in the Old World; the preference for the neatness of exit over the messiness and pain of voice has run through its national history. Britain's referendum on whether to stay in or leave the

European Union is another example. The Leave camp argued that, freed from EU "meddling," a fully sovereign Britain would thrive. The Remain camp argued that Britons would be better off staying put and trying to reform EU institutions from within. We know who won.

Albert O. Hirschman

Born in 1915 in Vienna to Jewish parents who baptized him a Lutheran, Hirschman enrolled at the University of Berlin just as Hitler was coming to power. His anti-Nazi views prompted him to flee to Paris, where he completed a business degree before studying at the London School of Economics. He fought on the Republican side in the Spanish civil war, and in 1938 gained a doctorate in economics at the University of Trieste. During World War Two he enlisted in the French Army, but found himself in Marseilles helping to smuggle thousands of Jews and intellectuals, including Hannah Arendt, Marcel Duchamp, and Marc Chagall, to safety in America.

In the United States Hirschman took up a fellowship at the University of California, Berkeley, and worked for a precursor of the CIA, translating at the first Allied war crimes trial of German generals. From 1946 to 1952 he worked for the Federal Reserve Board in Washington DC on the Marshall Plan, then for several years as an economic adviser to the government of Columbia, which made him an in-demand development economist. Academic postings included Yale, Columbia, Harvard, and Princeton's Institute for Advanced Study.

Key books include The Strategy of Economic Development *(1958),* The Rhetoric of Reaction *(1977), on conservative ideology, and* The Passions and the Interests *(1977), on how early capitalism subverted basic drives into moral values. Hirschman died in 2012, aged 97.*

1968

The Economy of Cities

"At the war's end, many people had, in fact, predicted severe economic distress and depression for Los Angeles. They would have been right if the city had had nothing to grow on but its export work and the multiplier effect of that work. But as it turned out, work and jobs in Los Angeles did not decline; they grew. In 1949 Los Angeles had more jobs than it had ever had before. The city's economy had expanded while its exports had been contracting! What was happening, of course, was that Los Angeles was replacing imports at a great rate."

In a nutshell

Cities have always been the main driver of development and wealth, and will be even more important in the future.

In a similar vein

Henry George *Progress and Poverty*
Friedrich Hayek *The Use of Knowledge in Society*
Michael E. Porter *The Competitive Advantage of Nations*
Hernando de Soto *The Mystery of Capital*

CHAPTER 18

Jane Jacobs

Well over half (55 percent) of the world's population now lives in cities, compared to 34 percent in 1960, and the figure keeps rising. Much of the growth is occurring in developing countries, where cities seem to offer something compelling. Big cities in rich countries, such as London, New York and Sydney, only seem to become more important to their national economies, and thus grow larger. The internet was meant to reduce the need for such concentration of population, but virtually the opposite has happened.

Today, the benefits for firms basing themselves in cities are the networks of knowledge they can be part of being near similar firms, and the ability to hire the right people. In places like Silicon Valley (part of the larger conurbation of San Francisco and the Bay Area), these knowledge workers feed off each other's ideas, cite each other's research, and create new companies drawing on their intellectual capital.

This "triumph of the city" (the title of a book by Harvard economist Ed Glaeser) was wholly expected by Jane Jacobs, whose popular *The Death and Life of Great American Cities* (1961) helped persuade the American public against the fashion of the time for grandiose urban planning schemes and expressways that destroyed neighborhoods. Her campaigns seemed to make her a paragon of the urban left, but in fact she believed that the self-renewing dynamism of cities rested on freedom of the market; they were hardly ever government creations. One only had to compare New York with Washington DC, Rio de Janeiro with Brasilia, or Sydney with Canberra, to appreciate this.

All roads (and ideas) lead to the city

When she started researching *The Economy of Cities*, Jacobs did not question the current theory that cities grow up from a rural base. It was *just common sense* that towns and cities grew out of villages, which became centers of administration for a settled farming area and so grew more complex. Or, it was claimed, cities arose as the base of a warrior class who protected peasants in the countryside in return for protection. In either case, the food provided by the land around was vital to the existence of the first towns.

Her own research led her to the surprising, opposite conclusion: rural economies "are directly built upon city economies and city work." This basic mistake, or dogma, of agricultural primacy, has clouded our understanding of cities ever since. Cities are seen as simply larger and more complicated towns—not as a phenomenon in their own right. This logic has shaped economic development and planning in both capitalist and communist countries, often with awful results.

What changed Jacobs' mind was the simple fact (which even Adam Smith had noticed) that big rises in agricultural productivity *follow* the growth of cities: "The most thoroughly rural countries exhibit the most unproductive agriculture. The most thoroughly urbanized countries, on the other hand, are precisely those that produce food most abundantly." In the earliest times, there was no such thing as rural agriculture. Food production was developed in cities, and everywhere else was simply hunting and gathering. Only later did agriculture "become a rural occupation," Jacobs says, with meat and wool production (which needed more land than grain growing) moving more than a day's journey from cities. When, as often happened, the parent city was destroyed in war, these villages would be orphaned, reverting to subsistence and without any more of the technological or agricultural development formerly provided by cities.

For centuries Japan only barely got by from the rice grown by its farmers, and had to import 25 percent of its supplies. This all changed in the 1950s, when agricultural productivity soared thanks to new access to fertilizers, farm machinery, refrigeration, and plant and animal research—all developed in cities. Despite a leap in population, Japan not only became self-sufficient in rice, but provided a more varied and richer diet with a growing production of eggs, fowl, fruit, and vegetables. If Japan had waited for an agricultural surplus to develop and grow the nation, Jacobs writes, "it would be waiting still." Jacobs gives many American examples which challenge the rural primacy paradigm. The real advances in farm machinery there, such as the McCormick horse-drawn reaper, arose from new developments in industrial metal production in the cities. The great Californian fruit and vegetable industries did not "evolve" from the original wheat farms and animal pastures there, but grew out of the demand of owners of preserving plants and canneries in San Francisco for farm produce that could be profitably packaged and sold in cities and for export.

It is easy to assume that new forms of rural work develop from older ones, but this is like saying that the dessert evolved from the main course instead of coming out of the kitchen, Jacobs writes. The city does not rest on the land, rather the land and its population depends directly on the changing needs and wants of the city; indeed, this is the only way the land can develop.

Ingredients and conditions for growth

People mistakenly believe that cities grow through a simple enlargement of what is already there, yet the growth of cities is not the same as the growth of towns; the growth is often explosive or exponential rather than incremental. On the surface, such an explosion occurs through the creation of an export industry, yet surges in the economies of early Rome, thirteenth century Paris, London in Shakespeare's time, or New York in the twentieth century, for instance, can't be accounted for by growth in exports alone. They happened in combination with booms in import-replacing local industry, that is, the creation of goods and services for the local market which had previously been imported. Jacobs cites Japan's bicycle industry, which began when local bike repair shops, who had simply been servicing imported bikes, began producing cheaper parts, and then bicycles themselves. These enterprises became part of a larger engineering ecosystem which would later support big companies such as Toyota and Sony. When cities engage in import replacement, Jacobs says, there is rapid growth in jobs thanks to the new work required, the rural sector is developed because of the need for new or more raw materials, and there is a fast expansion in the *sum total* of economic activity, because these elements support each other.

Jacobs' "import replacement" sounds a lot like the import substitution of economics textbooks, but whereas the latter is usually part of a government "nation-building" project, import replacement is an organic process that takes place in the free markets of cities, the result of millions of insights and decisions by entrepreneurs and traders reacting to conditions.

Jacobs argues that you cannot explain the success of cities according to location or other resources, rather "Their existence as cities and the sources of their growth lie within themselves, in the processes and growth systems that go on within them." It doesn't matter if a town is situated on the finest harbour in the world, or has been designated as a customs station or trading depot by a government; if an ecosystem of growth, and what economists call "knowledge spillovers," is absent, there will be no flourishing. Los Angeles and Tokyo were not promising places as trading sites, but boomed anyway. Many say that New York prospered after it was connected to the Erie Canal (which linked the Great Lakes with the Atlantic) but Jersey City was also connected and stayed small. It was only New York's development of a variety of industries that allowed it to capitalize on the canal when it came.

The "valuable inefficiency" of great cities

"The greater the sheer number and varieties of division of labor already achieved in an economy," Jacobs says, "the greater the economy's inherent capacity for adding still more kinds of goods and services." Cities can reinvent themselves and have several boom periods in which the labor, knowledge and capital from "old" work and industries is applied to the creation of new products and services. At the time she was writing, Jacobs observed that New York was in decline, but she would not have been in the least surprised to learn that, although it lost much of its garment-making industry thanks to cheaper labor in other countries, its huge intellectual capital in clothing design and distribution would see it add thousands of new jobs in the decades to follow. One of her key points is that to develop new kinds of work, a place needs to have many different sources of finance, since what people consider a good investment differs hugely. This "inefficient" deployment of capital is actually what makes a city grow.

Cities have always seemed impractical, Jacobs notes, filled with many problems of sanitation, pollution, the supply of water, congestion, and the risk of fire. Yet it is only cities that seem to come up with the solutions, and the new goods and services, which can alleviate these things. A government may feel justified in directing investment to a part of the country to "develop" it, when it makes more sense to allow private capital to decide where a new industry is best located. With the rise of the internet it was thought that work could and would be performed anywhere that had an online connection. That hasn't happened, because people still like to feel they are part of an intellectual ecosystem, which is always centered on a city. Despite cities' problems, people know that this is where new things happen. Their unproductivity is a myth.

Final comments

Jacobs predicted that the cities of the future will be larger, more complex, more diversified, and even more interesting, their size accommodating a vast range of old and new urban landscapes, cultural attractions, and intellectual buzz. What a contrast, she notes, to the "bureaucratized, simplified cities so dear to present-day city planners and urban designers," whose schemes inevitably poisoned natural city growth and development. In the 1950s she succeeded in halting the New York city planner Robert Moses' scheme for a lower Manhattan expressway that would have cut through Washington Square; later, her opposition to public tower blocks (she instead favored instead low-rise, mixed income housing) became accepted wisdom.

A key lesson from Jacobs' work is that, because great cities grow organically, the main job of government is simply not to ruin what is already there, including the "inefficient" streetscapes which prevent crime by increasing visibility, and which provide the vital social interaction that makes city life so interesting and productive.

Her message is that economic dynamism comes from people being engaged in the "unroutine business of economic trial and error," that is, experiments which create new ways of doing things, and therefore new work. If this process is absent, a city, despite its size, can decline. Great cities do not simply produce more things, but *new* things.

Jane Jacobs

Born in 1916, Jane Butzner grew up in Scranton, Pennsylvania. At 19 she moved to New York and worked as a stenographer and freelance writer, and took courses at Columbia University's School of General Studies.

During World War Two she wrote for Amerika, *a State Department magazine, and met her architect husband Robert Hyde Jacobs. They bought a house in Greenwich Village, and in 1952 she began writing for* Architectural Forum. *Her criticism of the "revitalization" of East Harlem, and plans for the new Lincoln Center, put her in opposition to wealthy developers and pro-development politicians. Funding from the Rockefeller Foundation enabled her to research and write* The Death and Life of Great American Cities.

An early opponent of the Vietnam War, in the 1960s Jacobs relocated with her family to Canada to prevent her sons being drafted. She played an important role in debates about city developments in Toronto and Vancouver. Jacobs died in Toronto in 2006. For more information, see Life on the Street: The Life of Jane Jacobs *(2016) by Robert Kanigel.*

1936

The General Theory of Employment, Interest, and Money

"The composition of this book has been for the author a long struggle of escape, and so must the reading of it be for most readers if the author's assault on them is to be successful—a struggle of escape from habitual modes of thought and expression. The ideas which are here expressed so laboriously are extremely simple and should be obvious. The difficulty lies, not in the new ideas, but in escaping from the old ones, which ramify, for those brought up as most of us have been, into every corner of our minds."

"Our criticism of the accepted classical theory of economics has consisted not so much in finding logical flaws in its analysis as in pointing out that its tacit assumptions are seldom or never satisfied, with the result that it cannot solve the economic problems of the actual world."

In a nutshell

Elegant models of how economies work are often wrong. Markets are not self-correcting, but need constant intervention and management to ensure high consumer demand, investment, and employment.

In a similar vein

Liaquat Ahamed *Lords of Finance*
Alfred Marshall *Principles of Economics*
Hyman Minsky *Stabilizing an Unstable Economy*
Thomas Piketty *Capital in the Twenty-First Century*

CHAPTER 19

John Maynard Keynes

On New Year's Day, 1936, John Maynard Keynes wrote a letter to his friend George Bernard Shaw. The book he was working on, he said, would "largely revolutionize—not, I suppose, at once but in the course of the next ten years—the way the world thinks about economic problems." On this occasion, Keynes' famous self-confidence was justified, for *The General Theory of Employment, Interest, and Money* would change the landscape of his discipline, create modern macroeconomics, and shape the post-war world economy.

Depending on your point of view, Keynes was the savior of capitalism, or the man who allowed for the great post-war expansion of government. Though many economists hoped that Keynes' influence had waned in the 1990s and 2000s, the financial crisis of 2007–08 saw "The Return of the Master," as a 2009 biography of Keynes by Lord Skidelsky was titled. It was only heavy intervention by governments, most people now accept, that averted another Great Depression. Keynes's ideas came back with a vengeance.

The philosopher Isaiah Berlin described Keynes as "certainly the cleverest man I have met in my life." Shaw said similar. But what were his ideas exactly, and what was the paradigm he sought to upend?

An elegant theory that doesn't work: wages and the economy

Keynes begins the book by noting that as a young economist he had fully accepted the economics paradigm of his day. This "classical" economics, a term coined by Marx to describe the intellectual basis of capitalism, seemed to explain the workings of the modern economic world, but it had slowly dawned on Keynes that it did not. With rare exceptions, for instance, it was simply uninterested in the issue of unemployment.

The classical economists assumed that, because the use of resources in a society was efficient (in the long term), employment would always take care of itself. If an economy slackened, Arthur Pigou said, the price of labor would go down, and that low price would prompt manufacturers to hire again, as it would allow for a profit. This self-balancing system ensured full employment. But in the real economy, Keynes observed, there will be times when a person is between jobs, looking for work, unable to work, or discouraged from trying to get work by the state of the economy. In addition, there is not always a perfect matching-up between demand and supply in terms of labor and wages, because wages can be "sticky;" that is, they stay too high or low for too long, lagging behind what is happening in the rest of the economy. For instance, although there may be a lot of people out of work, unions may resist any fall in wages, because they have long fought for a certain wage level.

Moreover, workers and employers bargain over nominal wages (i.e. an actual figure such as $200 per week), not on "real" wages, that is, the relative purchasing power of a wage relative to prices and inflation. The result is that, if the price of labor across a whole economy went down, so would prices, so in fact not much in the economy would change; there would be no self-correction. Lower money wages would not boost the whole economy, but make workers worse off in relation to other people in society. This is because wage-earners tend to spend most of their income (on housing, food, and transport) while others (owners of capital and landowners) spend less of their income on consumption, and save more. Therefore, "wage flexibility" may not cure an ailing economy, but simply make the rich richer and the poor poorer; you get an economy driven not by wages, but by assets—and if those assets stay in the same hands, there is no dynamism and no social mobility.

There was another reason why Keynes distrusted lower wages as a solution to a stalled economy: anyone owing money (assuming the amount of the debt stayed the same) would have less ability to repay it. A person with a stall or a small shop, for instance, could not increase their prices, but they would still have to pay the fixed debt. The result could be mass insolvencies.

Rather than getting an economy back on its feet by restoring equilibrium in production and consumption, declining wages could lead to a spiral of deflation, anaemic consumption, and a "credit crunch," where lending is considered too risky. Perhaps in the long run, the situation might correct itself, but only at the cost of millions of livelihoods. In such situations, Keynes concluded, the government had a responsibility to act.

An elegant theory that doesn't work: the psychology of demand

Yet the heart of Keynes' thinking was not employment as such, but the problem of demand. Classical economics was built on J. B. Say's observation that "supply creates its own demand." There can never be a lack of demand in an economy, or a glut of anything, because any money a producer (say, of nuts and bolts) earns is spent on buying more raw materials (iron, for example) and other goods he needs (such as food and clothing). Of course, that same producer could grossly overestimate the number of nuts and bolts the market wants, and as a result spend too much on his costs and go bankrupt. Though a setback for him, overall it ensures society's resources are put to more efficient use, preventing any future gluts or shortages of goods. Therefore, supply and demand are not working to different dynamics, but are more like two sides of the same coin, and this applies to savings too. If not spending, a person is saving, and their savings are used for investing back into society's increased productive value.

But what happens, Keynes asks, when not all savings that a society accumulates are poured back into productive investment? Fear of uncertainty in the economy could make people hoard cash, or make bankers hesitant to lend and borrowers afraid to borrow. The economy would slump and unemployment lines grow. This is where Keynes made his crucial break with classical economics: because of the role of uncertainty, and perhaps ungrounded fears, there won't always be a perfect dance between production and consumption. Consumer spending and the desire to save depends on subjective or psychological factors such as a person's view of the future, their wish for independence, or their desire to leave assets to their children, together with objective factors such as current income and interest rates. For businesses, decisions to invest in new plant and equipment depend on the expected rate of return on capital and interest rates. If rates are high, this investment may not happen. Expectations play a big role. If a business owner is confident about the economy, she will expect high future rates of return; if pessimistic, expecting lower rates of return, she may not invest.

Keynes wished to replace the classical "natural" rate of interest with a rate that was optimized to achieve full employment. Such an "optimum" rate would ensure that any benefits to capitalists and savers from rates were not at the expense of full employment. Keynes believed that making full employment the objective of interest rate policy was a sure-fire way to keep an economy healthy, because demand would remain high. The answer was clear: to ensure adequate investment and full employment, the interest rate could not be allowed to float naturally, but should be regulated by government (or central banks) in the national interest.

For Keynes the classical view of the economy was a *Candide*-like belief that "all is for the best in the best of all possible worlds provided we will let well alone." It may have been the view of how we would *like* an economy to work, "but to assume that it actually does so is to assume our difficulties away," he writes. Yet why, if the classical view of demand is so wrong, had it continued to be the dominant economic model? This "consistent logical superstructure," Keynes says, served another purpose: under the guise of being a natural, organic system, it preserved the status quo. It allowed huge amounts of social injustice and even cruelty to go on, while the vested interest of capital and the ruling class were furthered.

What to do: getting the economy going

Keynes jokes that in bad economic times a government might as well bury banknotes in jars underground, then employ thousands of people to dig them up. Paying the workers may be a "waste" in conventional terms, but it wouldn't matter as the overall effect—full employment which gets aggregate demand back to a normal level—outweighs the cost. A government could and should do virtually anything to jumpstart the economy.

There is a definite ratio, Keynes writes, a "multiplier," between the funds a government ploughs into employment and the positive effects on the wider economy, in that people can afford to keep buying goods and services. The problem is that nineteenth-century thinking about "prudence" and "waste" stopped policy makers from seeing that such public expenditures could have a positive effect on economies.

Even as he was writing, Keynes' shocking idea was being proved correct. In his famous first 100 days in office, Franklin D. Roosevelt took a scattergun approach to America's near-dead economy, passing measures that shored up the banking system, cut red tape, devalued the dollar to help exports, and funded huge infrastructure programs (including dams, bridges, and roads). Some of these measures had questionable economic value, but they provided a psychological boost and put money in people's pockets. Roosevelt also (to the consternation of advisers) took America off the gold standard, devalued the dollar and increased the money supply. As there was more money around, Americans felt freer to spend, and recovery began. In contrast, the more prudent measures of FDR's predecessor, President Hoover, had got the country nowhere. Later, the United States' massive war effort powered its economy, again demonstrating Keynes' point that big stimuli have big effects.

For Keynes, governments had a responsibility to use the levers of monetary policy (central bank creation of money and regulating interest rates) and fiscal policy (taxing and spending) to ensure aggregate demand stayed healthy and evened out the business cycle. This meant running budget deficits in bad times, effectively becoming "spender of last resort". When good times returned, governments could afford to cut back spending and get the public finances in order.

Adam Smith said that every thrifty individual is a public benefactor, since it is only through private savings that a nation has a pool of funds for investment. This was mostly true, Keynes says, but not to an *indefinite* degree. After all, if every person lived like a miser, there would be no demand for new clothes, housing, or entertainment which powers an economy. What is good for an individual or a family, is not necessarily good for society. Economic growth needs a lot of spending as well as saving.

Keynes' legacy

Towards the end of the *General Theory*, Keynes notes that if his proposed "central controls" succeeded in stoking economic output such that full employment was achieved, there was no reason why a national economy should then not default to the classical model of the economy being left to market forces. This is in fact what happened in the post-war era: central banks chose inflation targets and governments ran fiscal policies designed to keep demand high, but prices and investment were left up to individuals and companies. As long as the central controls achieved a good balance between "the propensity to consume and the inducement to invest," then "there is no more reason to socialise economic life than there was before," Keynes writes.

The Great Depression was just a case of "magneto trouble," (an engine problem) Keynes said, that needed a specific, mechanical fix. There was no case for a wholesale reorganization of production in any communistic sense, simply a need to create the environment that would ensure that all people who wanted to work could be productively employed. Indeed, it is only by enlarging government's role in the way he outlines that capitalist democracies can remain healthy, warding off the prospect of totalitarian revolution. Keynes admits that authoritarian states solve the unemployment problem, but "at the expense of efficiency and freedom." Keynes' system offered a lifeline, a chance "to cure the disease whilst preserving efficiency and freedom."

The world would grab Keynes' lifeline with gusto, so much so that by the early 1970s President Nixon would say, "We are all Keynesians now." Post-war Keynesian national economies seemed to succeed in producing humane capitalism that put people rather than capital first, and which resulted (as Thomas Piketty has demonstrated) in less inequality than the long historical norm, with wage-earners holding their own against the interests of capital.

Final comments

What motivated Keynes to become an economist, when he could have excelled at any number of professions, was that wrong thinking in economics could have devastating consequences. Countries could wither because of irrational attachments to ideas such as the natural rate of interest or the necessity of the gold standard, and vested interests could keep an economy and its people from reaching their full potential. By exposing the anomalies of this paradigm, he created a new one, and despite many detractors, the Keynesian approach is still at the heart of today's world economy.

John Maynard Keynes

Keynes was born in 1883 in Cambridge. His father was a logician and economist at Cambridge University, and his mother a social reformer who became mayor of the city. Keynes won scholarships to Eton and Cambridge, where he was exposed to some of the great minds of the time: G. E. Moore in philosophy, Alfred Marshall and Cecil Pigou in economics, and Alfred North Whitehead in mathematics.

Keynes took the civil service entry exam, and came second in the country. He took up a post at the India Office, but found it dull and returned to Cambridge to teach economics. While still in his twenties he became editor of the prestigious Economic Journal, *and in 1915 was drafted to the Treasury to negotiate loans for the British government's war effort. After the war, Keynes was included in the British delegation at the Versailles peace conference, and was a strident opponent of German war reparations. With his arguments lost on Prime Minister Lloyd George and the American delegation, he wrote* The Economic Consequences of the Peace *(1919). It was a surprise bestseller and made him a celebrity. His* Tract on Monetary Reform *(1923) argued that to prevent inflation and deflation from wrecking economies, central banks should control the money supply rather being tied to the gold standard. After World War Two, Keynes played an important role in establishing the Bretton Woods system, a flexible regime which would stop the epidemic of currency devaluations which had caused so much animosity before the war. Keynes also helped establish the International Monetary Fund and the World Bank.*

Keynes was part of the "Bloomsbury Set," which included Virginia Woolf, and married Russian ballerina Lydia Lopokov. He supported the Royal Opera, secured funding for Britain's Arts Council, and was a collector of modernist paintings. He very successfully managed the investments of Kings College, Cambridge, and made a fortune for himself from stock investing. On his death in 1946, caused by heart failure and the stress of negotiating post-war terms for Britain, he left an estate worth £479,000, or around £18 million in today's money.

2007

The Shock Doctrine

"Since the fall of Communism, free markets and free people have been packaged as a single ideology that claims to be humanity's best and only defense against repeating a history filled with mass graves, killing fields, and torture chambers. Yet in the Southern Cone [Chile, Argentina, Brazil], the first place where the contemporary religion of unfettered free markets escaped from the basement workshops at the University of Chicago and was applied to the real world, it did not bring democracy; it was predicated on the overthrow of democracy in country after country. And it did not bring peace but required the systematic murder of tens of thousands and the torture of between 100,000 and 150,000 people."

In a nutshell

If not checked by democracy, capitalism can become a coercive ideology.

In a similar vein

Ha-Joon Chang *23 Things They Don't Tell You About Capitalism*
Milton Friedman *Capitalism and Freedom*
Friedrich Hayek *The Use of Knowledge in Society*
Paul Krugman *The Conscience of a Liberal*
Dani Rodrik *The Globalization Paradox*

CHAPTER 20

Naomi Klein

In the 1990s, Naomi Klein became a figurehead of the anticapitalist movement, and a scourge of "neoliberals." She defines neoliberalism or neoconservatism as a policy trinity of the attempted elimination of the public sphere, total corporate freedom, and "skeletal" public spending. Wherever it is applied, she argues, you get a new elite which merges politicians and corporate power, and which brings big transfers of public wealth into private hands and increasing inequality. Yet ironically, the state does not disappear, but emerges as "an aggressive nationalism that justified bottomless spending on security," accompanied by increased surveillance and the shrinking of civil liberties.

Her term "disaster capitalism" refers to "orchestrated raids on the public sphere in the wake of catastrophic events, combined with the treatment of disasters as exciting market opportunities." The second Iraq War was used by the Bush administration as a means to privatize the provision of America's security, making some people very rich in the process, and Hurricane Katrina was seized on by right-wing think tanks as a chance to take over New Orleans' public school system. The title of the book comes from a paragraph in the 1982 edition of Milton Friedman's *Capitalism and Freedom,* in which Friedman seems to say that the point at which shocks occur (whether political or natural), was the time to bring in extreme capitalist measures which normally would not be tried. In Klein's view, this longing for a "clean slate" is not the innocent wish of an economist, but carries sinister political implications. From Latin America to Russia, she argues, ideological capitalism has been installed on the back of political shocks, not through democracy. Just as communism required authoritarianism to bring it to its conclusion, so "fundamentalist capitalism" requires the erosion of democracy to achieve its ends, to be replaced by a cabal of public and private sector elites. Both forms of political economy are ideologies that either end in violence, or which require violence to uphold the ideology.

I focus here on her analysis of the imposition of free-market capitalism in Latin America, but Klein also applies her thinking to Poland, China, South Africa, and Russia. *The Shock Doctrine: The Rise of Disaster Capitalism* is an unashamed polemic, with all the evidence-selecting that polemics involve, but it is heavily researched and a compelling read, and may have you questioning your beliefs.

Shock and awe: Chile and the Chicago Boys

For John Foster Dulles, the secretary of state in the Eisenhower administration, and his brother Allen Dulles, head of the new CIA, emerging "developmental" states (combining capitalism with an active government role) represented proxy Marxism. In a Cold War geopolitical reality, they determined to overthrow them. In 1953, a CIA plot overthrew the Mossadegh government in Iran and replaced it with the Shah, and the following year the CIA sponsored a coup in Guatemala that got rid of the democratically elected Jacobo Arbenz.

But some right-wing American economists, such as Theodore Schulz at the University of Chicago, believed that free market capitalism would only triumph over "pink" development economics if it was taught at universities. Schulz hatched a plan, supported by the US State Department, to have Chilean economics students taught by University of Chicago professors. From 1956 to 1970, scores of Chileans were sent to Chicago at American taxpayers' expense, and educated to become free market "ideological warriors," Klein says. The Chilean students were taught to disdain their country's efforts to create a social safety net, provide universal health care and education, and protect national industries, and instead embrace monetarism, deregulation, privatization, and free trade. In 1965, Ford Foundation funding enabled the program to be extended to students from across Latin America, including Brazil, Argentina, and Mexico.

In Chile's 1970 elections, Salvador Allende's party won on a socialist platform of nationalization that would involve fair compensation to foreign owners. But American companies (including big copper miners and ITT, which ran most of Chile's phone network) saw Allende as the start of a socialist takeover of Latin America, and worked with US authorities on an economic "dirty tricks" campaign to undermine the President.

In 1973, a military coup led by General Pinochet not only killed Allende himself, but over 3,000 other "subversives." 80,000 were put in prison, and 200,000 left the country. While business interests, the military and the CIA had been co-operating to overthrow Allende, a group of University of Chicago-trained young economists were drawing up plans for a massive reset of Chile's economy. These plans, codified in a 500-page document known as "The Brick," involved privatization of state-owned companies, financial deregulation, and the end of price controls that had kept the cost of bread and cooking oil low. Pinochet was told that following these measures would see the end of inflation, and largely adopted the plan.

Inflation in fact reached 375 percent in 1974, twice what it was under Allende. The end of import tariffs meant the country was flooded with cheap imports, local companies went under, unemployment ramped up and hunger became a problem. But when Milton Friedman visited Chile in March 1975, his opinion was that the government had not gone far enough in removing state intervention in the economy. More "shock treatment" was needed to jolt it onto the right course. As well as his talks to banks and lectures at universities, Friedman had a 45-minute meeting with Pinochet himself. In a follow up letter to the President, he advocated a further 25 percent cut to public spending, and complete free trade. "Gradualism is not feasible," he wrote. "Chicago Boy" Sergio de Castro was appointed the new Minister of Finance, privatizing 500 state-owned companies and ending the last trade barriers. In the depression that followed, the price of bread skyrocketed, but there was no longer any democracy to vote the junta out. It ruled by terror. Public schools were replaced by a voucher system and social security was privatized, as were kindergartens and cemeteries.

By 1976, Argentina, Uruguay, and Brazil, which had all been showcases of the post-war development state, had copied Chile's "reforms," which in each case resulted in Chicago School economics along with US-backed military governments.

Chilean miracle?

The "Chilean economic miracle" that economists often herald only gained steam in the mid-1980s, Klein points out, a decade after the coup. Pinochet was forced to renationalize many companies, and sacked de Castro and other "Chicago Boys" who had been in key government posts. The only thing that prevented Chile going into complete meltdown was that Pinochet had resisted privatizing Codelco, the state copper mining company that provided the bulk of Chile's export revenues.

If the Chilean economy did get onto an even keel and grow, it was not because it became a free market paradise in the Friedman and Hayek mold, Klein argues, but because it became a "corporatist" state in which government, business, and landowners colluded to retain power. A few people got very rich, thanks to the privatization of state industries, while the workers lost out.

Chile under the Chicago School, in Klein's view, foretold what would happen in much of the rest of the world in the ensuing decades: frenzies of asset speculation, rampant privatization, the hollowing out of the middle class, decimation of industry thanks to free-trade deals, and increasing inequality. Various forms of "shock therapy" around the world simply allowed a few to make a lot of money quickly. For instance, the attempted coup in Russia in 1993 gave Boris Yeltsin the opportunity to lock up opposition leaders and implement "the fire-sale privatization that created the country's notorious oligarchs." The shock of Tiananmen Square gave the Communist Party space to ramp up the market economy, without providing complementary worker's rights or political freedoms.

A torturous record

The problem, Klein says, is that you cannot advocate massive economic change in a country without that change having big political consequences. It may well be that Friedman met Pinochet only once, but his people had been training Latin Americans for years and were hell-bent on using Chile and other countries as the lab for their theories. When it happened that those theories were taken up by governments, including brutal ones, Friedman could not simply say, "that's politics." Friedman saw himself as a physician ending a plague in Chile, "the plague of inflation," yet removing disease, Klein notes, justifies a doctor in doing just about anything. She heads one chapter with a quote from the writer Eduardo Galeano: "People were in prison so that prices could be free." Anyone considered to be part of the Chilean left, from economics professors to journalists to students, was fired, imprisoned, or killed.

The world soon knew about Pinochet's executions and torture centers, and there was outrage, but critics put his *economic* plan into a different basket. Even as the junta was being showered with loans, it was ordering the murder, in 1976, of Allende's ex-finance minister Orlando Letelier in New York. Only the week before Letelier's death by car bomb, he had penned an article saying that Friedman could not be defended on the grounds that he had offered mere "technical" advice to the Pinochet regime.

It should also be noted that free-market economist Friedrich Hayek controversially defended Chile's Pinochet regime on the grounds that it was a transitional dictatorship, and was also an adviser on its free-market reform program.

Final comments

Some uncomfortable facts get in the way of Klein's narrative. For one, Chile under Allende was hardly the democratic socialist nirvana she makes it out to be, with constant political and economic turmoil and super-high inflation. Yet neither was Chile's eventual economic success simply the result of Chicago

School policies. The "Chilean Miracle" was only witnessed after Pinochet had changed economic course several times, renationalizing companies and putting in place expensive "socialist" social programs. As economist Brad DeLong concluded in a blog about "who was right" on Chile, "Chilean history from this period is as much a 'state-building' miracle as a 'free-market' miracle."

Klein posits the Chilean experiment as being the first installment of a neoliberal takeover, and that "disaster capitalism" has led to a more unequal, riskier and generally nastier world. Yet as Johann Norberg argues in "The Klein Doctrine: The Rise of Disaster Polemics" (2009), economic liberalism, wherever it has been applied, tends to increase wealth across the board. Where would you prefer to live, he asks: the failed state of socialist Cuba—or Chile, the best economy in South America?

Klein does not deny that markets bring prosperity; her fury is for the neoliberal form of capitalism, which seems only to advance at the barrel of a gun. And her point about ideology is important. If we know full well the horrors unleashed by ideologies of the left (communism under Stalin and Mao, for instance), we must also be very careful not to support extreme laissez-faire capitalism if it requires the suspension of political freedoms, even if only "temporarily", which open the door to obscene human rights abuses. She relates the story of an Argentinian television crew stumbling upon a torture chamber used during the country's junta (and free-market) phase, when 30,000 people were "disappeared." The gruesome rooms had been walled up when a gleaming new mall was built on top of it.

Naomi Klein

Klein was born in 1970 in Montreal. Her parents had moved to Canada in 1967 to escape the Vietnam War draft. At the University of Toronto she became editor of the student newspaper, and left before finishing her degree to work at the Toronto Globe and Mail.

Klein has been an outspoken critic of US foreign policy. She has been involved in Occupy protests and demonstrations at the G-20 summits. Her first book was No Logo *(2000, see* 50 Politics Classics*); her most recent is* This Changes Everything: Capitalism vs. the Climate *(2015).*

2007

The Conscience of a Liberal

"The New Deal did more than create a middle-class society. It also brought America closer to its democratic ideals, by giving working Americans real political power and ending the dominant position of the wealthy elite . . . Liberalism, in other words, isn't just about the welfare state: It's also about democracy and the rule of law."

In a nutshell

Growing inequality is not simply the result of technological change or globalization, but is the product of political values and decisions which can be reversed.

In a similar vein

Robert J. Gordon *The Rise and Fall of American Growth*
John Maynard Keynes *The General Theory of Employment, Interest, and Money*
Naomi Klein *The Shock Doctrine*
Hyman Minsky *Stabilizing an Unstable Economy*
Thomas Piketty *Capital in the Twenty-First Century*

CHAPTER 21

Paul Krugman

Paul Krugman is something of a superstar economist, holding forth in his columns for *The New York Times*. Yet many of the issues he writes on today—an ideological hijacking of politics, protecting the welfare state, the role of unions, the role of race in America, the best ways to create economic growth—were explored in greater depth in *The Conscience of a Liberal*.

The title is a play on Barry Goldwater's 1963 *The Conscience of a Conservative*, a manifesto for the "New Right" of American politics. Goldwater ran unsuccessfully against Lyndon B. Johnson in the presidential race of 1964, but many of his ideas would be taken up by Ronald Reagan. With *The Conscience of a Liberal*, Krugman sought to do for the center-left what Goldwater had done for the right—except that, as explained below, Krugman does not consider his views left-wing at all, but mainstream.

Krugman lays much of the blame for America's problems on a political and economic ideology that by its nature increases inequality. This is in stark contrast to the post-war decades, he recalls, when there existed a political consensus that sought to bring prosperity for all.

The not-so-good old days

Krugman goes to some length to remind the reader what America was like before Roosevelt's New Deal, in the period from the 1870s to the 1930s. He describes it as "a land of vast inequality in wealth and power, in which a nominally democratic political system failed to represent the economic interests of the majority."

There was also a strong anti-government ideology. Taxation was evil, the market was always right, and centralized government was painted as a European plague. True, living standards were rising—Krugman admits that there was "a vast improvement in the quality of life" in many areas in this period (see the commentary on Robert J. Gordon for details), yet most American lives were marked by economic insecurity. If you fell ill, were disabled, or lost your job, or if you grew old without children to support you, you would face poverty. There was no safety net, because taxation was very low: the wealthy paid only 1 percent of income compared to 20 percent today.

So why, Krugman asks, wasn't there a lot more political demand to help the worse-off? One reason was political disenfranchisement. In 1910, 14 percent of adult males were not eligible to vote because they were non-naturalized immigrants, and of course Southern blacks were disenfranchised by Jim Crow laws. The result: a quarter of the population, pretty much the poorest quarter, were cut out of the political process.

Krugman observes that "Middle-class societies don't emerge automatically as an economy matures, they have to be *created* through political action." It was only the election of Franklin Delano Roosevelt (FDR), in the depths of the Great Depression, and his "New Deal," including the Social Security Act of 1935 providing for federal unemployment and old age insurance, that made America less unequal. The New Deal, Krugman argues, "brought America closer to its democratic ideals, by giving working Americans real political power and ending the dominant position of the wealthy elite."

The Great Compression

In the post-war era, a new affluence flooded America. The massive inequality and political polarization of the 1920s seemed a thing of the past. The majority could afford to live decently, with their own home and car, and stable jobs, all of which provided "a new sense of dignity amongst ordinary Americans." In the 1920s, workers lived in fear of their bosses. Now they had decent pay, safe conditions, and health and employment insurance. That wages and conditions were good for the average person could be traced back to FDR's Fair Labor Relations Act of 1935, which supported the right of workers to organize themselves and unions to strengthen. The class consciousness of the 1920s was gone, because the rich were few and far between. One family might have a Chevy and another a Cadillac, but "there were no big differences in where people could go and what they could do," Krugman writes. Why were there many fewer rich people? In a word, taxation. In the 1920s there had never been more than a 24 percent tax on income. Roosevelt ramped this up, and taxation stayed high into the 1950s and 1960s to pay for welfare provision and the Cold War.

Standard economic theory, Krugman notes, says that you can't mess with the laws of supply and demand, and that any attempt to narrow pay differences is counterproductive. High taxes on profits would destroy incentives and cause business investment to collapse, while big increases in wages lead to mass unemployment. In fact, none of this happened—unparalleled government intervention coincided with an economic boom that lasted until the oil shocks of the 1970s.

Supply-side (i.e. tax cutting) economists find this so disturbing, Krugman notes, that they have tried to rewrite history. For them, prosperity began with Ronald Reagan. But income growth during the Reagan, Bush, and Clinton administrations did not come close to that enjoyed from World War Two to the mid-1970s. Krugman's point is that while the Great Depression still looms large in the collective memory, the "Great Compression" (when America created a great middle class and rapidly decreased inequality, with much credit to government action) is now forgotten.

A new Gilded Age?

Krugman admits that America is much more productive and richer than it was in the early 1970s, but gone is the sense that prosperity is *widely shared*. Average income (the income of the nation, divided by the number of its people) has gone up and up, but this is thanks to a huge increase in the wealth of the rich, skewing the numbers. The more telling measure is median income, the income of people who are neither very rich nor very poor, but in the middle. Adjusted for inflation, the median income of adult males in their 30s and 40s is 12 percent lower than it was in 1973. The drop explains why in so many families both parents are having to work, and why people generally work for longer hours than they did a generation ago.

Why have the earnings of the top 1 percent pulled away from the top earning 10 percent? The safe answer, which economists favor but for which there is little evidence, is that technological change increases the rewards going to the highly skilled. This answer sidesteps what may be the real cause: what Krugman calls "institutions, norms, and political power."

Some of the increased inequality can be attributed to the decline of unions, thanks to a well-funded right-wing crusade against them. The Republican party's antagonism, and hardball tactics by big business, resulted in a massive drop in the number of unionized workers, from 30 percent of the workforce in 1960 to 11 percent today. By way of comparison, Canada's workforce remains above 30 percent unionized, and has much greater equality of income. Growing income inequality in America, therefore, had little to do with technological change, but a lot to do with political change.

The politics of inequality

For Krugman it is no accident that right-wing conservatives took over the Republican party in the mid-1970s, and the well-documented increase in inequality began in the early 1980s: "polarizing political change came first, and rising economic inequality followed." But if that is true, why did Americans twice elect George W. Bush, who embodied the new kind of conservatism? One of the features of the new Republicans, Krugman says, is the use of national security issues as distractions from what is happening in the economy. Bush would probably not have been re-elected were it not for 9/11, and the subsequent Iraq War boosted his appeal until it became clear that it was based on false premises. Bush also tried (and failed) to privatize Social Security, a ploy consistent with the new kind of Republican party that exploited race issues for electoral gain. The civil rights movement of the 1960s and 1970s created a "white backlash," Krugman says, which became focused on opposition to universal health care and the welfare state, of which black Americans are sizeable beneficiaries.

Despite the increased intellectual influence of the right, thanks to generous funding of conservative think tanks, Krugman cites data showing Americans shifting to the left on a number of issues. The US is not in fact a conservative nation, he argues, or even a center-right one, but center-left. This new political reality has been driven partly by immigration. Most new immigrants are Hispanic or Asian, and feel no connection with the anti-state ideology of New Conservatism; and being non-white, they are instinctively repelled by the whiteness of the Republican Party and its apparent willingness to exploit "white backlash" in the service of winning power.

Indeed, many argue that this is exactly what Donald Trump did to win the 2016 Republican nomination. He energized the white Republican voter base, and inspired other white Americans to vote who felt hard-done-by in an increasingly multicultural America. Yet Trump's ultimate victory in the presidential race also casts doubt on Krugman's theory that the US is inherently "center-left" nation. Looking at the results of the election, only half of Americans fit this description.

Final comments

Given the image that many non-Americans have of the US as a haven for right-wingers who are willing to let the levers of government grind to a halt to make an ideological point, Krugman's notion that the US is inherently progressive takes some selling. And yet, Obama's election in 2008 and 2012, along with the enactment of the "Obamacare" universal health insurance regime, provides support for this. Krugman is most convincing when he argues that only politics can take the lead in reducing economic inequality, with all its bad effects. Whereas wealth tends to arise of its own accord, prosperity—evenly shared—has always required political action.

Paul Krugman

Krugman was born in 1953 and grew up on Long Island, New York. His father worked in insurance and his paternal grandparents emigrated from Russia in the 1920s. He won a place to Yale University, and went on to do a PhD in economics at Massachusetts Institute of Technology. He became a full professor at MIT in 1984, and from 2000 to 2015 was at Princeton University. He is currently professor of economics at the Graduate Center of the City of New York.

Krugman's 2008 Nobel Prize for Economics was awarded for his work on "new trade theory," which was an evolution of Ricardo's theory of comparative advantage, and "new economic geography," or how production is organized across the globe; he is also known for his work on income inequality, macroeconomics, and currency crises. In 2007–08, Krugman was among the most prominent economists urging Keynesian stimulus to revive the US economy, instead of austerity measures. "The Conscience of a Liberal" is also the title of his New York Times *blog on political and economic matters.*

Other books include End This Depression Now! *(2012),* The Return of Depression Economics and the Crisis of 2008 *(2008),* The Great Unraveling *(2003),* The Age of Diminished Expectations *(1990), plus many academic works.*

2005

Freakonomics

"Economics is, at root, the study of incentives: how people get what they want, or need, especially when other people want or need the same thing . . . An incentive is simply a means of urging people to do more of a good thing and less of a bad thing. There are three basic flavors of incentive: economic, social, and moral."

"Whatever the incentive, whatever the situation, dishonest people will try to gain an advantage by whatever means necessary . . . Cheating may or may not be human nature, but it is certainly a prominent feature in just about every human endeavor."

"Morality, it could be argued, represents the way that people would like the world to work—whereas economics represents how it actually does work. Economics is above all a science of measurement."

In a nutshell

We want a world based on morality; we have a world based on incentives.

In a similar vein

Albert O. Hirschman *Exit, Voice, and Loyalty*
Richard Thaler *The Making of Behavioral Economics*
Thomas Schelling *Micromotives and Macrobehavior*

CHAPTER 22

Steven D. Levitt & Stephen J. Dubner

In 2003, journalist Stephen J. Dubner went to interview Steven D. Levitt, an up-and-coming economist at the University of Chicago who had a popular *New York Times* column. To his surprise, Levitt spoke in plain English and was, in contrast to every other economist he had spoken to, fascinating. Levitt was hopeless at mathematics and uninterested in macroeconomics, and claimed to know little about the stock market, inflation, or the economics of taxation. What he was fixated on, Dubner recalled, "were the riddles of everyday life."

Levitt's abiding interest in cheating, corruption, and crime were outside the mainstream of economics—but the thinking behind them was based on a fascination for the supreme power of *incentives* in the decisions people make in life. Economics, Levitt explained, is essentially about "explaining how people get what they want, or need, especially when other people want or need the same thing."

Levitt was too intrigued by his work and experiments to write a book, and agreed to do so only if Dubner got involved. In *Freakonomics*, the combination of startling research and sparkling prose produced a surprise hit; economic analysis was suddenly interesting to millions. In "stripping a layer or two from the surface of modern life and seeing what is happening underneath," including freakish curiosities not normally studied in Economics 101, the authors spawned a new genre of popular economics.

Incentives to cheat

We all know individually whether we have or have not committed an act considered as cheating. What's more interesting than the act itself is the incentive behind it. The book provided interesting examples: Why would a teacher cheat on a school testing standard? And why do ordinary workers steal bagels?

There are several, understandable, reasons why teachers might cheat. The authors discuss "high-stakes testing," an educational initiative in which if a school tests poorly, federal funding can be stopped and teachers can be fired. If a teacher's students do well enough, the teacher is praised and may be promoted and even rewarded with cash. At one point, California handed bonuses of $25,000 to teachers producing high test-score gains. There was just one problem: there was no system in place for detecting teacher cheating, and so it was rarely detected or punished. "A cheating teacher may tell herself that she is helping her students," Levitt and Dubner point out, "but the fact is that she would appear far more concerned with helping herself." Alarmingly, an analysis of Chicago public schools' test scores found that, "It was the teachers with low-scoring classrooms who were most likely to cheat." Eventually, big cash bonuses for teachers were scrapped, in light of evidence that "classrooms with the teachers identified as cheaters scored worse, by an average of more than a full grade." The fact that teacher cheating fell by over 30 percent after the incentives were scrapped tells us something about the power of incentives.

White-collar crime costs billions of dollars a year, but it is more difficult to detect than other forms of crime. Embezzling, for instance, is harder to discover than bank robbery. Then there is the problem of who the victim is. When you take some copier paper from the office stores, who exactly is the victim? Occasionally, we do get an insight into white-collar thievery and its victims. Paul Feldman was a former economist who started supplying fresh bagels to offices. He would drop off a basket of bagels in the morning, and return later to collect the empty basket and the cash that people had left. Unfortunately, only 87 percent of bagel eaters left money for what they consumed. People were more honest in smaller offices than in large firms, and less honest when the weather was bad than on nice days. Feldman found that morale was a decisive factor. When people liked their boss and their work, they nearly always paid for what they ate. And contrary to what we might expect, people higher up the corporate food chain were less likely to pay. Did these executives have a greater sense of entitlement or, Levitt wonders, did they make it to the top *because* of their cheating? Perhaps the main point, though, is that most people *do* pay, despite the fact that payment was by honor system.

Economics is above all science of measurement, Levitt and Dubner note, and what we measure frequently confounds expectations, sometimes in a negative way. Whereas "morality represents the way that people would like the world to work," they write, "economics represents how it actually *does* work." Changing the moral code of a society can be difficult and take generations; changing incentives, by contrast, is often an easy and quick way of achieving socially positive outcomes.

Asymmetric information

Asymmetric information—when one party in a situation has more information about the situation than the other—is one of the keys to individual or organizational success. Whether it involves a person selling real estate, life insurance, or cars, or even an organization like the Ku Klux Klan increasing membership, the possession of asymmetric information is often decisive in achieving our goals. The advantage of the expert rests on the belief of his clients that they lack his crucial knowledge: "Armed with information," Levitt and Dubner write, "experts can exert a gigantic, if unspoken leverage: fear." However, once this information becomes public, their advantage is wiped away and the leverage changes hands.

When employing a real estate agent to sell and achieve the best price for your home, you would expect that your interests are the same as the agent. The higher the sale price obtained, the higher the fee received by the agent. Levitt questioned whether this is really the case. His research found that agents, instead of waiting for the highest price, look for a quick sale and accept a lower fee so they can move on to the next sale. Not only this, but agents advertise their own homes more attractively than clients' homes, and leave their homes on the market for longer (on average ten days), achieving a higher average price (roughly three percent). "The point here is not that real-estate agents are bad people," Levitt points out, "but that they simply are people—and people inevitably respond to incentives." Since the birth of online real estate sales platforms, the gap between the clients' and agents' sale prices has shrunk by a third.

Behind the obvious

One of the biggest difficulties when analyzing data is whether there exists only correlation between variables, or actual causation. Causation can sometimes be very difficult to find and it can come from the most unusual of sources. "Dramatic effects often have distant, even subtle, causes," Levitt notes. His famous paper on abortion, published in 2001, suggested that the large reduction in crime in the 1990s "was, in the language of economists, an 'unintended benefit' of legalized abortion." With such a controversial claim, Levitt came under sustained attack in the media and "managed to offend nearly everyone." However, he does provide a highly logical and persuasive argument for his opinion.

He dismisses the idea that crime fell because the economy improved. There are reliable studies showing "virtually no link between the economy and violent crime." Neither did the death penalty lower crime, since its deterrent effect is mainly limited to homicide. What about the hiring of more police? This only accounted for 10 percent of the fall in crime levels, Levitt says, and the crash of the crack cocaine market accounted for only a 15 percent fall. Some said that the greying of America was causing less crime, but the data did not suggest this, nor was regulation of the gun market a big factor, since if there is demand for something, a strong black market always provides it. Levitt went beyond such obvious explanations and instead suggested that the reduction in crime was set in motion a whole generation before it even occurred, with the 1973 Roe v. Wade Supreme Court decision in favor of legalized abortion.

But how did one's woman's legal right to abort her foetus "trigger the greatest crime drop in recorded history"? Two factors, Levitt says: childhood poverty, and single-parent households. He found these to be the strongest predictors that a child will have a criminal future, along with the limited education of the mother. The very factors that drive American women to abortion also predicts that their children, had they been born, would possibly have had criminal lives. Or as he puts it: "Legalized abortion led to less unwantedness; unwantedness leads to high crime; legalized abortion, therefore, led to less crime." Since 1985, in those states that had high abortion rates, there has been a 30 percent drop in crime compared to low-abortion states.

Levitt also looked into the black–white income and education gap, and the baby name phenomenon. He found that "black children who perform poorly in school do so not because they are black but because a black child is more likely to come from a low-income, low-education household." Interestingly, black students test similarly to white students when coming from comparable backgrounds and schools, making the distinction between correlation and causation even more challenging. Regarding baby names, Levitt found that a person with a distinctively "black" name is likely to have worse life outcomes than a person with a white-sounding name. He does, however, suggest that a black name is not the *cause* but is only an indicator of his or her outcome. Economists, he notes, have to be very careful in separating causation from mere correlation, and should simply be led where the data takes them. Not only is this more interesting, but it prevents the economist from being able to push an ideology or moral stance.

Final comments

Levitt likes to think of himself as outside the box of orthodox economics, when it could be argued that his work is simply orthodox economics taken to its extreme. The discipline is, after all, based on the idea of human beings as self-maximizing units who act according to the incentives in their environment to get what they want. He assumes that 87 percent of people pay for their bagels, even if it is an honor system, because of some threat of social sanction if they are discovered, and imagines the office workers thinking, "What would happen if I didn't pay and was found out?"

Such a reductionist view of human action (we are *only* our drives or instincts, or *only* the result of social conditioning) overlooks the fact that most people also have a conscience or moral compass—what Adam Smith called an "impartial spectator," that makes us do the right thing *whether or not* anyone is looking. People choose to live according to chosen ethics which have little to do self-maximization—indeed, many people in history have died for what they believed was right. People act from a range of motivations, including irrational quests for beauty, love, or truth, which are for the most part beyond the pat explanations of economists—even very good, impartial ones. Yes, we respond to incentives, but as the psychologist Albert Bandura has noted, these incentives are often ones we have fashioned *ourselves* as part of a desire to transcend our situation or live up to some goal. Moral purpose can be the highest form of rationality.

That said, *Freakonomics* created a template for a new kind of engagement between economists and the public, and for that reason alone the work is commendable. Get it for the many fascinating examples we have not space for here, or read the follow-up work *Superfreakonomics* (2009).

Steven Levitt & Stephen Dubner

Born in 1967, Levitt graduated in economics from Harvard University and received his PhD. from MIT in 1994. He is an economics professor at the University of Chicago. In 2003 he was awarded the American Economic Association's John Bates Clark Medal, given to the best US economist under 40. Dubner, born in 1963, is a graduate of Appalachian State University and Columbia University.

Levitt and Dubner's other books include Think like a Freak *(2014) and* When to Rob a Bank . . . And 131 More Warped Suggestions and Well-Intended Rants *(2015). They write a popular blog, freakonomics.com, and Dubner hosts Freakonomics Radio.*

2010

The Big Short

"Thousands and thousands of serious financial professionals, most of whom, a few years ago, had been doing something else with their lives, were now playing craps with money they had made off subprime mortgage bonds. The subprime mortgage industry Eisman once knew better than anyone on the planet had been a negligible corner of the capital markets. In just a few years it had somehow become the most powerful engine of profits and employment on Wall Street—and it made no economic sense."

"No Wall Street firm would be able to extricate itself, as there were no longer any buyers. It was as if bombs of differing sizes had been placed in virtually every major Western financial institution. The fuses had been lit and could not be extinguished. All that remained was to observe the speed of the spark, and the size of the explosions."

In a nutshell

Despite their "masters of the universe" image, investing professionals often fail to understand the risk of the assets they trade in, with awful social consequences.

In a similar vein

J. K. Galbraith *The Great Crash 1929*
Benjamin Graham *The Intelligent Investor*
Hyman Minsky *Stabilizing an Unstable Economy*
Robert Shiller *Irrational Exuberance*

CHAPTER 23

Michael Lewis

People talk of the greed of bankers, but bankers are also prisoners to intellectual paradigms which, if wrong, can produce catastrophic losses. Lewis' book is about the handful of people who not only pointed out that there was something wrong with the subprime mortgage system, but who actively bet against or "shorted" it. All were outsiders, even misfits, and Lewis's fascinating psychological portraits make this arguably his best book. As with *Flash Boys* (2014), his exposé of high-frequency stock trading, *The Big Short* is deeply researched and opens a window onto a realm of finance which had deliberately been made obscure to the public. Indeed, Lewis is so good at explaining the 2007–08 crisis that he was asked to speak several times before the US Congress' Financial Crisis Inquiry Commission.

Adam McKay's 2015 film version of *The Big Short* is enjoyable, but cannot replicate the pace and sheer detail of the book. It involves a cast of characters; we look here at the two most important, Steve Eisman and Michael Burry.

Just helping the poor: the evolution of subprime

Steve Eisman had cut his teeth on Wall Street in the 1980s, writing reports on a new breed of financial company specializing in housing loans for people with little earnings history or collateral, and who did not qualify for government mortgage guarantees. Often it was a second mortgage they were taking out, and not necessarily to buy a house, but to release the equity in their existing house because they needed the money, or to receive a large mortgage loan that they could use to pay off credit card debts, but at a lower interest rate.

Eisman thought that this "subprime" market was a natural response to growing income inequality, and served a social purpose by helping poorer Americans pay less for their debt. The subprime loan companies were another matter. Thanks to a nascent market in mortgage bonds (which pooled thousands of mortgages into securities which could be bought and sold), lenders could quickly sell on the loans they made, as soon as they made them. They did not have to think about the likelihood that a borrower could service the loan, since it would no longer be their problem. To some it seemed strange, if not a little wrong, to turn people's homes into an asset that anyone could buy and sell. But Wall Street provided a public-good rationale: in creating this market, it would attract a lot of capital that would result in lower interest rates for lower-middle class Americans.

The problem with subprime lending, Eisman saw, was that it was a "fast buck industry" made up of unscrupulous characters. In 1997, he wrote a report exposing the practices of the subprime lenders, and most of them subsequently went bankrupt. By 2002, however, a new subprime lender, Household Finance Corporation, had emerged, selling second mortgages at high interest rates (12.5 percent), when they had been deceptively advertised as being 7 percent. Class actions resulted in Household paying a big fine, but the government did not shut it down. Its big portfolio of loans was sold to the British bank HSBC, and its CEO Bill Aldinger, instead of going to jail, pocketed $100 million.

Eisman was shocked that the authorities hadn't done anything to protect the most vulnerable kind of borrower. People were taken in by loan offers which would allow them to pay off their car loans and credit card loans as they remortgaged, but the interest rate on offer was just a teaser rate, low for a couple of years then suddenly shooting up. At this point, many people could no longer cope with the repayments. Eisman gave a name to the consumer finance and subprime system: "Fuck the poor."

By 2005, when Eisman was running his own hedge fund, FrontPoint, focused on consumer finance, subprime lending had made a triumphant comeback. His team heard of migrant Mexican strawberry pickers with an income of $14,000 being given over $700,000 to buy a house, no money down. Eisman's nanny, no less, was offered loans to buy several houses in Queens, New York.

In the 1990s subprime lending had averaged $20–30 billion a year; in 2000 it was $130 billion; by 2005 it had reached $625 billion, and $507 billion of this was converted into mortgage bonds. Yet now, floating interest rates instead of fixed ones made the chances of default much higher. The subprime "lenders" were not lenders in any conventional sense, but were simply "originators" of loans, which were then bundled and sold to Wall Street investment banks including Bear Stearns, Merrill Lynch, Goldman Sachs and Morgan Stanley, who promptly turned them into mortgage bonds to sell to their customers. These banks became increasingly exposed to the subprime market.

Give it a rating, any rating

Lewis profiles Michael Burry, a one-eyed neurologist who left medicine to set up a Californian hedge fund. In 2004 Burry had begun studying the mortgage bond market. He noticed in the fine print for one bond brochure that, in the course of 2004, the percentage of mortgages which were described as "interest-only" increased from being 5.85 percent of the pool to 17.48 percent. By the late summer of 2005 this kind of mortgage had grown to 25.34 percent of the pool. Interest-only mortgages, obviously, appealed to people with a low ability to make repayments, but there was another kind of mortgage where people did not even have to pay back the interest; it kept rolling into a bigger snowball of principal, which made eventual repayment more unlikely and default almost certain. Such loans made no sense against traditional lending practices, but the point was that a growing loan book could be sold on to Wall Street banks to be made into bonds. Liking the combination of safety and high interest, institutional buyers snapped up the bonds without questioning the underlying assets. Was it not, after all, solid real estate, and were not the bonds given a good rating by the rating agencies, Moody's and Standard & Poor's?

Smelling an elaborate Ponzi scheme, Burry hatched the idea to sell mortgage bonds short, that is, bet that they would suddenly drop in value when the weakness of the underlying mortgage assets was revealed. There was no facility to do this (who bet against the American housing market?), but he persuaded financial institutions to develop "credit default swaps" for mortgage bonds. A credit default swap is an insurance policy against a bond going bad. Burry could see that if there was an epidemic of mortgage defaults, the bonds representing them could become worthless, and if that happened the owner of the credit default swap could make a fortune: having paid $200,000 in insurance, for instance, you could make $100 million. It was a zero-sum game in which banks, if they got their risk analysis wrong, could be ruined.

Bizarrely, banks selling mortgage bonds had not done their homework on the quality of the home lending that underpinned them, and were willing to sell Burry this insurance. He bought swaps from Deutsche Bank, Goldman Sachs, and Bank of America on bonds representing the riskiest pools of mortgages, the "no-doc" loans issued without proof of income. The banks were happy to sell the insurance because they were relying on ratings from Moody's and Standard & Poor's, but these ratings did not distinguish properly between the riskiness of one mortgage bond and another. "It was as if you could buy flood insurance on the house in the valley for the same price as flood insurance on the house on the mountaintop," Lewis writes. Triple-B rated bonds indicated that there was only a 1 in 500 chance of default, but Burry assessed that they would be made worthless if there was a default rate of only 7 percent. Given that borrowers shifted after two years from teaser rates on their mortgages to higher floating rates, defaults weren't just possible, Burry thought, but highly likely.

Burry liked to ask a question: why, after the tech stock crash of 2000, did house prices around Silicon Valley not collapse (as you might expect) but keep rising? The answer was that the money being thrown at subprime borrowers, fed by the rise of mortgage bonds as an asset class, was fueling a real estate bubble which kept the American economy motoring along. Chairman of the Federal Reserve Bank, Alan Greenspan, kept saying that there was no bubble, and therefore there could be no housing price collapse. Yet as Burry pointed out in a letter to his investors, the 1930s saw a house price collapse of 80 percent. Another collapse was coming, he wrote, which could wipe *half the value* from American real estate.

Weapons of mass destruction

It was Goldman Sachs who created the security which would become famously identified with the crisis of 2008: the "collateralized debt obligation" (CDO). Just as mortgage bonds pooled mortgages, CDOs pooled mortgage *bonds*. The idea behind them was that risk was further spread and minimized, but they actually represented a bonanza for banks selling them: triple-B rated mortgage bonds could now become a triple-*A* rated CDO. It was a brilliant piece of financial engineering built on a lie: for if the housing market soured, the structure of subprime loans ensured that defaults would come not in a trickle, but a tidal wave. CDOs were being sold to German banks, Taiwanese insurance companies, European pension funds—any entity that was required to only buy higher-rated securities which had virtually no chance of losses. In fact, they had bought financial time bombs.

House prices began to fall in 2006, and defaults began to increase, but those shorting subprime bonds, including Burry and Eisman, could not work out why the bonds kept holding their value. At a conference of subprime professionals in Las Vegas in January 2007, Eisman finally realized why the subprime bond market hadn't yet gone bad. The credit default swaps that he and others had bought had prompted the banks involved in subprime to generate even more mortgage bonds, to keep the money coming in and the juggling act going. For several years mortgage bonds had become the driver of profits on Wall Street; now, all that mattered was keeping those profits going.

Yet as 2007 wore on, the bonds did start falling in value, many dropping 30 percent. The CDOs composing triple-B rated subprime bonds should have collapsed too, but did not. Shockingly, Wall Street bond traders, including Bear Stearns and Lehman Brothers, were still publishing glowing reports so as to pass them off to unsuspecting institutional buyers as being quality securities. They were selling, as Lewis puts it, "juice from oranges that were undeniably rotten."

Fallout

In early April 2007, New Century, the biggest subprime lender in the United States, filed for bankruptcy thanks to a swamp of defaults. Another lender, Fremont Investment & Loan, began to see 40 to 50 percent of their loans go sour. Goldman Sachs quickly changed its position from being long on subprime to betting against it. Between 2005 and 2007, Wall Street had created in the vicinity of $240–300 billion worth of subprime-backed CDOs, which were now mostly worthless. Bear Stearns' bets on subprime were so big that its share price dropped to $2 a share, before it was sold to JP Morgan. Lehman Brothers filed for bankruptcy, and Merrill Lynch, after announcing losses of $55 billion on subprime-backed CDOs, was sold to Bank of America.

Bear Stearns and Lehman Brothers collapsed (other banks would have followed if not for government bailouts and guarantees), Lewis points out, because of their ridiculous leverage. In five years, for example, Bear Stearns had gone from making bets representing $20 for every dollar of capital they had, to bets worth $40 for each dollar of capital. Even with a modest decline in their assets, collapse was virtually assured.

When Michael Burry had bought his credit default swaps, they were worth 2 percent of the value of the CDOs he was betting against. In the end, Wall Street banks paid him 75–85%. In a fund with a portfolio of $550 million, he would add $720 million in pure profit. By the end of 2007, Steve Eisman's bets against the subprime market had rained money down into his FrontPoint fund, doubling its size and making him very rich.

Final comments

In the aftermath of 2007, Eisman was sickened by a view common on Wall Street that it was the grasping of the American public that had led to the subprime crisis. In truth, banks encouraged people to lie about their income so they could shovel money at them (the bigger the mortgage, the better to sell on), without reminding them of the consequences should they not keep up payments. Where was government in all this? Lewis tells how the Securities Exchange Commission, the regulator meant to police Wall Street, barely understood the exotic derivatives (financial instruments such as CDOs) that had vastly increased risk in the financial system, and so was in no position to do its job. Meanwhile, the ratings agencies were chasing ratings fees and lived in the pocket of the Wall Street bond market. The crash also exposed the massive conflict of interest in Wall Street banks, who were trading bonds and derivatives for their own account (proprietary trading) but also selling bonds to external investors. By making bets against their own customers' positions, they made fools of them.

Secretary of the Treasury Hank Paulson persuaded Congress to supply $700 billion to buy the distressed subprime mortgage assets of banks, including huge debts on the losing end of credit default swaps, and directly bail out failing banks including Citigroup, whose assets were guaranteed to the tune of $306 billion. The US Federal Reserve bought bad subprime mortgage bonds off banks, so that by 2009, "the risks and losses associated with more than a trillion dollars' worth of bad investments were transferred from big Wall Street firms to the US taxpayer," Lewis writes. While very few bankers lost their jobs, and none went to jail, subprime borrowers were left to default and live in tent cities and gymnasiums while they rebuilt their lives. During a lunch meeting with his old boss, John Gutfreund, ex-CEO of Salomon Brothers, Lewis was given the legendary financier's take on the crisis. "It's laissez-faire until you get in deep shit," he was told. The throwaway remark may stand as the best one-line summary of the crisis, and indeed American finance.

Michael Lewis

Born in 1960, Lewis grew up in New Orleans. He studied Art History at Princeton University and on graduating worked for an art dealer. He studied at the London School of Economics, gaining an MSc in Economics in 1985, then joined Salomon Brothers to work in bond sales, in New York and then in London.

Books include Liar's Poker *(1989),* The New New Thing *(2000),* Moneyball *(2003),* The Blind Side *(2006),* Flash Boys *(2014),* and *The Undoing Project* (2016). *As a financial journalist, he has written for* The New York Times Magazine, Vanity Fair, Slate, The Spectator, New Republic *and* Bloomberg.

2016

Bourgeois Equality

"The Great Enrichment is not to be explained . . . by material matters of race, class, gender, power, climate, culture, religion, genetics, geography, institutions, or nationality. On the contrary, what led to our automobiles and our voting rights, our plumbing and our primary schools were the fresh ideas that flowed from liberalism, that is, a new system of encouraging betterment and a partial erosion of hierarchy."

"Thank God, then, for the Bourgeois Deal, and its democratic test of consumer satisfaction, and the private profit that so lucidly signals its success. And thank God for too for the social gain from reasoning by commercial cost and benefit rather than by national glory or the interests of the aristoi *or the number of souls entering heaven."*

In a nutshell

Capitalism on its own did not create the prosperity of the modern world, but a new philosophy of egalitarian liberalism which unleashed the potential of unprivileged people.

In a similar vein

William J. Baumol *The Microtheory of Innovative Entrepreneurship*
Robert J. Gordon *The Rise and Fall of American Growth*
Karl Polanyi *The Great Transformation*
Ayn Rand *Capitalism: The Unknown Ideal*
Adam Smith *The Wealth of Nations*
Max Weber *The Protestant Ethic and the Spirit of Capitalism*

CHAPTER 24

Deirdre McCloskey

McCloskey is one of an increasing number of economic historians (others include Joel Mokyr and Paul Romer) who emphasize the power of *ideas* over physical inputs or institutions in growth and development. She argues that the modern world cannot be explained (as economists from Adam Smith to Marx to Piketty have said) from the accumulation of capital, "from piling brick on brick, or bachelor's degree on bachelor's degree, or bank balance on bank balance." The bricks, degrees and money were necessary ingredients, but it was equality before the law and human dignity (bourgeois ideas) that explain how things came together in such a powerful fashion in Northern Europe two centuries ago. This combination of "legal liberation and social honoring," McCloskey says, is a timeless wellspring of prosperity. It worked superbly for nineteenth- and twentieth-century Europe and America, and given the chance will have the same positive effect in twenty-first century China and India.

That is the basic argument, but it becomes truly forceful in McCloskey's prose. Her dual background in economics and English literature makes this an unusually delightful, amusing, and page-turning read, as if she had set out to write a book on economics for people who only read fiction. With the text flowing with references to Ibsen, Jane Austen, Chekov, Balzac, and Shakespeare, you feel you are being not just educated, but elevated.

The Great Enrichment

A billion people out of seven billion today live with poor food, sanitation, schools, and housing. That is a tragedy, yet we shouldn't forget that most people, through most of human history, lived like this, in a hand-to-mouth existence, living in a hovel under the thumb of a local lord, and seeing half their children die before the age of five. Not so long ago, an English poet like John Keats could suffer and die from tuberculosis in his 20s because antibiotics hadn't been invented, and as late as 1917, people in a part of rural Sweden could starve to death when their potato crop failed. Books, shoes, furniture and horses were all expensive in terms of the hours of labor you had to work to get them. Today, such things (replace a horse with a car) are either free, cheap, or easily attainable through a regular salary. One American farmer can feed 300 people, and life expectancy has doubled.

The average per capita world income in 2016 is almost that of America's in 1941, or present day Brazil ($33). In the next generations, the rest of the world will approach incomes and standards of living similar to those of the Organisation for Economic Co-operation and Development (OECD) countries, who enjoy per capita income of over $100 a day. "We're on our way to a pretty good material paradise," McCloskey says. The fact that people now consume 70 times more goods and services than they did in 1800 allows for much bigger economies of scale in production, which means cheaper goods and services. A larger population means more minds working on the problems of better medicines and transportation, not to mention environmental quality. Believing that the Great Enrichment we have seen over the last 200 years is just a riot of environmental degradation and consumerist excess is a betrayal, McCloskey says, "of the remaining poor in the world."

How and why did it happen?

Though the Great Enrichment will end poverty, McCloskey reckons that neither economists nor historians, from any political persuasion, can really explain it. They look at "factors," when it is *ideas* and shifts in thinking that enabled a sudden take off in growth and living standards from the late eighteenth century onwards.

Modern economics says that prosperity came from the division of labor, or the accumulation of capital, or the expansion of international trade, or the lowering of transaction costs and increasing economies of scale. These all played their part, but everything from the spinning jenny to the insurance company to the autobahn, along with new political and social constructs such as the American Constitution and the British middle class, arose mainly from a new egalitarian liberalism that began in late sixteenth century Holland, and was later adopted in England, Scotland, and New England. The upsurge in invention and innovation came from new freedoms given to commoners, and new equality of recognition and rights. "What led to our automobiles and our voting rights, our plumbing and our primary schools," McCloskey writes, "were the fresh ideas that flowed from liberalism, that is, a new system of encouraging betterment and a partial erosion of hierarchy." In short, more people were being allowed to "have a go," and to have society value them for their efforts. Capital accumulated *in response to* life-improving and bettering ideas; it was not a cause of them. Capitalism had been around in various guises throughout history, McCloskey notes. It was more specifically *liberalism*, applied to trade and politics, that massively increased wealth.

It was, then, not the aristocracy or rent-seeking bureaucrats who made the modern world, but everyday producers reacting to what people wanted, and providing it. Our heroes became Henry Ford, with his assembly line, or Steve Jobs, with his iPhone. This shift was only possible because bourgeois values of prudence, efficiency, and simply "doing what works" overtook in our estimate the grand aristocratic gesture or the general's glory. The test of any new thing was now not whether it amused or gained the favor of the king, but whether it made the lives of millions easier and better. This is the essence of commerce and bourgeois civilization, and quite different to the pre-bourgeois ethic of simple conquest, sacking, or thievery. The bourgeois paradigm also rests on the dignity of the individual. Formerly, dignity was a simple equation with one's rank, position or station in the social order (hence the English word to denote people of rank, "dignitaries"). The freedom to do and to be recognized, combined with a new dignity of the person, are things we take for granted now, but such bourgeois equality was very liberating when it emerged.

Anti-commercialism

The bourgeois desire to please the customer is arguably more moral, and better for the advance of all people in a community, McCloskey writes, than the mindset of "a haughty aristocracy or an envious peasantry or a proud clerisy." The clerisy—the class of intellectuals and journalists who form public opinion—in its ethical superiority and dislike of commerciality has often turned against technological and commercial progress, favoring antiliberal utopias such as socialism and central planning, nationalism, or more simply ever-increasing regulation. Yet this class, says McCloskey, forgot the one "scientifically proven, social discovery of the nineteenth century . . . that ordinary men and women do not need to be directed from above, and when honored and left alone become immensely creative . . . Liberty and dignity for ordinary people made us rich, in every meaning of the word."

It is equality and dignity before the law that has brought all the comforts of modern life to larger numbers of people (a "paroxysm of betterment"), without restricting their liberty. Of course, a society in which people must compete, and in which a person ventures their savings in some new business that fails, can be desperately sad. But at least all competitors "face the same democratic test by trade." That is, do people want what is being sold? Better that there is this kind of test governing society, than one based on birth, class, ethnicity, or gender. Joseph Schumpeter's concept of "creative destruction" may be fearful, but it is fairer than any communitarian system (socialism, communism) which claims to have solved the human condition.

Liberal civilization is a civilization of rhetoric, discussion, and persuasion. This means that questions are not already settled, that the reins of power and pots of money and whatever might constitute society's prizes are still up for grabs. Much better to have rhetoric, and its expression in advertising and PR, than Plato's "Truth," Marx's "ideology," Derrida's "deconstruction," or some other supposed intellectual key to a better, clearer, or purer world.

Final comments

In the worldview of Adam Smith, which McCloskey admires, people are not the self-maximizing robots that today's orthodox economics imagines we are, but human beings who simply enter into commercial transactions when they see a benefit. The rest of life is about pursuing or cultivating virtues including faith, justice, courage, and love. Smith appreciated that people in the modern economic world, while needing to make money, still remain citizens, spouses, parents, neighbors, and friends. Indeed, the "business civilization" of the modern era has not corrupted the human spirit, McCloskey argues. Rather, its prosperity has enabled hundreds of millions more families and individuals to exist and maintain themselves. The "greed is good" ethic, McCloskey argues, is a caricature of capitalism that is not consistent with the moral political economy of exchange observed by Adam Smith, John Stuart Mill, or Alfred Marshall.

McCloskey's point is that capital, technology, or resources, are on their own never quite enough. An ethical environment must exist that allows individuals to push the potential of each such "factor" to its creative limits. This requires personal freedom, and proper recognition of value when it is created. Such equality is the real causative factor in rising wealth and living standards.

Deirdre McCloskey

McCloskey was born in 1942. She studied economics at Harvard University, where her father Robert was a professor of government. In the 1970s McCloskey became an associate professor in economics, and later history, at the University of Chicago, and between 1980 and 1999 was John Murray Professor of Economics and of History at the University of Iowa. Since 2000 she has been Professor of Economics, History, English, and Communication at the University of Illinois in Chicago.

As well as her "Bourgeois" trilogy, including The Bourgeois Virtues: Ethics for an Age of Commerce *(2006)* and Bourgeois Dignity: Why Economics Can't Explain the Modern World *(2010), McCloskey is the author of the classics* Economical Writing, *a guide to clear prose for economists, and* The Rhetoric of Economics, *arguing that the discipline is a blend of science and the humanities, and involves the art of persuasion.*

For much of her career McCloskey was known as "Donald McCloskey," and changed gender in 1995. Her book Crossing: A Memoir *(1999) covers this period of her life. She is an advocate of LGBT equality and rights.*

1798

An Essay on the Principle of Population

"Population, when unchecked, increases in a geometrical ratio. Subsistence increases only in an arithmetical ratio."

"Must it not then be acknowledged by an attentive examiner of the histories of mankind, that in every age and in every state in which man has existed, or does now exist, that the increase of population is necessarily limited by the means of subsistence."

In a nutshell

Restrictions on population growth are crucial for prosperity. We let it get out of control at our peril.

In a similar vein

David Ricardo *Principles of Political Economy and Taxation*
Amartya Sen *Poverty and Famines*
E. F. Schumacher *Small Is Beautiful*
Julian Simon *The Ultimate Resource 2*

CHAPTER 25

Thomas Malthus

Some writings achieve fame because they capture the spirit of the times, others because they sensationally go against that spirit. Thomas Malthus's *Essay*, published anonymously, was of the latter kind. His pessimism about the possibilities for human advance, given unchecked population increase, is what is said to have inspired Thomas Carlyle to call economics the "dismal science." Charles Darwin was also influenced by Malthus's ideas. The natural struggle for survival to which Malthus drew attention helped Darwin to imagine a mechanism (natural selection) that allowed species to adapt and prosper.

Until Malthus, population growth had been seen as a natural blessing, but Malthus was darkly realistic, seeing the sex drive as the great shaper of humanity. Social reformers like William Godwin or Robert Owen could come up with all the schemes they liked for improving the lot of the poor, but this was just playing with effects. The root cause of all social problems was simple: too many people for the amount of food available. Malthus was determined to put the issue of population at the center of political economy; his ideas fueled public and governmental concerns that led to the passing of the Census Act of 1800.

The *Essay* is written in a flowery, unscientific style that was common in the early days of economics. Indeed, Malthus was, like his dear friend David Ricardo, not a professional economist; he was an Anglican minister and gentlemen amateur attempting to put the world to rights. Even if his premises are somewhat mistaken, his influence on economic thinking has been great, perhaps as great as Adam Smith or Marx. It was Malthusian fear of the inability to feed the population that spawned China's one child policy (which with greater prosperity is only now being wound down), and his spirit is at any environmental summit where overpopulation is fingered as the culprit for resource depletion.

Irrefutable links between population, food, and prices

At the start Malthus makes two statements that he says can't be refuted: first, that "food is necessary to the existence of man," and second, that "passion between the sexes is necessary and will remain nearly in its present state."

People's desire for sex and coupling had not changed over the millennia, and was unlikely to lessen in the future. And here lay the problem. For while "subsistence" (or the ability of a person to cover their needs with their income) only increased incrementally, if it went unchecked, population could increase "geometrically."

Malthus notes that for every 25 years of its existence, the population of North America had doubled, because it had virtually unlimited arable land to support such growth. But Britain's conditions were quite different. Even assuming that the yield from the land could double in the same period, it would be "contrary to all our knowledge of the qualities of land," Malthus says, that it could quadruple during a 50-year period. Thus he imagines that during a 75-year time span, the population of Britain would increase from 7 million to 28 million to 56 million, but because agriculture could not double and then double again in output, but only increase incrementally, there would be a shortfall in food supply so as only to be able to feed 28 million. If Britain's population was not held back there could be starvation on a mass scale.

Malthus claims that no state in history has existed which did not try to limit the growth of population in some way, either by preventing early marriage among the lower classes, or limiting it amongst the better off, for fear that they could not maintain their standard of living. He draws a picture of a man weighing up whether to get married and have a family. Will he be able to provide for them at the standard that he himself has enjoyed? If not, his deferment of marriage produces a natural check on population. The downside is that, to satisfy his natural wants, he will turn to prostitutes. From this equation, Malthus concludes that the desire for sex can lead to only one of two things: poverty, or "vice."

Poverty happens, he explains, when higher food prices are combined with lower wages. A state of low wages arises because there is a surplus of labor, which is a product of overpopulation. Landowners do what they can to keep the price of labor down, so that they keep more of the benefits when times of plenty return. The laborer feels lucky just to have some work, and his family only just gets by. There is one other reason why agricultural output rises more slowly than population: taking a leaf out of David Ricardo's theory of rents and land use, Malthus notes that cultivation of marginal land is in theory the answer to food supply problems, but the cost of developing it is often not worth it to the landowner. Thus land lies fallow while prices rise and the poor go hungry.

The welfare delusion

Malthus argues that England's Poor Laws, a social relief system distributed through local parishes, had two effects. The first was to increase dependence and reduce personal responsibility. Knowing there would always be some basic food provision, the poor felt they could afford to have more children. Yet because the quantity of food being produced could not keep pace with the population increase, causing prices to rise, people became further dependent on what relief was available. Echoing today's debates about welfare provision, Malthus thunders that "A laborer who marries without being able to support a family may in some respects be considered as an enemy to all his fellow-laborers."

The Poor Laws might have helped the people in genuine acute distress, but they had reduced the total sum of happiness among the lower classes, chiefly because of the problem of moral hazard (I will take undue risks, because someone else will pay the final bill). If they were abolished, Malthus says, people would individually make better decisions about "family planning," and the nation would be better off.

Taking down the Utopians

Malthus spends a significant portion of the *Essay* refuting voguish ideas from French Enlightenment thinker Marquis de Condorcet and social philosopher Robert Godwin about the advance of humanity and the "organic perfectibility of man."

For Malthus, such notions took little account of the facts of nature (desire for sex and need for food), and took away the responsibility of the individual. Malthus laughs off the idea that man's basic nature was changing. As for helping the poor, this was naïve at best, and at worst dangerous. His idea that helping the poor, through charity or through legislation, actually worsened their condition by increasing the number in poverty, was horrifying to the chattering classes of early nineteenth century Britain, who were eager to "do something" about the terrible conditions of the working class. Yet for a silent majority, perhaps, it seemed to have a perfect logic, expressed by the character of Ebenezer Scrooge in Dickens' *A Christmas Carol.* Scrooge refused to give money to the poor on the grounds that it only kept them alive, and increased the "surplus population."

Malthusian theology

Having presented himself as the objective social scientist, by the end of the *Essay* Malthus seems to remember he is a clergyman, and provides a lengthy theological justification for evil and inequality in the world.

The idea that God had created a world of plenty for man to enjoy, Malthus writes, was too simplistic. The Deity had in fact formed a Law of Nature that "population should increase faster than food," and it made perfect sense. For without the pressure to come up with more food, there would be little motivation to develop land, make products to sell or organize industry: "The exertions that men find it necessary to make, in order to support themselves or families, frequently awaken faculties that might otherwise have lain for ever dormant." In contrast, in parts of the world where humans find abundant food growing on trees, there is no incentive to till the land, grow crops, develop animal husbandry, or advance civilization generally.

This big historical process created winners (those who used their heads and hands to provide for themselves), and those who gave in to natural human laziness. The variety found in nature, including human beings, all worked to a higher divine good, and the general current of the river is not contradicted by a few whirls and eddies of poverty and vice. It is up to the individual to lead a righteous and productive life, fulfilling the will of the Creator.

Final comments

In 1803 Malthus published a substantially revised edition of the *Essay* (with his name on it) which recorded attempts at limiting population in various countries (he had traveled around Europe collecting population data), and which put more emphasis on "moral restraint" (not contraception) and later marriage to prevent the number of children being born, as opposed to natural checks such as famine or poverty. In later editions Malthus also left out the theological chapters in the original, probably because their notion of a divinely preordained struggle for survival seemed too harsh.

The main criticism of Malthus is that he did not foresee the huge advances in agriculture which broke the links between population, labor and food supply. When one tractor or harvester can do the work of 200 laborers, and fertilizers and chemicals can produce great yields on previously marginal land, food security is no longer a big issue. Moreover, in most countries the portion of a week's wages needed to feed a family has steadily decreased since Malthus' time.

Environmentalists recoil at the thought of 8 to 10 billion people on the planet, but they may be making the same basic mistake that Malthus did: it is not so much the number of people that matters, as much as their use of resources, which continually get easier and cheaper to produce. Just as Malthus did not take account of technology, neither are they.

Thomas Malthus

Malthus was born in 1766 in Surrey, in comfortable circumstances. His father Daniel was a gentleman intellectual. After a mix of home and private school education, Malthus was admitted to Jesus College, Cambridge, where he excelled in Latin, Greek, and mathematics. In his mid-20s he was made a fellow of Jesus College. He was keen to enter the Anglican church, and despite a speech impediment was ordained deacon in 1789.

In 1804, Malthus married a cousin, Harriet Eckersall, and the following year was appointed professor of history and political economy at the East India College, where he also preached. He would keep this position until the end of his life. He was well-liked by students and nicknamed "Pop" or "Old Pop" (referring to population) Malthus. In public debates he was opposed to David Ricardo on almost every economic issue, including theories of rent, value and demand, but they remained close friends. Malthus theorized that recessions were caused by insufficient demand (Keynes was an admirer).

Other writings include An Investigation of the Cause of the High Price of Provisions *(1800),* An Inquiry into the Nature and Progress of Rent *(1815),* Principles of Political Economy *(1820), and* Definitions in Political Economy *(1827), which sought to bring more rigor to economics. Malthus died in 1834.*

1890

Principles of Economics

"Just as the chemist's fine balance has made chemistry more exact than most other physical sciences; so this economist's balance, rough and imperfect as it is, has made economics more exact than any other branch of social science. But of course economics cannot be compared with the exact physical sciences: for it deals with the ever changing and subtle forces of human nature."

"Thus though it is true that "money" or "general purchasing power" or "command over material wealth," is the centre around which economic science clusters; this is so, not because money or material wealth is regarded as the main aim of human effort, nor even as affording the main subject-matter for the study of the economist, but because in this world of ours it is the one convenient means of measuring human motive on a large scale."

In a nutshell

The purpose of economics is not simply to study wealth, but to study man. Habits of earning, saving, and investing provide the data to do so.

In a similar vein

Gary Becker *Human Capital*
Friedrich Hayek *The Use of Knowledge in Society*
John Maynard Keynes *The General Theory of Employment, Interest, and Money*
Paul Samuelson & William Nordhaus *Economics*

CHAPTER 26

Alfred Marshall

When, in 1903, Alfred Marshall launched his "Economics Tripos," a three-year undergraduate degree at Cambridge University, it was the first in the world dedicated to the subject. Until this point, economics had been taught as part of a moral sciences or philosophy degree, or came under the broader "political economy" heading. The perception that the subject was "merely technical," relating to trade and business—and therefore not part of a proper education—was a prejudice that continued well into the 1960s and 1970s. When, in the comedy television series *Yes, Minister*, chief mandarin Sir Humphrey Appleby quotes a Latin or Greek phrase, and his ministerial boss looks nonplussed, it provides the opportunity for the Oxbridge-educated Sir Humphrey to remark smugly, "You went to the LSE, didn't you Minister?"

Yet Marshall's hunch that economics would become central to the modern world would lay the foundation for half a century of Cambridge pre-eminence in the discipline (with the new London School of Economics—"the LSE"—only increasing its popularity). Economics in Marshall's early career was still based on the theories of Ricardo and Adam Smith, and he felt it had to move on from "rent and the value of corn" to become an empirically grounded science. Indeed, it became such a different beast to the classical positions of Smith and Ricardo that the tag "neoclassical economics" stuck. Marshall would originate or popularize several basic concepts which are still taught today (see "Marshallian Concepts" below), and was the first to express economic concepts through curves and graphs.

Marshall's vision was of an economic science which could illustrate how the economy worked in detail, and which paved the way for later economists (such as his Cambridge pupil John Maynard Keynes) to move the discipline from one founded on the belief in natural equilibrium to one which envisaged taking a more active, policy-driven stance that sought specific social outcomes—like full employment. Marshall did have a social agenda, which made him more progressive than his contemporaries: he was devoted to the alleviation of poverty and the extension of education to the lower-middle and working classes. However, as a socially conservative Victorian, Marshall did not hold back from projecting morality onto his economics, like Malthus emphasizing self-control among the poor so that they did not have large, unsustainable families.

Marshall was an academic through and through, and reading the book may remind you of some long-winded professor you endured at university. Keynes is said to have remarked that economists should just read Marshall's footnotes and forego the main text. Still, it is because Marshall wrote in clear prose that the book was such a success. The original edition of 750 pages grew to 870 pages by the time of the eighth and final 1920 edition, and it continued to be a set text for students for decades.

What is economics for?

For Marshall, the great advantage of economics over other social sciences was that many aspects of it could be measured. Knowing what people earned, spent, saved, and invested was a window onto human behavior which could be graphically illustrated by curves showing demand and supply. The real meaning of money was the power it gave to achieve "all kinds of ends, high as well as low, spiritual as well as material." Human beings are driven by a range of things, including social approval, the desire to protect one's family, duty and patriotism, and the desire to alleviate the suffering of others. Many of their decisions are far from "optimal." It was therefore wrong to see economics as merely the science of selfish gain.

Marshallian concepts

Nineteenth century economists borrowed a lot from Jeremy Bentham's utilitarianism in seeing people as machines for seeking pleasure and avoiding pain. "Utility," so often used in economics, is a dry word disguising its true meaning: anything that delivers us more pleasure or gain. Society was imagined in terms of millions of individuals each seeking their highest utility, putting up with the disutility of working in order to buy goods and services they wanted. Firms, meanwhile, existed in a state of perfect competition to supply these wants. Marshall took such concepts and gave them his own twist. We now look at some of his key ideas.

The scissor action of supply and demand

Adam Smith and Ricardo had emphasized the costs of production and supply of a good as the determinant of its price. William Stanley Jevons held that price was mainly shaped by demand. Marshall instead imagined supply and demand acting like the blades of a pair of scissors, acting in concert to produce a price reflecting both. He showed supply as a rising line on a graph, demonstrating that when prices for a good rise, companies will increase their supply. His corresponding law of demand said that price decreases of the same good mean that more people will buy it. This constant self-adjustment of supply and demand resulted in an "equilibrium price" for the good concerned which ensured the best allocation of resources. The "Marshallian Cross" shows a point on a graph where the intersecting lines of supply and demand meet. Consumers are happy to buy a product at the price wanted, and producers are happy to sell at the same price.

Many factors could affect demand, including a rise or fall in incomes, demographic factors like population increase, the price of other goods (if food gets cheaper, we can spend more money on clothes), advertising, and expectations (for example, buying now to avoid a future price increase). Supply of a particular good was determined by the maker's simple desire for profit. He would only keep producing if the price of a good could cover his production costs including labor.

Price elasticity

Marshall is also famous for his concept of price elasticity.

Some goods, such as fuel, have relatively inelastic demand; people will still need to get around by cars and buses, and will keep filling up their vehicles even if the price of fuel rises significantly. Other goods, such as designer handbags, have more elastic demand. If the economy falters, the first thing people give up is luxuries. The same woman who in good times might have bought a Chanel bag, now settles for a nice-looking but cheaper one.

Marshall points out that elasticity of demand could change over time. The demand for fuel may be inelastic in the short term, because people need their car to get to work and do the school run, but in the long term changes in technology and resource use, such as the decreasing cost of electric cars, could make the demand for fuel more elastic.

Marginal utility

Though the concept of marginal utility can be credited variously to William Jevons, Carl Menger and Leon Walras, Marshall discusses it at length in the *Principles*.

Marshall categorized our wants in terms of "necessaries," "comforts," and "luxuries." The utility or usefulness to me in obtaining a car, for example, when I have to walk five miles to work each day (because there are no direct bus routes), will be great. Driving instead of walking will give me an extra couple of hours a day to spend with my family or do other things. If, subsequently, I can afford a second car for my wife or teenage daughter to get around, this will make life even more convenient, but the leap in utility will not be as great, as at present they can easily take buses to their work and college. Some time later again, I find that with a pay rise I can now buy a sports car to tool around in at weekends. Though long wished-for, it is hardly a necessity. Marshall tells us that with each successive car bought, the utility of it becomes more marginal: the first car made a massive difference to my life, the second car a mild difference, and the third made little difference (nice as it is, if I had to sell it tomorrow there would be no material change to my standard of living). This idea of "marginal utility" could apply to anything I consume, whether it is beer, bedding, a haircut, or even education. Finishing high school makes a big difference to my job prospects, as opposed to dropping out at 15, but getting a PhD may not make me a lot richer compared to having only a Masters degree.

Marshall saw a "law of increasing returns" (similar to marginal utility) operating in manufacturing. Once a plant is set up, it doesn't cost a manufacturer much more to create 1,000 steam irons than it does 900; in fact, as the owner has already forked out for machinery, finance, rents, and labor, he or she may only get profitable with the last 100 irons sold. A modern example: each additional unit of the MS Office software suite costs Microsoft virtually nothing to make, so after the point is reached at which all costs have been accounted for, each additional unit sold is pure profit, and the longer the life cycle of the product, the more profit increases.

Consumer surplus and purchasing power

Marshall used the term "consumer's surplus" to mean the difference between the price a person paid for a good or service, and the price she was *willing* to pay. The bigger the gap, the greater the welfare experienced.

This concept has particular resonance in today's economy, in which online platforms and utilities (for instance, web utilities like Wikipedia, Google search, and Facebook) can be very valuable to us, and yet they are free, or cost very little. Indeed, it can be argued that well-being can be measured according to the extent to which we enjoy consumer surpluses in a range of areas; this is the basis of welfare economics.

Marshall also said that there could be a "producer's surplus," in which a company will try to sell a product for a higher amount, even if it would have been happy to sell at a lower amount. Today, airlines sell tickets at different prices according to the time of day, the proximity to the time of travel, and even the kind of person they have identified is researching fares. If an airline's system knows that a person has to fly tomorrow, for instance, it might charge $400 for a seat that might have cost $100 if bought three weeks ago.

In a Marshallian world, it is not our absolute income that matters, as much what we are able to buy with what we have. Goods rise and fall in price, with some becoming dearer and others cheaper. If the same basket of goods and services is cheaper than it was five years ago, a consumer is richer regardless of changes in absolute income or wealth.

Perfect competition

Marshall developed a model of "perfect markets" or perfect competition to explain how an economy worked. He imagined a large number of producers and an even larger number of consumers, all trading in a particular product or commodity and all having good information about its quality and price. In such an environment, producers find it hard to set prices because another producer can ask for less, and sell more of the same good. Thus producers are generally "price takers," and can't make profits higher than the norm for any length of time. This ensures that the market frequently "clears," so there is equilibrium of demand and supply.

Marshall did not take account of the fact, however, that knowledge about prices is not always complete. If a company develops a monopoly, the public won't know what they might have paid if there was more competition. In addition, an industry may require high capital investment, or need to jump through regulatory hoops, so restricting the number of companies which can compete. Even in the fields Marshall gave as examples, currencies and agriculture, there is no perfect competition. Government shapes these markets through subsidies, for instance, or can be influenced by lobbyists. The other failing of Marshall's model of perfect competition is that most products today are not the same; in fact manufacturers strive to create differences or improvements, or dream up new things, which have little or no competition.

Final comments

In assessing his legacy, Robert Heilbroner (*The Worldly Philosophers*) noted that Marshall had little to say about the cataclysmic events in his own time, including the 1890s Depression, the Russian Revolution, or World War One. "*Natura non facit saltum*" (Nature makes no sudden leaps) prefaces every edition of *The Principles of Economics*, yet as Joan Robinson, perhaps the second most famous product of Marshall's Cambridge economics program after Keynes, argued in a famous article, "history" trumps "equilibrium" every time. The world is not an economic machine moving towards balance, but is frequently and unexpectedly convulsed by political and social events which change everything, including economies. The neat world (Heilbroner calls it a "well-mannered zoo") that Marshall saw had little to say about such events.

Ironically, by making economics into a proper discipline with greater rigor, Marshall's own theories were able to be more easily tested and shown to be wanting. He had developed an intellectual universe that would be challenged by his own pupil, Keynes, who knew that for economics to advance it had to take full account of politics and the unruliness of markets, in which the soft factors of psychology and expectations play as much of a role in outcomes as the rules of supply and demand.

Alfred Marshall

Born in 1842, Marshall's background was modest. His father was a clerk at the Bank of England, and his mother was a butcher's daughter. The family lived in working-class Clapham, South London, but his father pushed him to study hard. He won a place at Cambridge University and took the mathematics tripos, coming second in his year.

After a brief period teaching at a boy's school in Bristol, in 1865 Marshall returned to Cambridge and took up a fellowship at St John's College. He threw himself into the study of metaphysics, ethics and psychology, and in 1868 was appointed lecturer in moral sciences. In 1877 he took up a position as principal and professor of political economy at Bristol University College, which emphasized education of women and the working class, but in 1885 returned to Cambridge, where he remained for the rest of his career.

Marshall helped found what became the Royal Economic Society and the prestigious Economic Journal. *He provided evidence to royal commissions into the elderly poor, the Indian currency and local taxation, and his work on the royal commission into labor (1891–94) allowed him to research poverty in depth. Marshall thought of the* Principles *as "Volume 1" of a bigger work which would cover trade, money and taxation, but ill-health and time pressures meant further volumes were never completed. However, he did produce* Industry and Trade *(1919), written with his wife Mary Paley Marshall, and his contribution to monetary economics,* Money, Credit and Commerce *(1923).*

Marshall retired in 1908 and died in 1924. He left his huge library of economic literature to Cambridge University.

1867

Capital

"Hand in hand with this centralization, or this expropriation of many capitalists by few, develops . . . the entanglement of all nations in the net of the world market, and with this, the international character of the capitalist régime. Along with the constantly diminishing number of the magnates of capital, who usurp and monopolize all advantages of this process of transformation, grows the mass of misery, oppression, slavery, degradation, exploitation; but with this too grows the revolt of the working class, a class always increasing in numbers, and disciplined, united, organized by the very mechanism of the process of capitalist production itself. The monopoly of capital becomes a fetter upon the mode of production, which has sprung up and flourished along with it, and under it. Centralization of the means of production and socialization of labor at last reach a point where they become incompatible with their capitalist integument. This integument bursts. The knell of capitalist private property sounds. The expropriators are expropriated."

In a nutshell

When an economic system treats workers as mere objects, it is setting itself up for revolution.

In a similar vein

Erik Brynjolfsson & Andrew McAfee *The Second Machine Age*
Ha-Joon Chang *23 Things They Don't Tell You About Capitalism*
Thomas Piketty *Capital in the Twenty-First Century*
Joseph Schumpeter *Capitalism, Socialism, and Democracy*
Adam Smith *The Wealth of Nations*

CHAPTER 27

Karl Marx

Compared to the shorter and more sensational *Communist Manifesto*, *Capital* is often seen as the dull but worthy masterwork that underpinned Marx's thinking. There is a reason for this. *Capital* was in Marx's mind a continuation of *A Contribution to the Criticism of Political Economy* (1859) his critique of classical economics, and indeed the first chapters of the work read like an economics textbook, explaining in detail concepts such as "use value" and "exchange value."

Yet this objective tone soon gives way, as Marx provides a snapshot of the horrifying conditions in which men, women and children labored in early industrial Britain. In contrast to the rosy view of progress and prosperity of Victorian times that we get in, say, Samuel Smiles' *Self-Help*, in page upon page of examples Marx reveals the dark side of capitalism. England's industrial revolution had brought social disintegration, and would be a template for the rest of Europe, Marx tells his readers: "The country that is more developed industrially only shows, to the less developed, the image of its own future." Rather than bringing with it increased leisure time and comforts, technological wizardry combined with capital had turned Britain's workers and rural folk into a class of "white slaves." Its patriarchal society became one in which people were reduced to factors of production, with the whole system fueled by the desire for export profits.

Capital took years to write (mostly in the reading room of the British Library), and it shows. Marx wished to provide a damning case against laissez-faire economics, and even if you are an ardent capitalist it is hard to walk away from the book without thinking about the perennial question of labor versus capital, and whether things have even changed much since Marx's day.

All in the making: the labor theory of value

Marx's labor theory of value, borrowed from Ricardo, says that the value of something is simply the labor that has gone into it. A coat, for instance, is "congealed human labor."

Something created simply for its "use value," or its worth as that product (making a coat to wear it) is to be distinguished from things which are created to be a store of value, and to be traded, bought or sold as a commodity (making coats to sell, to get rich). Because one kind of commodity can be used to purchase other commodities, and labor is the basis of the creation of commodities, it means that all labor has an equivalence. Thus, a 20-yard roll of linen becomes exchangeable for two ounces of gold. When it is expressed in money form, labor becomes a kind of social utility, and every product becomes a kind of "social hieroglyphic," Marx says. We know what someone is "worth" by what they can exchange their labor value for, converted into money.

This sounds innocent enough. Take it to its conclusion, though, and you will see transitions from, for instance, a society of self-sufficient farmers, to one that has slavery as the basis of its economic relations. If everything in society becomes commoditized, and labor is the main input into the creation of commodities, Marx notes, people become objects to be bought and sold.

Money (which becomes capital) changes everything

Imagine an entrepreneur with some money savings who opens a shoemaking shop, and employs a leatherworker. The leatherworker owns his own labor, and cannot sell all of it at once, as he would be selling himself. But because he owns only his labor, and not any means of production (for example, machinery or leather to make shoes), he is immediately in a lesser position than the entrepreneur who does own such means; he can only sell his labor, and not the product of that labor. In this "unnatural economic relation," Marx says, the laborer will be paid only to the extent that he is kept in food, fuel and housing ("subsistence") so that he can renew himself each night in order to come back and work the next day. The price of his labor will be the sum cost of the commodities he must buy to keep himself and his children alive.

In modern societies, social relationships exactly shape themselves around economic relations, to the extent that one person's savings become the instrument of another's exploitation, Marx says. In a money economy, "social power becomes the private power of private persons." It was for good reason, Marx notes, that "The ancients . . . denounced money as subversive of the economic and moral order of things." While someone's initial savings may have been innocently made, they are soon deployed as capital, which becomes the instrument of exploitation.

Surplus labor-value: the secret key to capitalism

Capital contains large sections on the length of the working day, and Marx explains why he is almost obsessional about it. There is a portion of the day which is "necessary" labor time, because it both pays for the worker's subsistence, and for the owner's costs of running the factory. But there is a second part of the day which is not necessary, in that all costs have been covered; this surplus laboring is pure profit for the capitalist, while no extra value is gained by the worker. Thus "the laborer . . . works one half of the day for himself, the other half for the capitalist." It was precisely because most factories would have entered the profit zone only at the end of the day, that English manufacturers tried to stop laws mandating a ten-hour day in place of twelve. The only difference between a slave-owning society and a wage-earning one, Marx says, is in the degree of exploitation. The so-called "greatness" of a nation is not measured by the quantity of what is produced, he notes, but by how much surplus labor-value is generated: "Capital is dead labor, that, vampire-like, only lives by sucking living labor, and lives the more, the more labor it sucks."

Marx describes the "relay system," in which mills and factories were kept going 24 hours a day, and which saw ten-year-olds being made to work 15 hours a day for a few shillings a week. An 1863 physician's report on the Staffordshire pottery industry stated that workers had a range of pulmonary diseases, their growth as children and teenagers had been stunted, and they became prematurely old. Children in the match making industry were exposed to phosphorus and developed lockjaw. In even apparently benign industries such as baking, extreme overwork meant that bakers rarely lived past the age of 42. In sum, capitalists believed it was more efficient to use up a worker's labor-power for a few years, then discard them for new blood, than to keep that same worker on but in conditions which would give them a longer working life.

Marx provides a history of the Factory Acts in England, from 1833 to 1864. The opposition to them from industry, he says, is characteristic of the "spirit of capital." Yet if the engine of wealth was the ability of factories to coordinate large quantities of raw materials and labor, putting many workers all under one roof, this also created an opportunity, for "As the number of the co-operating laborers increases," Marx notes, "so too does their resistance to the domination of capital." The scene is set, with an emerging sense of collective identity, for a great struggle between capital and labor.

Final comments

For Joseph Schumpeter, the patron saint of capitalism, Marx presented his ideas as the articulation of grand impersonal forces of history, yet he somehow failed to see the most salient feature of capitalism: its dynamism and affinity to human aspiration. Marx ignored the reality that capital is built up in the first place through intelligence, energy, creativity, hard work, and saving—not accumulated by force, subjection, and exploitation as Marx believed. And rather than spending time developing "class consciousness", the average worker is instead looking to move up a rung on the social ladder. He accepts the rules of capital as long as there is some chance for him to use it to his own advantage. Marx did not take enough account of the role of technology and productivity in making things cheaper to buy for the average worker, or that through contributions to a pension fund, which invests in industrial stocks and real estate, the average worker becomes a capitalist himself; capitalism works because it ensures that labor retains a piece of the pie.

For all its flaws, Marx's "economic interpretation of history" did show how the economic environment and forms of production shape religion, art, philosophy, and institutions—the society we live in. One of Marx's achievements, Schumpeter admitted, is the reminder that "it is our daily work which forms our minds, and that it is our location within the productive process which determines our outlook on things." Whether owner, investor, or worker, our "location within the productive process" will be a major determinant of our happiness, and so warrants deep reflection. Our work and our relationship to capital may not define us completely, but it is a big part of who we are.

Reading *Capital* may make you stop and ponder how much of your day is spent earning money for yourself, and how much is spent enriching your employer—and whether this is fair. If your work involves use of your judgement and knowledge, why shouldn't you take charge of the "means of production" (your mind), and reap the fruits of your labor? In Marx's day business was very capital-intensive, whereas today there are many areas of business where one can begin with almost nothing. Technological advances, combined with the democratization of capital, mean that "surplus value" is more easily captured if an individual comes up with a winning product or service. But for capitalism to be humane, all who have worked to create the product or service must feel they are getting a proportionate gain. An unbalanced labor–capital equation may bring workplace mutiny, flight of talent, or at a societal level, rebellion against "the 1 percent" through the ballot box.

Karl Marx

Marx was born in 1818 in Trier in the Prussian Rhineland, one of nine children. Marx's grandfather and great grandfather were rabbis, but his liberal lawyer father Heinrich converted the family to Lutheranism to avoid anti-Semitic laws preventing him from practicing. Marx's mother Henrietta came from a wealthy Dutch Jewish family who would later start the Philips electronics company.

At Trier Gymnasium, Marx gained a solid grounding in Latin, Greek, French, and German. He attended university in Bonn and Berlin, then gained a doctorate from the University of Jena, but was considered too radical to be given an academic post. He married Jenny von Westphalen, of a Prussian aristocratic family, in 1843. They would have seven children.

In 1842 Marx began working for the radical New Rheinische Zeitung *in Cologne. After it was shut down by the authorities he moved to Paris, a center for socialist ideas, mixing with anarchists Pierre Joseph Proudhon (famous for saying "property is theft"), and Mikhail Bakunin, and becoming friends with his subsequent collaborator, Friedrich Engels. Forced to leave Paris in 1845 after pressure from the Prussian state, he continued agitating from Brussels, penning* The Communist Manifesto *(1848—see commentary in* 50 Politics Classics*). After being thrown out of Belgium and refused entry to Prussia, Marx moved to London in 1849. He was never granted citizenship, but lived there until his death in 1884.*

The English edition of Das Kapital *did not appear until 1887. Volumes 2 and 3 of* Capital *were put together by Engels from Marx's notes.*

1986

Stabilizing an Unstable Economy

"To be exact, our economic leadership does not seem to be aware that the normal functioning of our economy leads to financial trauma and crises, inflation, currency depreciations, unemployment, and poverty in the midst of what could be virtually universal affluence—in short, that financially complex capitalism is inherently flawed."

"What we seem to have is a system that sustains instability even as it prevents the deep depressions of the past. Instead of a financial crisis and a deep depression separated by decades, threats of crisis and deep depression occur every few years."

In a nutshell

Competitive market economies, it is held, naturally create efficiency and stability. Capitalism's booms, busts, and financial crises, which skew long-term investment and increase inequality, suggest otherwise.

In a similar vein

Ha-Joon Chang *23 Things They Don't Tell You About Capitalism*
J. K. Galbraith *The Great Crash 1929*
John Maynard Keynes *The General Theory of Employment, Interest, and Money*
Michael Lewis *The Big Short*
Robert Shiller *Irrational Exuberance*

CHAPTER 28

Hyman Minsky

In the 1980s, when most economists had cheered on financial innovation and deregulation, maverick economist Hyman Minsky had warned that these shifts turned capitalism into an accident waiting to happen. "In a world of businessmen and financial intermediaries who aggressively seek profit," he wrote in *Stabilizing an Unstable Economy*, "innovators will always outpace regulators." Markets may work most of the time in efficiently allocating resources, but the big issues of stability and equity that shaped people's lives and livelihoods had to remain a matter of *policy* and *politics*. The ultimate owners of economies were citizens and their governments, not banks and companies.

When the 2007–2008 financial crisis unfolded, Minsky suddenly seemed like a seer. The Federal Reserve Bank's Janet Yellen would write a 2009 article, "Minsky Meltdown: Lessons for Central Bankers"), and the phrase "Minsky Moment" (coined by fund manager Paul McCulley to explain the 1998 Russian financial crisis when debts exploded at the same time asset prices were falling) was now applied to the United States, where financial innovation had obscured the riskiness of the subprime mortgage bond market.

The financial system: help or hindrance?

The two decades after World War Two, 1946 to 1966, Minsky notes, were marked by steady growth and relative stability. The financial system had been robust and resistant to crisis, and had served the growing economy. From the late 1960s, however, there was increasing inflation, higher unemployment, and rising interest rates. Bankruptcies were on the rise, along with energy crises and urban problems. The credit crisis of 1966 was followed by financial "near crises" of 1970, 1974–75, 1979–80 and 1982–83, each one worse than the one before. Minsky argues that changes to the US financial system happened slowly in the post-war decades, gradually eroding its foundations and making it "amenable to crisis." He identifies 1982 as the start of an era of semi-permanent financial turmoil.

Minsky argues that decentralized markets are the best way to deliver growth and stability for most of the economy, most of the time, but there are important caveats. Finance and credit are the oil in this machine, and therefore are public goods which need strong regulation. Too little credit, or too much, can turn a correction into a depression. If asset values are in a constant cycle of speculation and collapse, and if employment goes up and down like a yo-yo, it's fatal for a capitalist economy. The uncertainty in business cycles means people will not invest for the long term, as they would in a more tranquil system. Because a more unstable economy provides opportunities to make money from speculation, speculation begins to dominate over long-term investment and enterprise.

Central to Minsky's thinking is that, "Economic systems are not natural systems. An economy is a social organization created either through legislation or by an evolutionary process of invention and innovation." Institutions run their course, and new events demand new institutions, or changes to existing ones. Following Keynes, Minsky argues that institutions and policy must work to bring about three things: economic efficiency, social justice, and personal liberty.

Riding with stabilizers

During the post-war Keynesian economic consensus, stability and prosperity were thought to have two important elements: the welfare state (or what Minsky calls "Big Government"), and a central bank acting as lender of last resort. The financial crises of the 1970s and early 1980s all led to recessions, but they did not become depressions because government stabilized the economy through entitlement programs (like Social Security), through securities (like bonds) which paid for deficits, and through central banks acting to defend and stabilize the system. The trade-off was, in each case, the ramping up of inflation.

By 1975, US government spending on welfare was 20 percent more than the government was spending on goods and services. This sounds alarming, but in fact if you have a significant portion of national disposal income (say, 15 to 20 percent) being independent of private enterprise (and a higher portion during a recession, when unemployment insurance rises) it will naturally have a stabilizing effect on the economy, as people will keep spending no matter what. If the government is in deficit spending mode, robust disposable income also means that corporate profits can be maintained, or even increase, in a recession. Big Government, with its potential for automatic massive deficits, "puts a high floor under an economy's potential downward spiral." This becomes particularly important in a world of high corporate and household debt, because it means that companies and families can continue to service this debt without bankruptcy or default.

While Big Government stabilizes output, employment, and profits through its deficit spending, the Federal Reserve Bank, and private institutions working with it, stabilize asset values and financial markets by buying, or accepting as collateral, financial assets that otherwise can't be sold—or if they were sold, would only realise precipitously low returns. In buying such "positions", the institutions exchange these assets for their riskless ones.

Driven by the panic of 1907, the "lender of last resort" function was a key reason for establishing the Federal Reserve system in 1913. The obvious problem with this function is that some of the risks involved in speculative finance are lessened. This in turn makes the financial system more unstable, as banks can engage in "casino capitalism" in the knowledge that they will probably be bailed out if it all goes wrong.

How instability grows

Minsky contends that the actual panics, deflations, and depressions that follow the ends of booms are not as important as how an economy changes during the years leading up to boom. "Instability emerges," he says, "as a period of relative tranquil growth is transformed into a speculative boom." Corporations, banks and other financial middlemen respond to the growing success of the economy. All manner of enterprises increase their exposure to riskier investments which, in the glowing rays of prosperity, do not seem risky. During this time of "tranquil expansion," banks seek to carve out greater profits by inventing new forms of money, securities, and financing. If the wheels of investment are well-oiled, demand for assets increases, and so do prices.

Yet this tranquil equilibrium of full employment with stable prices is never sustained, because financial innovation will always work towards the bumping up of asset prices beyond what an economy in equilibrium requires. Financial innovation therefore becomes the key *dis*equilibrating factor in capitalism, shunting an economy from healthy but modest growth into a speculative boom. The financial sector begins to move "too fast" for the real economy itself. A boom changes the investing landscape from one of stable, long-term investment horizons, to one geared towards shorter-term gains.

Minsky makes a distinction between two kinds of capitalism. The older type consisted mostly of people owning companies on their own. Trade in companies and capital assets was limited. The newer kind, the "corporate capitalist" economy we live in now, has vastly expanded the buying and selling of companies, their debt, and the capital assets they produce. This financialization of what was once essentially a market for physical goods and services has made the modern economy much more complex—and more risky. Keynes observed that the capitalist economy is underwritten by borrowing and lending using established rules of thumb about margins of safety. But Minsky notes that "A history of success will tend to diminish the margin of safety that business and bankers require." Catastrophic bets, born of overconfidence and hubris, are frequently made. This wouldn't be so bad if the effects were limited to the firm that made the bets, but it is usually society at large that ends up paying for the bailouts.

Debt isn't all the same

Minsky distinguished three types of borrower: the hedge borrower, who was able to pay back, from current cash flows, interest and principal over time on loans taken; the speculative borrower, who can afford to pay back the interest on a loan, but must periodically re-borrow the principal; and the Ponzi borrower, who can afford to pay neither interest nor principal, but takes out a loan on the basis that the price of the asset he has bought with the loan finance will keep on rising, so that he can at some point sell the asset, pay off the loan and still make a profit.

The second and third kind of borrowing characterized the housing bubble leading up to 2007, when real estate prices were rising so steadily that the idea of paying off a loan began to seem quaint. Instead of paying off their mortgages, people used their home equity as a cash machine—but when house prices began to fall, the outstanding debt finally mattered, and mass defaults occurred. With their fingers burnt, banks and lenders stopped lending even to people with sound finances and prospects.

What to do?

What Minsky got from Keynes is that the market is a good mechanism for resolving a lot of less important decisions and allocations, but is not to be relied upon for issues of equity, efficiency, and stability. Minsky's almost-shocking conclusion is that "capitalism is flawed mainly because it handles capital poorly." Because government is needed to offset swings in private investment, so that profits and employment remain stable, government has to be of a certain size, around 16–20 per cent of GDP, Minsky argues, or equivalent to the normal level of private investment. He calls for an activist central bank that does not simply act as lender of last resort, but actively guides the evolution of the banking and financial institutions so as to prevent cyclical instability.

At the end of his book Minsky warns of the conflict of interest in private banks, who are meant to be acting in the interests of their clients and depositors, yet who are tempted all the time to make money off this captive audience. As the natural profit bent of banks eggs them on to increasingly risky lending, he suggests the mandating of equity to asset ratios, to limit the risks of speculative bank activity. This is, of course, what governments the world over had to do after the 2008 financial crisis, with the implementation of greater capital buffers.

Final comments

Financial innovations, Minsky concludes, are likely to make instability a permanent feature of capitalism, and it is instability that brings unemployment, currency fluctuations, inflation and deflation, and poverty. Policymakers call for changes in tax law or central bank operations, but such things are really just tinkering. Credit crunches, inflationary spirals, and banking crises are seen as being due to "shocks" and "errors" rather than *systemic* causes which require public policy solutions. Believers in neoclassical "equilibrium" should not be allowed anywhere near the levers of government, Minsky says, because "Meaningful reforms cannot be put over by an advisory or administrative elite that is itself the architect of the existing situation . . . *Only an economics that is critical of capitalism can be a guide to successful policy for capitalism.*"

The real task is structural change to the financial system, but even then, Minsky warns, "instability, put to rest by one set of reforms will, after a time, emerge in a new guise." A truly sustainable capitalism would require that government never let finance zoom ahead of the needs of the productive economy. Otherwise, there will be more "Minsky Moments".

Hyman Minsky

Born in 1919, Minsky spent his formative years in Chicago, where his Belarusian immigrant parents were active in labor and socialist politics. He graduated from high school in New York City, but returned to Chicago to do his bachelor's degree in mathematics. His Masters and PhD in economics were from Harvard, where his teachers included Joseph Schumpeter and Wassily Leontief.

He began his teaching career as an assistant to Alvin Hansen, the Keynesian economist, moved on to Carnegie Tech (now Carnegie-Mellon University) and Brown University (1949–58), before taking up a post at the University of California, Berkeley. From 1965 to 1990 he was Professor of Economics at Washington University in St Louis.

Minsky's other main work was John Maynard Keynes *(1975). He died in 1996. For more information, see L. Randall Wray's* Why Minsky Matters: An Introduction to the Work of a Maverick Economist *(2015).*

1949

Human Action

"It is impossible to understand the history of economic thought if one does not pay attention to the fact that economics is such a challenge to the conceit of those in power. An economist can never be a favorite of autocrats and demagogues. With them he is always the mischief-maker, and the more they are inwardly convinced that his objections are well-founded, the more they hate him."

"It (the state) protects the individual's life, health, and property against violent or fraudulent aggression on the part of domestic gangsters and external foes. Thus the state creates and preserves the environment in which the market economy can safely operate . . . Each man is free; nobody is subject to a despot. Of his own accord the individual integrates himself into the cooperative system. The market directs him and reveals to him in what way he can best promote his own welfare as well as that of other people."

In a nutshell

The triumph of the market economy over traditional modes of political economy was the most important event in history, allowing the power of individuals to be unleashed.

In a similar vein

Milton Friedman *Capitalism and Freedom*
Friedrich Hayek *The Use of Knowledge in Society*
Deirdre McCloskey *Bourgeois Equality*
Ayn Rand *Capitalism: The Unknown Ideal*
Joseph Schumpeter *Capitalism, Socialism, and Democracy*

CHAPTER 29

Ludwig von Mises

If there were a museum of free-market economics, the main display should not be of Friedrich Hayek, Milton Friedman, or Ayn Rand, but the one who came before all of them: the Austrian political economist Ludwig von Mises.

His magnum opus, *Human Action*, was written when capitalism was exposed and under attack from Marxism and fascism, and he felt driven to provide a convincing philosophical rationale for what he believed was the only viable economic and political system. Spurring him on was the idea put forward in the "socialist calculation debate" of the 1930s, that "market socialism" (a blend of planned economy and limited markets) was the way of the future. Von Mises argued that you could have no calculation without the price system underpinning a free market.

Human Action, or in its original German version *Nationalökonomie: Theorie des Handelns und Wirtschaftens* (1940), which took von Mises five years to write during a spell in Geneva, aimed to provide a complete, unified theory of economics which became known as the "Austrian School." In normal times such a book (it runs to four volumes and over 800 pages) might have put von Mises in the limelight, but after the Anschluss of Austria by Germany in 1938, his ideas and anti-fascism put him in danger. The Nazis had ransacked his Vienna flat while he was in Switzerland, and his Swiss publisher could not sell the book in Germany. He and his wife decided to emigrate to America, but it turned out to be a blessing in disguise. With publication of a new, expanded, English version of *Human Action* in 1949, von Mises' ideas gained a much wider audience than if he had stayed in Europe. Transplanted to America, Austrian economics found its spiritual home.

The Austrian School's influence reached a turning point in 1974, when von Mises' disciple Friedrich Hayek won a Nobel Prize in economics. In a time of stagflation (the combination of economic stagnation and inflation) brought on by Keynesian economics, the ideas of von Mises, Hayek and Milton Friedman, for so long on the fringes of economics, now became mainstream.

What economics has done for us

Von Mises notes that throughout history, social problems were considered ethical problems. All you needed were enlightened rulers and good citizens to advance. But it became clear that market phenomena had their own logic, and that the old tags of "good" and "bad," or "just" and "unjust" were irrelevant to economic interaction. Success in the market arena seemed to proceed independently of what "ought" to be in a moral sense. Therefore, to understand society you had to examine how humans acted in the economic sphere. Economics deals with man as he is, not how he should or could be.

In its infancy, economics as a discipline had the image of being about the pursuit of wealth and profit; the rest of life was decidedly *not* about economics. But von Mises' great interest was choice and preference, or human action in general. In this scheme of things, economics simply becomes a part of a universal science, "praxeology," or a general theory of human choice.

At the time he was writing, socialists saw economists as "sycophants of capital," without realizing that economics, or at least a genuine science of human action, was culturally neutral. One could not describe action in the economic sphere as bourgeois, western, or Jewish, any more than one could describe a theory of physics in this way. In fact, the socialists, racists, and nationalists who tried to paint economics in this manner never succeeded, von Mises notes, because it constitutes a set of laws that transcend culture and time, and therefore is much more reliable and useful than grand theories of race, nation, or social progress.

The critics of economics argued that it had not ended starvation, unemployment, war, or tyranny. They fail to recall, von Mises writes, that the classical economists played a vital role in exposing the irrationality and rottenness of established customs, laws, and patronage, and promoted liberal values and forms of government which gave technology and innovation free reign, in the process making societies much richer and better off than they might have been. It was the economists who argued for the social benefits of business: that competition was good; that old methods of production should not be protected; that machines could create wealth rather than destroy it; and that government should not stand in the way of innovation. It was no accident that laissez-faire policies coincided with the Industrial Revolution; political liberalism was its foundation.

Von Mises believed that it was not the job of any science to dictate the ends or goals to which humans should aspire, but simply to describe how things are and work in reality. In economics, it is not the job of government to say what human action should be for, only to be a good midwife for human ingenuity.

Human action

The goal of human action is to remove an uneasiness, which could be anything from a desire for food or sex, to concern for the plight of one's fellow man, and this need to act is what builds civilization. People are born into a particular set of circumstances, and what matters is how a person acts within their milieu to achieve their ends. Humans are not just the playthings of their environments, but can change their environment through their action. Marx was all about "historical forces," as if individuals did not make choices on their own account, but for von Mises it is the individual that dreams and builds, not "society." Government exists only for basic physical protection and defense, and must restrict its wish to "elevate" its citizens by controlling them. The beauty of a liberal market state is that each person gets to choose their own path. Any other form of political economy is wrong, because "Nobody is in a position to decree what should make another man happier."

The discipline of economics "is not about goods and services," von Mises says, "it is about the actions of living men". It is about reason over ideology. For this reason, von Mises put the entrepreneur, who has to make rational calculations about possible futures, at the center of his philosophy and political economy.

The rational discipline

In the section, "Revolt Against Reason," von Mises argues that Marxism, racism, and nationalism are all ideologies which try to ignore or supplant rationality. "A theory is subject to the tribunal of reason only," he says, and if proven correct must be as valid for a capitalist or a Marxist, and for an American as much as for a Chinese.

Economic law was as valid in ancient Rome or the empire of the Incas as it is today. There are no "special circumstances" of culture or religion or politics that have got around it. Every leader and government seems to have the conceit of power, when in fact, "economic history is a long record of government policies that failed because they were designed with a bold disregard for the laws of economics." The advisers and philosophers serving the powerful come up with any number of schemes to act in an economically irresponsible way, but they are always exposed. Given this, von Mises writes, a true economist "can never be a favorite of autocrats and demagogues. With them he is always the mischief-maker, and the more they are inwardly convinced that his objections are well-founded, the more they hate him."

Final comments

All ideologies involve a compelling purity of thought. Socialists believe that *if only* the world was rid of destabilizing market forces and wealth redistributed from greedy individuals, it would be a great place. Libertarians plead that *if only* government got out of the way and let the individual rule we would live in paradise.

The truth is always more nuanced, as von Mises himself discovered after becoming a citizen of the United States. He flourished there, but only because its many freedoms and protections were guaranteed by a strong state, fed by significant taxation. For someone who had always argued that civilization had happened despite the state, not because it, it was interesting that his resurgence as a philosopher was thanks to political freedom, not capitalism per se. He admitted as much in later editions of *Human Action.* Such a paradox is reminiscent (in reverse) of Marx, who was able to live as a scholar thanks to the capitalist largesse of his partner Engels and his wife Jenny's wealthy family.

Still, the book stands as a great monument to the Austrian School, an ideological pole of capitalism in a similar way that Marx's *Capital* is for socialism. If you believe that government has crept into too many areas of life, or that individual agency has been forgotten amid calls for a greater "society" or communalism, reading von Mises is the antidote.

Ludwig von Mises

Von Mises was born in 1881 in Lemberg, then part of the Austro-Hungarian empire and now Lviv in Ukraine. His family later moved to Vienna, where he studied economics and law, graduating in 1906. He began working at the Vienna Chamber of Commerce and Industry, and from 1912 would be its chief economist. During World War One he was an artilleryman and an economic adviser for Austria-Hungary's war effort. He also worked as an adviser to Engelbert Dollfuss, the Austrian chancellor, and to Otto von Habsburg, whose imperial family lost power in 1918.

The original German version of Human Action *was written while von Mises was chair of International Economic Relations at Geneva's Graduate Institute of International Studies. He came to the United States in 1940 with the help of a Rockefeller Foundation grant, and from 1945 to 1969 was an unsalaried visiting professor at New York University (NYU). One of his students at NYU was Murray Rothbard, later to write the libertarian classic,* Man, Economy, and State *(1962). He knew Friedrich Hayek from when the two were colleagues in Austria's finance administration, and was part of the New York intellectual circle that included Ayn Rand. In 1947 he co-founded the free-market Mont Pelerin Society.*

Other books include The Theory of Money and Credit *(1912),* Liberalism *(1927),* Omnipotent Government and Bureaucracy *(1944) and* The Anti-Capitalist Mentality *(1957). Von Mises died in 1973.*

2010

Dead Aid

"What is clear is that democracy is not the prerequisite for economic growth that aid proponents maintain. On the contrary, it is economic growth that is the prerequisite for democracy; and the one thing economic growth does not need is aid."

"As hard-hearted as it sounds, it is better to face economic hardship in a thriving economy with prospects than to be confronted by it in an aid-dependent economy, where there are none."

In a nutshell

Aid is like a drug, and as with any drug, pushers and addicts find it hard to kick the habit.

In a similar vein

Ha-Joon Chang *23 Things They Don't Tell You About Capitalism*
Niall Ferguson *The Ascent of Money*
Naomi Klein *The Shock Doctrine*
Hernando de Soto *The Mystery of Capital*

CHAPTER 30

Dambisa Moyo

The "pop culture of aid" (Make Poverty History, Live 8, the Millennium Development Goals, Bono, Bob Geldof) as Zambian economist Dambisa Moyo calls it, has provided an outlet for the belief that "something is being done" about African development. We are bombarded with requests to give, because the only thing stopping people from dying or having a better life is our generosity. There is a deep, almost unquestioned assumption that the better-off have a responsibility to help the poor in this way. Aid is "one of the biggest ideas of our time," Moyo says, and so it takes courage to second-guess the big institutions, governments, multinational charities, and celebrities who support the aid paradigm.

But has aid actually worked? When so many other developing countries have emerged into prosperity in the last 50 years, why have many of Africa's countries largely failed or been left behind?

Moyo stresses that she does not have anything against emergency and humanitarian aid (supplied by the likes of Oxfam and Médecins Sans Frontières), but notes that this kind of aid is actually "small beer" compared to the size of government-to-government transfers and aid from the World Bank and other financial institutions. A large chunk of this aid is in the form of loans at below-market interest, and for very long repayment periods. Given such easy terms, and the fact that loans are often forgiven, in the minds of Africa's leaders the distinction between outright grants and loans has become less defined. Moyo therefore puts concessional loans and grants under the same "aid" umbrella.

Dead Aid is a polemic rather than a scholarly work, and so can be accused of cherry-picking facts to suit its argument, but the evidence Moyo does provide is disturbing. Big influxes of aid money reduce the incentive to save, increase inflation and corruption, and prevent the hard work of building institutions and industries and attracting foreign direct investment (FDI). Yet her book is "not a counsel of despair." In fact, the very awareness of the aid delusion is liberating, she says, and is the beginning of African prosperity.

A brief history of aid

In the 1950s and 1960s, 31 African countries achieved independence from colonial rule, and the future looked bright. The old colonial powers were anxious, however, to retain financial footholds in the countries into which they had poured so many resources, and aid looked like a good way of achieving this. There was also a geopolitical dimension: the dynamics of the Cold War required newly-independent countries to choose their allegiances, which meant choosing between capitalist or socialist models of political economy. The US and the Soviet Union were both happy to prop up dictators, from Idi Amin to Samuel Doe to Mobutu Sese Seko, and aid was the crucial means of keeping a country onside; whether or not any actual development was occurring was secondary.

Through the 1960s aid kept increasing, and there was a shift towards funding of big industrial and infrastructure projects; by the mid-1970s, half of aid went towards the building of roads, ports, sewerage, power, and water projects. This gave way to a new focus on projects involving agriculture and rural development, housing, education, health, mass inoculation, adult literacy, and the prevention of malnutrition. By the early 1980s, the emphasis changed again, to poverty alleviation; half of aid money went on this, where the decade before it had been only 10 percent. Why the shift? The growth and industrialization strategies had largely failed, and the situation was made worse by rising interest rates thanks to oil price shocks. Many African countries had aid loans with floating interest rates, and these debts now became crippling, especially as higher interest rates in the rich world caused recession and hence lower demand for exports from poor countries. Most debts were restructured to avoid defaults and therefore global financial meltdown, but the result was only further aid-dependence.

Africa's outright economic failure, despite record levels of aid, prompted a swing to neoliberal ideas. The only sensible route to prosperity now seemed laissez-faire economics, as evidenced by the market-centered and outward looking policies of the "Asian tigers." Meanwhile in Britain and America, the ideas of Milton Friedman and the Chicago School of economics had been adopted and seemed to be working well, after years of creeping socialism. These intellectual winds now blew through the world of development economics, taking the form of "stabilization and structural adjustment" regimes involving new fiscal and monetary rigor, and fixing a country's import–export ratio. Structural adjustment meant greater trade liberalization and the removal of tariffs and subsidies. The World Bank and the IMF spearheaded an aggressive new regime which tied aid to free-market solutions including the reduction of the role of the state, privatizing nationalized industries, and cutting back the civil service.

This "Washington Consensus," backed also by the might of the US Treasury, created such a big change in how poor countries operated that it amounted to "shock treatment," to borrow a phrase from Naomi Klein. Did it work? Countries were now free to succeed on their own terms, but they were also, Moyo notes, free to fail. With massive debt mountains to service, the odds were stacked against them. A tragic situation emerged in which interest paid out on loans to rich countries was dwarfing the inflow of foreign aid. Meanwhile, corruption continued unabated. Moyo tells of Zaire's President Mobutu who, fresh from a meeting with President Reagan to get better terms on his country's $5 billion in foreign debt, leased a Concorde to fly his daughter to her Ivory Coast wedding.

As the millennium drew near, there was a feeling that if Africa's debts could just be forgiven, it could finally achieve prosperity. At the Jubilee Debt Campaign's conference in 2005, Tanzania's President Mkapa said it was a scandal "that we are forced to choose between basic health and education for our people and repaying historical debt." Such sentiments only increased the moral handwringing in the West over poverty, and the message to give, give, give continued with new strength. Many debts were indeed canceled, but the culture of aid dependency remained. It was not politically correct to question the aid model itself, even if, as Rwandan president Paul Kagame noted, after 50 years and $2 trillion, there was "little to show for it in terms of economic growth and human development."

An institutional and democratic problem?

Moyo goes through possible explanations for Africa's difficulties.

The first is the idea that Africa's abundance of natural resources and good land has not proved a great advantage—in fact, a curse. History shows that countries depending on natural resources will see their economies boom or bust depending on commodity prices, while little investment happens in more sustainable areas. Some have argued that the legacy of colonialism has held back African countries, and there is even the insidious suggestion that Africans themselves are simply not up to the discipline of development. Another view is that Africa is held back by its 1,000 different tribal identities; Nigeria alone has 400 tribes among its 150 million population, and indeed intertribal rivalry has often led to war and genocide, such as in Rwanda in the 1990s. Then there is the "institutional" argument: evinced by Douglass North, Dani Rodrik (and more recently Acemoglu and Robinson in *Why Nations Fail*— see *50 Politics Classics*) this is the idea that the absence of clear property rights, a lack of constraint on executive power and generally poor governance are the underlying causes of Africa's malaise. Finally, there is the democracy argument: democracy will be Africa's savior because it exposes inefficiency and corruption, and stops leaders from being able to appropriate national wealth. As Amartya Sen argued in *Development as Freedom*, democratic leaders have a strong incentive to avoid economic disaster in order to get re-elected.

Moyo doesn't have much time for these arguments; they are excuses rather than causes. Proponents of democracy first have it the wrong way around, she says. Consider Chile, which was transformed into a democratic state only *after* it had developed clear property rights, functioning institutions, and growth-promoting economic policies under the decidedly *un*democratic leadership of Pinochet. The Western view is that such countries are an anomaly and somehow succeeded despite not being democratic, but Moyo says it is an uncomfortable truth that multiparty democracy can actually get in the way of development, at least in the early stages of a country's growth. "No one is denying that democracy is of crucial value" Moyo says, "it's just a matter of timing." It doesn't matter a great deal to an African family on the breadline whether it can vote. What matters is whether it can put food on the table, and this requires a growing economy and some stability. "What is clear is that democracy is not the prerequisite for economic growth that aid proponents maintain," she writes, "and the one thing economic growth does not need is aid."

The International Development Association is a club of developing countries who have been successful, including China, Turkey, Chile, Columbia, South Korea, and Thailand, and in Africa, Botswana and Swaziland. None of these countries have been aid gluttons, Moyo notes; all have kept to aid contributions of less than 10 percent of GDP. Botswana did receive aid of up to 20 percent of GDP in the 1960s, but its growth and stability (it has four times the per capita income of the rest of Sub-Saharan Africa) came from economic openness, monetary stability, fiscal discipline, and probity in government. By 2000, the share of aid in its national income was only 1.6 percent. "Botswana succeeded," Moyo says "by ceasing to depend on aid."

Aid and corruption

The big problem with aid, Moyo says, is that however much you give, it gets diverted into unintended areas ("more grants means more graft"), or the aid distorts local markets and affects local businesses who are in a vulnerable stage of growth. Influxes of aid money reduce the incentive to save and stop the hard work of building institutions and industries, thus diminishing exports.

Moyo refers to a study by economist Bill Easterly which concluded that if Zambia had invested wisely all the aid it had received, its current per capita income would be around $20,000, instead of the $500 it is today. African leaders have a penchant for glory projects, but the greater the project, Moyo says, the larger the opportunity for leaders to give the contracts to favored people instead of choosing the best provider. It wouldn't be so bad if the proceeds of corruption were spent in the home country (as in, for instance, China and Indonesia), but looted funds and rents in Africa usually end up in foreign bank accounts.

Foreign aid props up bad governments by providing the cash for them to be maintained and to grow in power. These governments' disrespect for the rule of law, for serious development policies, and for fiscal discipline means local investment dries up and foreign investment becomes unattractive, which perpetuates a cycle of poverty. A 1997 World Bank study found that 72 percent of its lending was going to countries that had a poor track record in compliance and in meeting the conditions of the loan.

If aid to Africa's poorest countries continues to be misused and abused, why do donors keep on giving it? The first reason is simply pressure to lend. The World Bank employs 5,000 people, the IMF 2,500 and other UN agencies 5,000. Add another 20,000 for aid charities, NGOs, and government aid bureaucracies, and you have an aid industry that is keen to perpetuate itself.

Moyo also argues that African governments have become more accountable to the big aid donors than to their own middle class, yet it is only a growing middle class, paying taxes, that can make a country truly economically independent. When governments stop bothering to collect taxes because they can rely on aid money, the link between people and state breaks down. And of course, by reducing incomes and national growth, aid makes a country inherently riper for revolution and war. Rebel groups may organize under a political banner, but much of the time they want to seize the state so that they can siphon off aid money.

Alternatives to aid

If aid doesn't work, what does?

Part of the solution, Moyo contends, is bonds, whereby a country raises money to pay for infrastructure or services from the international market, paying a return on funds invested over a certain period of time. There is in fact a healthy appetite for African bonds from pension funds, mutual funds, and private investors, looking for higher returns than they might be able to get at home, or to diversify their portfolios. Bonds are more likely to induce responsible behavior from the bond-issuing country, since the interest rates payable are higher than aid loans (and so there is an incentive to make good use of the funds), and there are punitive terms in the event of a default in payments. The successful issue of a bond confers credibility in international markets that African countries crave. They can move from being aid basket cases to having a credit rating and the ability to raise more money, rather than having to beg for it. The African bond market still has a long way to go (in 2015 it was only worth $7–8 billion), but offers an alternative to aid which properly engages countries with the international financial system and increases responsibility.

There is another area which could make a huge difference to Africa's fortunes. Africa's share of global trade is a scandalous 1 percent (it was 3 percent in the 1950s), even though it is chock-full of commodities and resources the world needs. Its countries lose out big time to the agricultural subsidies, worth hundreds of billions a year, given to farmers in rich countries. EU subsidies make up over a third of European farmers' incomes, and EU tariffs on food imports can be as high as 300 percent. Annual US farm subsidies amount to $20 billion. Trade reform, not aid, would make the world of difference to Africa.

Final comments

There has been plenty of criticism of China's role in Africa, principally because it does not attach the labor, environmental, and human rights conditions that the World Bank, IMF, and UN bodies invariably tie to aid, grants, and lending. Yet many African leaders prefer to be partners of the Chinese government and Chinese companies, rather than debtors being told what to do. Of course China is self-interested, Moyo notes, compared to the altruistic aid agenda, but if average Africans are also benefiting from Chinese investment, who cares? Better than the years of stagnation and decline under the aid paradigm.

In fact, African states can choose to do deals with a number of big powers, notably Japan and India, thus seizing control of their destiny. As Senegal's President Wade said in 2002, "I've never seen a country develop itself through aid or credit. Countries that have developed—in Europe, America, Japan, Asian countries like Taiwan, Korea, and Singapore—have all believed in free markets. There is no mystery there. Africa took the wrong road after independence."

Dambisa Moyo

Moyo was born in Lusaka, Zambia, in 1969. She began a chemistry degree at the University of Zambia, but transferred to the American University in Washington DC, graduating in 1991. She worked at the World Bank for two years, contributing to its World Development Report, and spent nearly a decade as a research economist at Goldman Sachs, working in bond markets, hedge funds and global macroeconomics.

Moyo has a Masters in Public Administration from Harvard's John F. Kennedy School of Government and an DPhil in economics from Oxford University (St Anthony's College). She is a director on the boards of Barclays Bank, Barrick Gold, Chevron and Seagate Technology. She is a regular speaker at conferences such as the World Economic Forum in Davos and the Aspen Institute.

Other books include How the West Was Lost: Fifty Years of Economic Folly—And the Stark Choices that Lie Ahead *(2011), and* Winner Take All: China's Race for Resources and What It Means for the World *(2012).*

1990

Governing the Commons

"What one can observe in the world . . . is that neither the state nor the market is uniformly successful in enabling individuals to sustain long-term, productive use of natural resources systems. Further, communities of individuals have relied on institutions resembling neither state nor the market to govern some resource systems with reasonable degrees of success over long periods of time."

In a nutshell

Natural resources like water and forests do not necessarily require government or laws to be well-run. Stakeholders with a long-term interest in the resource can police each other.

In a similar vein

Ronald Coase *The Firm, the Market, and the Law*
Friedrich Hayek *The Use of Knowledge in Society*
Thomas Schelling *Micromotives and Macrobehavior*
E. F. Schumacher *Small Is Beautiful*

CHAPTER 31

Elinor Ostrom

We frequently hear about some natural resource, such as a fishing ground, that is threatened with destruction or depletion. Government blames the fishers for overfishing, they in turn say too much or poor regulation is to blame. Either way, the phrase "tragedy of the commons" is used, and its emotiveness helps those in favor of strong central government regulation make their case.

In fact, Elinor Ostrom said, neither the state nor the market is the answer to many natural resource issues; people have been solving them for a very long time without recourse to either. She was the first to collate thousands of case studies across many disciplines, including rural sociology, anthropology, history, economics, political science, forestry, and ecology, and from around the world, which showed how people had created self-governing institutions to manage "common pool resources" (CPRs).

The assumption that "common-pool problems are all dilemmas in which the participants themselves cannot avoid producing suboptimal results, and in some cases disastrous results" had given rise to models, she noted, that did not fit what was actually happening on the ground. Nor was there a theoretical framework to guide people in situations where they simply wanted to organize themselves to manage a resource well. *Governing the Commons* provided the theory, and helped her win a Nobel Prize in Economics in 2009, the first woman to do so.

The commons don't have to be tragic

From Aristotle to Hobbes, many have noted that people pursue their own self-interest at the long-term expense of the whole, and that when a resource is free, it is not valued. In a famous 1968 *Science* article, Garrett Hardin gave the example of herders gaining in the short-term from use of common grazing land, while only sharing a small cost in resultant overgrazing. This "use today, worry-about-the-future tomorrow" attitude results in destruction of the very resource they are using. The "tragedy of the commons" warning is made not just in relation to natural resource depletion, but also to issues of overpopulation, regional wars, and overspending governments.

Such thinking, Ostrom says, assume that humans are helpless in the face of their own selfish drives, and that left to their own devices, they will destroy the world's natural resources. The obvious solution seems to be tight government regulation and coercion, yet very little attention is given to the significant costs of creating and maintaining a government agency to police and govern natural resources, even assuming it would be good at doing so. The other solution put forward to prevent tragedies of commons is to replace all commonly used resources with private property rights. The common meadow, for instance, would be divided into two, with each herder being awarded rights to their half. Now, they will not be competing against each other, but will be playing a game against nature itself. The herder begins to see that any gain has wider costs, and so adjusts his use of the resource accordingly in order that the value of the land is maintained. This seems sensible, until it's appreciated that that each parcel of land is part of a bigger natural resource *system* covering many parcels of land. And even if privatization could work on land, how is it possible to divide up the seas?

In sum, both the high-regulation and the privatization models assume a central role for government, either as crafter of the laws or as policer of the property rights, but this role always has real and often underestimated costs to the public.

Look at the alternatives

Ostrom's alternative is the slow and often difficult process of creating institutions (which are usually neither state nor private, but may involve elements of both) for managing a specific resource, taking account of the history of its use and the people involved. The parties design contracts reflecting their intimate local knowledge of the resource and its current state. While the process will involve conflict, the outcome normally brings lower costs in terms of not having to resort to the judicial system to gain the upper hand, or attempting to get legislation enacted. The successful ones also deal with the free rider issue—of everyone enjoying the resource without contributing to its maintenance.

Parties often agree to use and abide by a private arbitrator or monitor, the costs of which are shared. This arrangement is already used in business life, Ostrom notes, and of course sports teams abide by referee decisions. While state regulation would be too much at a remove from the situation, the parties and the arbitrator are there on the scene, and are able to see and report any infractions of the deal agreed. Of course, many problems can happen with the self-regulating approach, just as they can with central regulation and privatization, but self-regulation is an option that gives resource users the feeling of ownership.

Ostrom gives many examples of institutions developed to govern common natural resources, including Törbel, a mountainous village in Valais canton, Switzerland, which has arrangements going back to the thirteenth century to regulate use of five types of communally-owned property: alpine grazing meadows, forests, unproductive land, irrigation systems, and paths and roads running through private and communal lands. All citizens could vote on the village statutes which regulate use and misuse of common land, arrange for manure distribution, maintain alpine roads and huts, and allocate certain numbers of trees for families for construction and heating. There is a wide variety of such agreements in Alpine areas of Switzerland and Germany, but the basic principle of having private property for agricultural activity, and communal property for meadows and forests, is well-observed. Such communities, from long experience, know what kind of land suits private ownership, and what does not.

Los Angeles and its water

Ostrom devotes a chunk of the book to her study of the evolution of institutions to manage groundwater use in the city where she grew up, Los Angeles. Thanks to its surrounding foothills and mountains, LA's water has always drained into underground sand and gravel beds, creating a valuable source in addition to surface water. However, as the city grew, the aquifers became overused and levels began dropping below the level of the neighboring Pacific Ocean. This raised the possibility that seawater would fill up the wells. In such a dry city, it was a ticking environmental time-bomb.

The law provided that the owner of a parcel of land (the "overlying landowner") only had access to the water flowing under the land. This right did not provide much security, however, as extraction could obviously be affected by a neighbor's more rapid withdrawal of water. If the parties went to court about it, each would be assigned "proportional" use, which usually meant a cutback to both. Private and public water companies were allowed to extract "surplus" water in the basin not being used by overlying landowners, and the larger they were, the more rights they had. Yet most of the time no one really knew whether there was a surplus, and what the "safe yield" of the basin was. Despite the laws, the system amounted to an open access CPR, in which extractors did not have to factor in the cost of their actions to others. The likely end result of this "pumping race" would be overexploitation and salination, undermining the very basis of a growing city.

With the prospect before them of litigation and lengthy and expensive court proceedings, parties drawing water in the Raymond Basin and West Basin of Los Angeles, including municipal water providers and industry, came to agreements which limited the total withdrawal of water to a safe yield to prevent salination and depletion, with a court appointing a watermaster to ensure the agreements were kept to. An additional effect of the agreement was to see a market for water rights emerge, properly taking into account the costs and benefits of the resource.

Such proportional-use agreements were driven by the idea of "no one left a sucker," in contrast to the previous pumping race regime in which one user's excess water extraction came at another's loss. Yet once the model was established, groundwater levels rose again to healthy levels, users and producers of water got security of flow, and legal costs dropped. The result was that stakeholders learned much more about the resource they were using, it was better managed, and through taxation (to pay for monitoring and any legal costs) they had greater control.

Keeping it local

Ostrom accepts that the ability of people to create self-governing common-pool resource institutions will depend on the autonomy allowed under the political regime they live under. In so many places, the use of resources is governed not by the interests of local users or the nation at large, but by the rent-seeking of corrupt officials and private organizations in league with each other. Or, national officials presume that there is an absence of arrangements to manage common-pool resources, when in fact there are longstanding informal tenures and boundaries among local peoples. In many developing countries, forests were nationalized with the rationale that local people couldn't manage them in a productive and sustainable way, even though they had done so for generations. Nepal's Private Forests Nationalization Act was designed "to conserve the forests for the entire country," but led to free and damaging logging because local people believed they had lost control of their forests; if they were no longer owners or custodians, it seemed rational to become free riders themselves, taking what they could. Only when the Nepal government reversed the policy in 1978 did reforestation begin to occur.

Final comments

It can be argued that Common Pool Resource agreements are usually not as good as competitive markets in driving efficiency, because they represent a system not driven by the power of price signals. For an individual, focusing on the rules of a CPR agreement could seem a much fuzzier and uncertain strategy than simply adjusting to and taking advantage of changes in market prices. On the other hand, if a party to an agreement engages only in short-term profit maximization in response to market price, it can mean serious damage to the resource. Indeed, the prospect of losing a resource can make people even more willing to extract use from it before it collapses. Yet what is "selfish" depends on one's timeframe; do I want to get something out of the resource today, or do I want to hand it over to my children in good condition? Such decisions involving time, family, custom, and locality may not seem efficient in the short term, Ostrom noted, but over a longer timeframe they are indeed rational, and have the potential to deliver better results than market solutions or solutions imposed by the state.

Elinor Ostrom

Ostrom was born in 1933 in Los Angeles. Her mother was a musician and her father designed stage sets. After Beverly Hills High School she majored in political science at UCLA, and worked in business for several years before returning to do her Masters degree and PhD.

In 1965 her husband was offered a professorship in political science at Indiana University, and she took up a post teaching American government there, becoming a professor in 1974. The couple established the Workshop in Political Theory and Political Analysis, which still provides research and teaching on democratic institutions, incentives and self-governance. In 2006, Ostrom established the Center for the Study of Institutional Diversity at Arizona State University.

Ostrom did field work in many countries, and received research grants from the National Science Foundation, Andrew Mellon Foundation, Ford Foundation, the United Nations, and the US Geological Survey. She was included in a "100 Most Influential People" list by Time *magazine, which noted, "Virtually all the world's most urgent problems require collective action. Be it environmental protection, the international financial system or the dimensions of inequality, Ostrom's work sheds light on the direction society must follow to avoid misuse of shared resources." She died in 2012.*

2014

Capital in the Twenty-First Century

"Thus throughout most of human history, the inescapable fact is that the rate of return on capital was always at least 10 to 20 times greater than the rate of growth of output (and income). Indeed, this fact is to a large extent the very foundation of society itself: it is what allowed a class of owners to devote themselves to something other than their own subsistence."

"The world to come may well combine the worse of two past worlds: both very large inequality of inherited wealth and very high wage inequalities justified in terms of merit and productivity (claims with very little factual basis). Meritocratic extremism can thus lead to a race between supermanagers and rentiers, to the detriment of those who are neither."

In a nutshell

Unless governments introduce new forms of taxation and ways of increasing social mobility, we are heading for levels of income inequality not seen since the nineteenth century—and possible political upheaval.

In a similar vein

Robert J. Gordon *The Rise and Fall of American Growth*
Paul Krugman *The Conscience of a Liberal*
Karl Marx *Capital*
Hernando de Soto *The Mystery of Capital*
Dani Rodrik *The Globalization Paradox*

CHAPTER 32

Thomas Piketty

Like many bestsellers, no one really expected *Capital in the Twenty-First Century* to do so well. The 700-page work did not make a big splash when published in France in 2013 as *Le capital au XXI siècle*, not even making the top 100 books of the year. It was the English version, translated by Arthur Goldhammer, that caught the public's imagination and turned it into an unlikely economics blockbuster. Why?

Piketty's worldview was naturally different to the East Coast American academics that shape the economic consensus. Issues of inequality had long been part of the French political debate, but it had now become a hot issue in America and Britain too—and here was a work of deep scholarship in an area that had "long been based on an abundance of prejudice and a paucity of fact," as Piketty puts it. In particular, Piketty sought to expose the canard of orthodox economics that "a rising tide raises all boats." In fact, he argues, this was true of only a relatively short period in human history, the "Trentes Glorieuses" (or thirty-odd years following World War Two), when national politics favored labor over capital. As this period has long since ended, only big public policy gestures (recall the impact on social mobility of the GI Bill, as one example), he argues, can save Western countries from being dominated by a combination of meritocratic elite ("supermanagers") and the inherited rich.

One advantage of being French, Piketty writes in his introduction, is that economists do not have high esteem in his country, which prevents hubris and forces them to work with other social scientists. Indeed, *Capital in the Twenty-First Century* almost seems written for his friends in the Paris intellectual elite who turn their noses up at economics. Piketty admits that he admires historians and sociologists like Fernand Braudel, Claude Levi-Strauss and Pierre Bordieau more than he does other economists. Economics should never have tried to remove itself from the other social sciences, he says, and he goes out of his way to bring literature and history into his analysis, including references to the novels of Jane Austen and Balzac, which he says tell us a lot about the distribution of wealth in Britain and France between 1790 and 1830 and how it affected every aspect of social life and opportunity. "In my mind," Piketty writes, "this book is as much a work of history as of economics." Looking at data only from a period of a decade or two or three, as most economists do, hides the long-term trends in the ratio between capital income and wage income, he says. But economic data from the past three centuries has become more accessible in the last 15 years, providing the foundation for Piketty's 300-year survey, which includes over 120 tables, graphs and illustrations to back up the arguments being made.

Like Stephen Hawking's *A Brief History of Time*, Piketty's *magnum opus* threatens to become one of those books everyone has, but few have actually read (or listened to: the audiobook runs to 26 hours). It is certainly very long and requires concentration, but is not especially difficult. Make it one of your projects this year and you will be richly rewarded.

When the past rules the future

Piketty's basic question is, does capitalism inevitably lead to greater inequality of income? Or do competition, growth, and advancing technology bring about greater equality of incomes in the long term?

He devotes several pages to discussing the work of American economist Simon Kuznets, who was the first to properly measure the distribution of income in the United States. Kuznet's 1955 paper, "Economic Growth and Income Inequality," gave rise to the "Kuznets Curve," the observation that in the early stages of industrialization, it is capital rather than labor that brings the most benefits, because capital is able to profit from new technologies. But as industrialization matures, a greater proportion of society can partake of its fruits in terms of higher real wages: "A rising tide lifts all boats."

Piketty agrees, but notes that real incomes did not expand for Britain's factory workers until the last third of the nineteenth century, *generations* after the Industrial Revolution had begun. Most of the early gains went to industrialists and landowners, despite accelerating economic growth. The scenes painted by Dickens in *Oliver Twist* and by Hugo in *Les Misérables* were historically correct: working class incomes had stagnated, while others had enjoyed some fantastic wealth increases. If World War One had not happened, Piketty says, inequality between capital and labor would have continued to increase. It took a shock as big as the Great War to change things.

His point is that the Kuznets Curve is not an inexorable law, but was an ideologically driven notion promoting the benefits of capitalism to poor countries during the Cold War. But if the Kuznets curve isn't real, where does it leave our societies? The signs in our own era are not good; new information technologies including the internet have created massive fortunes for a few, while wages for the majority have gone up very little.

Labor's share of national incomes has shown no sign of increasing even with advancing technology (indeed, some jobs have disappeared altogether). The real problem, Piketty says, is that increasing inequality can happen even in a world of adequate education, skills, and training, and in which there is market efficiency.

He points to the uncomfortable mathematical fact that, in periods of slow economic growth (such as the rich world is in now), the share of capital in national wealth grows faster. Instead of doing the hard work of building a company and investing in people, it is more profitable for the better-off to become rentiers, collecting dividends on real estate, shares, and other capital. Moreover if not much new wealth is being created, existing wealth takes on greater importance. When the return on capital outpaces the national rate of economic growth—expressed in the formula $r > g$, in which the return on capital (r) is greater than the rate of growth (g)—it is very easy for the rich to get richer, even as the wages of the poor or middle class stagnate or fall. Greater property rights, freer markets, or increased competition won't make the situation any better, Piketty says, because more perfect markets tend to help capital more than they do labor.

Capital's comeback

Economic growth is composed of two things: growth from population increase, and growth from increased productivity per worker. For most of human history, there was virtually no growth in productivity, only from population. The Industrial Revolution changed all this. The period 1700 to 2012 saw a 1.6 percent growth rate, half of which was due to actual growth in productivity per head. That doesn't sound like much, but consider that over a 30-year period, a growth rate of only one percent will see an increase of standard of living of about a third. A growth rate of two percent will see a doubling.

The 30-year period after World War Two saw very high growth thanks to a lucky combination of a baby boom, advances in technology, and rebuilding efforts after the war. But this "Trente Glorieuses", which people took to be the start of a normal high-growth pattern, now seems like the exception to the rule. With world population growth slowing, and indeed declining in some countries such as Japan, the chances for high growth for rich countries are small.

But what has falling population growth got to do with Piketty's main subject, inequality? One of the consequences of faster population growth is that it lessens the power of inherited wealth. If you are from a family of seven, for instance, your share of the family's wealth is not likely to be great.

Better to rely on your own labor to build wealth. And in a fast-growing economy (in terms of both productivity and population), the earnings of your parents or great-grandparents will not amount to a great deal compared to what you can earn today. A society with a growth rate of only one percent annually will over a generation change dramatically. Modes of production change, creating new kinds of jobs, which in turn increase social mobility, which favors income over capital, and so on. In contrast, a society that does not grow retains the same social structures and patterns of ownership and production from generation to generation. A high-saving, slow-growing country (Piketty uses the term "quasi-stagnant") will see the balance tip towards capital and away from wage income over time.

Before World War One, the bulk of Europeans worked their whole lives for a pittance for people who never had to work. The wealthiest one percent of the population in France and Britain owned fully *half* of each nation's wealth. The rise of a propertied middle class, comprising 40 percent of the population, was therefore one of the great changes of the twentieth century, which resulted in this demographic grabbing a third of the wealth in Europe. It happened partly because the wealth of the top 10 percent was cut in half (due to war, depression, and pro-labor government policy). Many more people now had to work, and wages became more important as the source of wealth.

But in the early twenty-first century, Piketty notes, wealth has made a comeback, and we are returning to the capital/income ratio seen in the eighteenth and nineteenth centuries. In 1970, the stock of private capital in rich countries (the US, Japan, Germany, Britain, France, Italy, Canada, and Australia) was worth between two and three-and-a-half years of national income. By 2010, private capital was worth between four and seven years of national income. Of course, in the short run, the capital/income ratios can vary a lot, because the prices of real estate and stocks are often volatile. However, "bubbles aside," Piketty writes, "what we are witnessing is a strong comeback of private capital in the rich countries since 1970, or, to put it another way, the emergence of a new patrimonial capitalism." The world is beginning to resemble Europe at around 1900, when class and wealth divisions were at their height prior to the First World War. In short, a new Gilded Age.

The structure of inequality

There are two kinds of inequality, Piketty stresses. One sees a "society of rentiers", with people basically living off accumulated and inherited wealth, and with an upper class employing very low-paid people. This is *Ancien Regime* France, or Europe in the *Belle Époque*. The second form was virtually invented by the United States, a "hypermeritocratic society" or society of "supermanagers," with a tiny percentage of people earning vast sums from their labors. Since 1980, three-quarters of the income gains in the US have gone to the top 1 percent, which includes people making more than $1.5 million a year. The result has been a greater inequality in income from labor than at any time in human history. What may well be happening, Piketty says, is that hypermeritocratic earning transforms into a new rentier class, or complements it. This would mean that unless you inherit wealth, or you are some kind of superstar in your domain, your economic outlook is modest at best.

Piketty believes that increasing inequality was a cause of the 2008 financial crisis, for the simple reason that the wages of the middle and lower classes had stagnated, and to maintain their standard of living people had to take on more debt. In terms of purchasing power, the American minimum wage was at its highest in 1969, at around $10 in 2013 money. By 2013, the purchasing power of the minimum wage had sunk to $7 an hour—considerably less than minimum wages in France, and less than Britain's. What is incontrovertible is that in the 30 years leading up to the crisis, 1977 to 2007, the incomes of the bottom 90 percent of Americans grew only 0.5 percent per year. Meantime, the richest 10 percent of Americans enjoyed 60 percent of total income growth.

Merit and inheritance

By 2020, Piketty notes, the share of inherited wealth in France will be 70 percent of total wealth, with only a third coming from savings, from wages, or from capital gain. In other words, inherited wealth is becoming significantly more important than wage earnings in determining who is well-off and who is not. Rich societies have not become more meritocratic, nor has education created the intergenerational mobility that was expected of it. Although today there are proportionately fewer really big estates inherited in the manner of the nineteenth century fortunes, there are thousands of medium-sized and smaller estates of the value of $200,000 to $2 million. These estate sizes do not stop education and skills being valuable for the inheritors, or mean they can stop earning a living, but it does mean that there is a sizeable chunk of society (Piketty calls them "petits rentiers") who move ahead of the rest thanks to the genetic lottery. In 2010, the people who received a legacy amounting to a lifetime of labor income, or more, amounted to 13 percent of the French population. This is hardly the "just inequality" you would hope to see in a truly meritocratic society, particularly in "egalitarian" France.

His point is that a just society must never only be concerned with regulating markets or upholding law and order, but must continually be seeking to increase social mobility and minimise the effects of "lottery by birth."

The case for a global wealth tax

Piketty assumes that the rate of growth at a world level will drop to just over 3 percent until 2050, then from 2050 to 2100 fall to 1.5 percent, which was the global growth rate in the nineteenth century. Meantime, the rate of return to capital will stay steady at between 4 and 5 percent, as it has done throughout history. Therefore, he suggests, the only thing stopping the domination of capital over labor would be a global tax on capital: a progressive annual tax on individual wealth, or the net value of assets a person has minus any debt. Such a tax, which would need to be combined with new laws and compliance on banking transparency, and clampdowns on tax havens, would stop the "endless inegalitarian spiral" facing the world.

Piketty admits the idea is utopian, yet not impossible to implement. If governments avoid it, they may be forced to deal with inequality anyway through political shocks. The alternative is the rise of nationalism, which brings with it protectionist policies and capital controls. A tax on capital wouldn't replace progressive income taxes or property taxes, but serve the purpose of getting more tax from very wealthy people, who at the moment are mainly taxed on income, which they can easily minimize. It doesn't matter whether you tax them at 98 percent, he notes, they are not paying a tax proportional to their wealth.

Piketty leaves the reader with a dark thought: "If you have free trade and free circulation of capital and people but destroy the social state and all forms of progressive taxation, the temptations of defensive nationalism and identity politics will very likely grow stronger than ever in both Europe and the United States." An economically more extreme polity leads to extreme political outcomes.

Final comments

Critics say that Piketty's solution focuses too much on redistribution, when simple growth can lessen inequality, or government efforts to increase the capital of the less well-off (for instance, through the topping up of pensions contributions or savings, or making it easier to own a home). Economic historians such as Deirdre McCloskey note that Marx's pessimism about capitalism led him to wrong prophecies about its demise, and the same is true of Piketty. Perhaps he is wrong too, to see the past as a guide to the future; capitalism may turn out to be much more dynamic than he gives it credit for being.

Recent research on the fabled "elephant chart," a graph produced by economist Branko Milanovic in 2012 which seemed to show global inequality on a steep rise since 1980 (imagine the elephant's trunk reaching into the air), now shows the trend is not as steep as was thought. The middle class is not disappearing in rich countries, and is growing fast in poorer ones. We may never see a return to the income-equalizing era of the Trentes Glorieuses, but neither, perhaps, is increasing inequality, either within or between countries, the inevitability that Piketty fears. We can only hope.

Thomas Piketty

Piketty was born in Paris in 1971. After taking his Baccalaureate he won a place to the prestigious École Normale Supérieure, and studied mathematics and economics. By 22 he had a PhD in economics jointly from Paris's EHESS (School for Advanced Studies in the Social Sciences) and the London School of Economics. His thesis on wealth distribution won a "best in year" prize from the French Economic Association.

After a period in the United States at the Massachusetts Institute of Technology, he became a full professor at EHESS in 2000, and in 2006 he became the first head of the newly created Paris School of Economics. With Emmanuel Saez and Gabriel Zucman he is a co-director of the World Wealth and Incomes Database, which furnishes some of the data in the book. In 2015 Piketty was awarded an honorary doctorate from the University of Johannesburg, but refused to accept France's Legion D'Honneur, saying "I do not think it is the government's role to decide who is honorable. They would do better to concentrate on reviving growth in France and Europe."

Other books include Les hauts en France au XXe siècle *(2001) on income inequality in France over the course of the twentieth century,* The Economics of Inequality *(2015),* Why Save The Bankers? And Other Essays on our Economic and Political Crisis *(2015) and* Chronicles of Our Troubled Times *(2016) which collates his articles for the French newspaper* Liberation. *A documentary film based on* Capital in the Twenty-First Century, *by New Zealand director Justin Pemberton, is released in 2017.*

1944

The Great Transformation

"No society could, naturally, live for any length of time unless it possessed an economy of some sort; but previously to our time no economy has ever existed that, even in principle, was controlled by markets. In spite of the chorus of academic incantations so persistent in the nineteenth century, gain and profit made on exchange never before played an important part in human economy. Though the institution of the market was fairly common since the later Stone Age, its role was no more than incidental to economic life."

In a nutshell

"Free" markets, far from being a natural force, are very much a human invention which must serve the interests of the larger society and humanity, not vice versa.

In a similar vein

Liaquat Ahamed *Lords of Finance*
Deirdre McCloskey *Bourgeois Equality*
Henry George *Progress and Poverty*
Friedrich Hayek *The Use of Knowledge in Society*
Paul Krugman *The Conscience of a Liberal*
Karl Marx *Capital*
Ludwig von Mises *Human Action*

CHAPTER 33

Karl Polanyi

Today, such is the predominance of markets, pricing, efficiency, and output in the thinking of the contemporary person, no one can be blamed for seeing "'society'" as simply an element within an unstoppable global capitalist economy.

For Karl Polanyi, such thinking had it the wrong way around. Markets and economic systems are very much a human creation, embedded in society. They serve purposes of our choosing, and do not float free of social relations. There is nothing "natural" or inevitable about the rise of markets, and indeed there were longstanding alternatives, demonstrated in earlier human cultures, based on reciprocity and redistribution.

Polanyi's "great transformation" was from a world resting on social and cultural values to one driven by market thinking. The spread of market forces into every aspect of life had negative effects, and he saw history as a back-and-forth tussle (a "double movement") between the forces of the market and the balancing move for greater protections in society (for example, the welfare state, health and safety legislation, worker unions). His mission was to reclaim humanity from laissez-faire economic ideology.

Published in the same year as Hayek's *The Road To Serfdom* (see *50 Politics Classics*) Polanyi's book offered an alternative to Hayekian and von Miseian free-market economics, but also to the economics of Keynes, who never described himself as a socialist, as Polanyi did. Today, Polanyi is a sort of patron saint for critics of "neoliberal" economic orthodoxy (including Joseph Stiglitz, who wrote a lengthy Introduction to one edition of *The Great Transformation*), and is considered a pioneer of economic anthropology, influencing scholars such as David Graeber (*Debt: The First 5,000 Years*). His arguments are less respected by economists and economic historians, who dispute his account of history, but in a post-Financial Crisis era in which some view markets as too lightly regulated, his ideas are worth analyzing.

Social, not economic beings

Adam Smith famously wrote of man's "natural propensity to barter, truck, and exchange." Most economists after him agreed, but Polanyi says there is little evidence for it. In most societies through history, resources were organized communally. It is only in modern times that markets have come to dominate societies, to become the main form of engagement and relation. Before then, in Europe at least, "the progress of civilization was . . . mainly political, intellectual, and spiritual." People, then and now, are not motivated by material goods on their own, but only to acquire them in order to safeguard social standing, social claims, and social assets. Economic activity is "a mere function of social organization." European feudalism was also a system of redistribution and reciprocity in which, however unbalanced, there was some protection for all and no one went hungry. In contrast, Polanyi (echoing Henry George) asserts that the richer a country gets under free-market principles, the more people will be found to be living in poverty.

Polanyi argues that the role of markets in societies has been exaggerated to suit current ideologies. For instance, in medieval Europe, towns arose around markets, but the authorities went to some lengths to ensure that what went on in towns did not spill over into the countryside. Venice, Hamburg, Lyon, and London were not Italian, German, French or English cities as such, but trading entrepots which had more in common with each other than their hinterlands. They allowed for marketization "in spots", while the color of the nation or kingdom remained the same, ensuring that its society and institutions did not change. Thus, Polanyi writes, "The economic system was submerged in general social relations; markets were merely an accessory feature of an institutional setting controlled and regulated more than ever by social authority." The Industrial Revolution changed all this.

Origins of the market religion

The Industrial Revolution (whose most active period, Polanyi says, was 1795–1834) required long-term capital investments in plant, machinery, and buildings, which had to be amortized. In reaction to an economy built on prices and unit production, labor simply became a factor within the formulae for capital returns. The "satanic mills" tore apart families and the traditional relationship of the poorer classes to the land; such people were shunted into ghastly conditions in cities. The only thing tying the industrialist to the people creating his products was a wage, and the lower it was, the better.

A commodity is anything that has been expressly produced *for* sale, Polanyi notes. But neither people nor land fall into this category. If you treat people as a commodity that can be shifted about or used at will, it causes acute misery and dislocation. The same happens when land, "which is only another name for nature," Polanyi writes, and which people have a close relationship to, is exploited only for monetary gain without recognizing its non-economic status and value. Foreshadowing the environmental movement, he observes that the commoditization of land can only result in defiled landscapes, polluted rivers, and the destruction of sustainable food production. Finally, the marketization of society also means that money itself becomes a commodity. Treat money as a commodity, Polanyi says, and it will mean that shortages of it, or too much of it swilling around, will be as ruinous to business "as floods and droughts in primitive society."

The nineteenth century seemed to bring a new age of prosperity, but figures such as the socialist industrialist Robert Owen and philosopher William Godwin pointed to a deepening of inequality and social alienation. Yet such men could not compete against the idea that there was a new set of "laws" in political economy, including the self-regulating market, which were as immutable as moral or theological laws. The "market system" began to take over society. Its promoters framed it as a natural, elegant process the logic of which no one could deny. Nineteenth-century liberalism seemed to be a political creed, but it became a mere skin covering the body of the beast: pure economic interest.

The countermovement

In fact, Polanyi argues, since the end of the eighteenth century there had been a natural countermovement to the apparently inexorable march of the market. An expression of this was England's Speenhamland Law.

In 1795 the laws of serfdom were loosened, paving the way for a national market of labor, which suited the new industrialists. But the Speenhamland Law reversed this, entrenching the system of labor organization that the Stuarts and Tudors had put in place. Under the law, people were effectively entitled to a minimum wage linked to the price of bread (a "right to live") so that their income could be topped up to this level (through rates paid by local ratepayers) even if they were working. Until its abolition in 1834, the Law was very popular amongst common people because it meant that no one could go hungry. Polanyi admits that it made people more dependent on handouts, but it probably prevented a revolution. When the Reform Bill of 1832 and the Poor Law Amendment Act of 1834 abolished this "right to live", it caused destitution to thousands, particularly those too proud to enter the workhouse. Ricardo and Malthus "passed over in icy silence," Polanyi says, the effects of the changes.

As life was pretty bleak for most factory and mill workers, it wasn't long before labor began organizing and reformers began agitating for social legislation. Yet nothing would stop the belief in the religion of the laissez-faire market system. The religion would only meet its demise with the failure of a key feature, the gold standard, which fell apart under the pressure of war debts, German inflation, British recession, and national deflations required to keep currencies on gold. Yet "no private suffering, no restriction of sovereignty, was deemed too great a sacrifice for the recovery of monetary integrity," Polanyi writes.

In the 1930s, as the Great Depression took hold, economic liberalism was finally recognized as a failure. It provided no protection for the health, safety, or livelihoods of people locked into the new forms of industrial organization, and it was only right that new legislation was brought in to make mines safer, prevent the deaths of chimney sweep children, establish fire brigades in towns and cities, and create forms of social insurance. This was not a case of creeping collectivism, as Herbert Spencer charged, or anti-liberal prejudice. It was rather a "spontaneous reaction" based on simple justice and humanity. These measures were not ideological, but a common-sense countermovement to the utopian principles of free-market liberalism.

The darker progeny of the system, Polanyi contends, were fascism and imperialism. Fascism was a reaction to the system's failure to create economic stability, and imperialism provided a convenient distraction to domestic woes including unemployment, balance of payments and currency crises. European societies became battle grounds for the competing claims of working-class and business interests. In America it brought a backlash in the form of Roosevelt's New Deal, and in Britain Labour Party governments that established a hybrid of socialist capitalism.

Final comments

You could argue that *The Great Transformation* was very much a product of its time, in that it was focused on explaining how laissez-faire economics led to an extreme counter-reaction—fascism—leading up to World War Two. Yet one could easily apply Polanyi's outlook to our time, too. Practices such as the bundling up of people's mortgages as "financial products", a cause of the 2007–2008 financial crisis, is a very good example of the "decoupling of markets from society."

The flipside of Polanyi's argument (so well expressed by Hayek), is that social freedoms only come about through economic freedoms. Polanyi admitted this, and in the last part of his book claims that Bills of Rights and other civic institutions could protect personal freedom even within a more planned economy. History has shown this view to be rather naïve, and therefore *The Great Transformation* rings hollow to many ears. Still, the book does provide an important warning about unregulated markets. Whenever you hear people urging that the state is an obstacle in the way of the economy, at least consider the argument that the marketization of all aspects of life can have a corrupting effect on state and society. Polanyi's ultimate, and very important, question is: are we citizens, or are we just consumers?

Karl Polanyi

Polanyi was born in 1886 in Vienna. His father was a successful Hungarian-Jewish railway contractor and his mother hosted a literary salon. At the University of Budapest he studied law and founded the Galileo Club for radicals; in 1914 he helped form Hungary's new Radical Party. During World War One he served on the Russian Front.

After the collapse of the Austro-Hungarian Empire, Polanyi was associated with the Hungarian People's Republic, but its fall to Bolsheviks in 1919 forced him to move to the newly social democratic Vienna. There he met and married another Hungarian émigrée, the political firebrand Ilona Duczynska. For a decade Polanyi was the editor of The Austrian Economist, *and from this platform began criticizing the free-market Austrian school of economics, engaging in a debate with Ludwig von Mises on the mechanics of how a socialist society would work. When the Depression and the rise of fascism put Polanyi out of a job he moved to England, mixing with Fabian socialists and surviving by teaching economic history through the Workers Education Association.*

From 1940 to 1942, when he wrote The Great Transformation, *Polanyi was at Bennington College, Vermont. The book was not an immediate success, but in 1947 it brought an offer to teach at Columbia University. Because of his wife's history as a communist she was barred from living in America, so Polanyi had to commute to New York from their home in Ontario. Polanyi won funding from the Ford Foundation to study pre-modern economic systems, which resulted in* Trade and Market in the Early Empires *(1957). He died in 1964 in Pickering, Ontario.*

1990

The Competitive Advantage of Nations

"Active feuds between domestic rivals are common, and often associated with an internationally successful national industry . . . Pride drives managers and workers to be highly sensitive to other companies in the nation, and the national press and investment analysts constantly compare one domestic competitor with the others. Domestic rivals fight not only for market share but for people, technical breakthroughs, and more generally, 'bragging rights'."

"A nation's industries are either upgrading and extending their competitive advantages or are falling behind."

In a nutshell

The best thing that governments can do to increase national economic advantage is to ensure there is lively competition in local industries, which pushes companies to create world-beating products and services that can be exported.

In a similar vein

William J. Baumol *The Microtheory of Innovative Entrepreneurship*
Gary Becker *Human Capital*
Ha-Joon Chang *23 Things They Don't Tell You About Capitalism*
Jane Jacobs *The Economy of Cities*
David Ricardo *Principles of Political Economy and Taxation*
Julian Simon *The Ultimate Resource 2*

CHAPTER 34

Michael E. Porter

If there were a pantheon of greats from the Harvard Business School, Michael Porter's bust would be placed higher than most. In looking at how companies could position themselves to succeed within an industry, his heavily-researched business classics *Competitive Strategy* (1980) and *Competitive Advantage* (1985) brought a degree of gravitas to a literature prone to fads.

But when, having spent his career looking at the microeconomics of industry and firm, Porter was appointed to President Reagan's Commission on Industrial Competitiveness, he was forced to think more about the *nation's* role in economic success. At a time when America felt threatened by the great success of Japanese firms, and there was a lot of talk about whether the US needed a more interventionist industrial policy similar to Japan's or South Korea's, Porter resisted the mania for a national industrial policy. He instead chose to focus on "national environment," that is, the investments in human and physical capital and the macroeconomic and legal environment that allow firms to flourish. And it *was* firms, not government, that drove national prosperity: "The outcome of thousands of struggles in individual industries," Porter wrote in *The Competitive Advantage of Nations*, "determines the state of a nation's economy and its ability to progress."

Yet some national environments were of course more helpful to the advance of firms and industries than others, and Porter's purpose was to uncover their features so they could be replicated. The ambitious synthesis of macroeconomics, microeconomics, and management produced an 800-page whopper of a book. Though written in a time when fax machines were the new thing and Japan was still exporting typewriters, the principles remain valid.

Part of Porter's motivation was seeing how bad economic ideas had relegated millions to poverty in the post-war period and made some countries islands of unfulfilled potential. From the outset, *The Competitive Advantage of Nations* set out to have a real impact on national economic policy. His "diamond" theory of the determinants of competitiveness was adopted by New Zealand, Singapore, Canada, and later applied to Norway, Finland, the Netherlands, and Hong Kong, and his thinking on the "clustering" of industry was much-followed by cities and regions within the United States and around the world.

Comparative advantage or competitive advantage?

Porter specifically chose the title of the book to distinguish it from existing theory on the *comparative* advantage of nations, as articulated by David Ricardo.

Ricardo's theory rested on the assumption that a nation's natural endowments of resources and labor, combined with sufficient capital, would be enough for a country to become a successful trader with other nations. Porter argued that such "factor inputs" became increasingly less important in a globalized economy, because it was not what you *possessed* that made for success, but what you *created.* A lot of countries with amazing natural resources remain poor and undeveloped, while countries which have virtually no mines or forests, and not many people, produce world-beating companies that increase the national standard of living. These countries create an environment which allows for constant upgrading of skills, technology, and infrastructure. Under Porter's theory of competitive advantage, success becomes a *choice*, no longer down to natural advantages.

Porter argues that the old choice, between government intervention in industry and laissez-faire economics, is redundant. The state's role, which cuts across left and right of politics, is simply to create an environment in which productivity per worker (perhaps the best measure of wealth) keeps on rising. This means reducing trade barriers—a traditional liberal position—but it also means actively ensuring that high-quality education and training are being provided to citizens, and that there is healthy competition in the economy. Strict antitrust or antimonopoly laws, tough health and safety regulation, and environmental statutes are all important in competitive advantage. Far from being a "race to the bottom" in terms of competition between lower labor costs, the global economy rewards those countries that help the environment and pays proper wages, because the steps taken to do so increases investment in productivity

Porter exposes the myths about the causes of productivity. In his mind low wages, rather than being a boost to competitiveness, were a sign of failure. "The ability to compete *despite* paying high wages," Porter writes, "would seem to represent a far more desirable national target." International success comes from creating and selling things of high added value, which means cutting edge research and design, the most advanced production techniques, and a highly skilled and educated workforce. These things don't come cheap, but the potential profit from, for instance, creating the best smartphone, driverless car, or solar panel, are vast.

The success diamond

Porter isolates four attributes that determine national advantage in an industry:

- Factors of production: including skilled and educated labor, infrastructure, physical resources, stock of scientific, technical and market knowledge, and capital resources.
- Demand conditions: that is, what demand exists for a particular product or service, and the general level of consumer discernment.
- Related and supporting industries: industries which can help build a cluster or ecosystem of production excellence, particularly if supplier industries themselves are internationally competitive.
- Microeconomic environment: the legal and political conditions affecting how firms are created and structured, and the degree of rivalry and competition between them.

The four factors form the points of a diamond which gets stronger as each point reinforces the other. Any nation can have a chance invention or breakthrough, but it is the ones that have an infrastructure of capital and technology development that will have the means to bring that invention to commercial application. Equally, many a nation will have industrial capabilities, or an educated work force, or pools of capital, but not all will have pressure from exacting local consumers to improve particular products or develop new ones. Porter argues, for instance, that the German consumer's passion for precision and quality was a key factor in its carmakers designing and engineering the best cars in the world. The key "demand factor" in America, in contrast, was the demand for millions of affordable, mass market cars which could get people comfortably from A to B.

Porter notes that "Social and political history and values create persistent differences among nations that play a role in competitive advantage in many industries." Italy's love of clothes and cars spawned Gucci and Ferrari; America's penchant for credit spawned global leadership in credit cards, notably Visa and Mastercard, and its talent for popular culture and entertainment pushed the movie industry to be world-dominant. Often, it is simple physical conditions that can shape success: Sweden's remote forests and mines required super-reliable trucks, and Volvo and Saab-Scania provided them, becoming key exporters in the process.

It is tempting, Porter says, to make the role of government the fifth aspect of the "diamond" in terms of national competitive advantage; consider the key role of the state in the success of post-war Japanese and Korean companies. But government's real role is in influencing the existing points of the diamond by being an important procurer, by establishing standards and regulations which push industry in a certain direction, or by creating education policies which can help industry. Government's role is not to create national advantage, but to raise the odds of it happening.

Clusters of competition

On the whole, Porter says, asking why a whole nation is competitive is asking the wrong question. Rather we must ask what is happening in the particular industries where the country's firms are competing, and how they are managing to keep up a high rate of productivity growth. Agglomeration of firms, suppliers, specialized skills and supporting institutions in a certain geographic location—what Porter calls "clusters"—bring multiple benefits to a nation. Information flows quickly between the leading companies, who leap upon new ideas and new technologies. One firm's success in global markets spurs the others to have a go.

Paradoxically, as globalization seems to lessen the importance of distance and geography, clustering becomes more valuable. Porter cites the City of London. Its banks, trading firms, insurance firms and other financial services are supported by a myriad of industries including information services (Reuters, for example), financial journalism and publishing, legal services, advertising and public relations, plus state institutions, notably the Bank of England. However, the City of London would never have flourished without stiff competition.

Competitive advantage, Porter says, "emerges from pressure, challenge, and adversity, rarely from an easy life . . . Among the strongest empirical findings from our research is the association between vigorous domestic rivalry and the creation and persistence of competitive advantage in an industry." This went against the accepted view that it is best to nurture one or two "national champions" in each industry which can bestride the world stage, and that too much competition reduces economies of scale. In fact, Porter found that even in small countries like Sweden and Switzerland, important industries like automotive manufacturing and pharmaceuticals had several strong local rivals, and achieved their economies of scale through worldwide sales. Switzerland's small size would suggest one dominant player in key industries. In fact, each industry tends to have several—for instance, Nestlé, Jacobs-Suchard, Lindt in chocolate, and Rolex, Patek Phillipe and many others in watches.

"It is rare," Porter writes, "that a company can meet tough foreign rivals when it has faced no significant competition at home." In pencils, Faber-

Castell dominated the German home market, so Staedtler found it hard to make headway. But this tough environment made it focus on the international market. Often a disadvantage in some factor pushes a nation to compensate by making it pursue advantages which will set it apart. The Netherlands today has a multi-billion dollar cut flower and vegetable growing industry despite its selective factor disadvantage of a cold, grey climate, which spurred it to invest in greenhouse technology, new strains of flowers and energy conservation, and develop value chains in flower handling and air freight.

Porter's notion that "pressure instead of abundance or a comfortable environment underpins true competitive advantage" is as true today as it was in 1990.

The blunting of competitive advantage

There is a natural human tendency, Porter says, for individuals and nations to stop creating new wealth and live off the capital already created. He describes a "wealth driven stage" of development—actually, decline—marked by increasing concentration of ownership and less competition, and the seeking of protection by established interests. Non-functional business activity such as mergers, takeovers, and acquisitions take the place of innovation and productivity. There are pockets of innovation, but increasing income inequality and societal drift. Government has to increase taxes to pay for social welfare provision that was justified in the more robust "innovation driven stage" of growth.

In 1990, Porter worried that the European Union was not fulfilling its promise. The single market should have unleashed new competition and innovation, but instead was evolving into a protectionist club which kept out Japanese cars and American television programs. "If these tendencies gain the upper hand," he writes, "the 1990s will prove to be the wrong kind of turning point in European economic history." Looking at Europe's poor growth performance over the last 25 years, compared to the United States, Australia, Canada, and East Asian countries, you could say he was right.

Final comments

Porter was no libertarian or ideologue, insisting that strict antitrust or anti-monopoly laws, tough health and safety regulation, and environmental laws were important in competitive advantage. The global economy rewards countries that respect the environment and develop human capital, not only because it is the right thing to do, but because the steps taken to achieve these things force companies to invest in greater productivity from the resources used, which means greater profits.

It might be said that Porter's book, which after all preceded the internet and the rise of great online corporations, is no longer relevant. In fact, the epicenter of this revolution, Silicon Valley, is the classic example of a self-reinforcing "diamond" where the output is greater than the sum of its parts, and a cluster *par excellence* which tends to become more important over time. That the online realm gives the appearance of transcending the nation is the greatest irony, for it is precisely domestic features unique to the United States (deep pools of venture capital, good universities, robust competition, and the early adoption and development of computer technology), and indeed to one smallish part of California, that gave rise to companies that have changed the world. Location, particularly stiff competition and rivalry within that location, matters.

Michael E. Porter

Porter was born in Ann Arbor, Michigan, in 1947. At high school he excelled in football and baseball and gained a place at Princeton University to study aerospace and mechanical engineering. After graduating he went to Harvard and did an MBA course, followed by a PhD in business economics, awarded in 1973.

Porter is Bishop William Lawrence University Professor at Harvard Business School, and helped found its Institute for Strategy and Competitiveness. As a private consultant he has advised many countries on competitiveness. In 2012 he co-founded the Social Progress Imperative, which publishes an annual Social Progress Index ranking nations by various measures of well-being.

Books include Competitive Strategy: Techniques for Analyzing Industries and Competitors *(1980),* Competitive Advantage: Creating and Sustaining Superior Performance *(1985), and* Redefining Health Care *(2006).*

1966

Capitalism: The Unknown Ideal

"No political-economic system in history has ever proved its value so eloquently or has benefited mankind so greatly as capitalism—and none has ever been attacked so savagely, viciously, and blindly. The flood of misinformation, misrepresentation, distortion, and outright falsehood about capitalism is such that the young people of today have no idea (and virtually no way of discovering any idea) of its actual nature."

"What they have to discover, what all the efforts of capitalism's enemies are frantically aimed at hiding, is the fact that capitalism is not merely the 'practical', but the only moral system in history."

In a nutshell

In capitalism, wealth is created by free, individual minds with no coercion involved. This makes it a more moral system of political economy.

In a similar vein

Milton Friedman *Capitalism and Freedom*
Friedrich Hayek *The Use of Knowledge in Society*
Deirdre McCloskey *Bourgeois Equality*
Adam Smith *The Wealth of Nations*
Ludwig von Mises *Human Action*
Julian Simon *The Ultimate Resource 2*

CHAPTER 35

Ayn Rand

Ayn Rand is the author of the famous 1400-page philosophical novel *Atlas Shrugged* (1957), which glorifies individual freedom and the ability to create wealth unhampered by government (see commentary in *50 Success Classics*).

Capitalism: The Unknown Ideal, is essentially a non-fiction version of the novel, laying out Rand's Objectivist philosophy of the importance of personal motives above any kind of collectivist or tribal outlook. The power of the book rests on Rand's surprising contention that capitalism (in stark contrast to Marx's dark pronouncements) is a system morally superior to any other, built on personal freedom and delivering astounding wealth—and which yet remains the most misunderstood system of political economy.

She wrote it because she was confounded by the fact that young people blamed every societal ill on capitalism, which was hardly surprising since they had not lived under any other system. Socialism and communism, at the time she was writing, had legions of promoters and defenders, but capitalist ideals seemed to be trampled on everywhere and held up as evil. An immigrant to America who had witnessed the economic misery and attacks on individual dignity that defined communist Russia, she had at an early age resolved to be capitalism's defender.

The 24 essays in the book originally appeared in Rand's *The Objectivist Newsletter*. While most are by her, there are two by her then-acolyte Alan Greenspan, who became the chairman of the US Federal Reserve Board, and a couple by Nathaniel Branden, whom self-development readers will know as the author of *The Psychology of Self-Esteem*.

Most of the thinking of the book is encapsulated in the first essay, "What Is Capitalism?" Its main points are discussed below.

Beware "the common good"

Rand rounds on what is usually considered a source of impeccably objective information: the *Encyclopaedia Britannica*. She had discovered its entry on Capitalism, which described it as simply another way that a society organizes itself to produce a "social surplus", and contained no mention of wealth being created by individual minds. Rather, wealth is described as an impersonal aggregate produced by the efficient allocation of resources.

This infuriated Rand, as in her view there is no such thing as a "social surplus". All wealth is created by *somebody*, and therefore belongs to them. In modern society, it is very clear who has contributed what. To see wealth as some social good produced by the tribe was "morally obscene".

In her words:

> *"When "the common good" of a society is regarded as something apart from and superior to the individual good of its members, it means that the good of some men takes precedence over the good of others, with those others consigned to the status of sacrificial animals."*

When the good of the majority overrides individual rights, Rand observes, you may as well have no rights at all, since what you are left with, taken to its logical conclusion, is regimes like the former Soviet Union, where "the greater good of all" means misery for almost every individual. In Russia, people were told to bear many hardships in the service of achieving some vision of a prosperous, industrialized state. Tough conditions were only temporary; soon they would overtake the capitalist West. But while they waited for tractors and generators, the government was spending fortunes on atomic power and putting men into space. In a socialist or communist society, Rand notes, everything gained comes at the expense of something else.

This does not happen in a capitalist system. America grew rich not by public sacrifices to some "common good", but by the freedom of people to use their brains in pursuing their own fortunes. No one had to starve for America to become industrialized. In fact, the freedom of innovators to do their thing led to ". . . better jobs, higher wages, and cheaper goods with every new machine they invented, with every scientific or technological advance."

She thought it wrong to consider society as an entity that advanced as one. Rather, the entity that advanced humanity was the *individual*. "A great deal may be learned about society by studying man," she observed, but ". . . nothing can be learned about man by studying society."

Give free reign to the thinkers

Civilization has been built on the thought of individuals, the "intransigent innovators" as Rand calls them. She describes the creation of new things as "the application of reason to the problem of survival." Prosperity requires people to have absolute freedom to think, and not to be held back by those who do not. The most truly successful cultures in an economic sense have always been the freest politically.

Property rights are so important to a capitalist system because thinking people need to be able to freely dispose of the products of their efforts in order to support their lives. They must not be accountable to the tribe, the state, the society, or collective. When people make money in a free market, she notes, "They did not take it from those who had *not* created it." The law must support their sovereign nature. The free world's economic progress came about precisely because no one was forced into doing anything by some method of central planning. Rather, the great achievements occurred through voluntary thought and action, not only in pursuit of financial fortunes, but motivated by individual *values*. Capitalism cannot only be seen as a practical system that works to deliver the greatest economic output for all, but as the most *moral* system of political economy.

Values cannot be determined by a majority or by some state dictate, but are always a personal matter. A free society allows for a myriad of individual values to exist, as long as others are not harmed by them. There are not many areas the state should be involved in, but protection against violence is basic to ensuring the right of everyone to pursue "life, liberty and happiness".

Final comments

Most of the "anti-capitalists" of today actually know little about the system into which they were born. They have eyes only for some actors within it (such as large companies) and their apparent greed, while being blind to the fantastic freedoms and prosperity they have inherited. Free markets, they believe, will mean a "race to the bottom" of greater and greater exploitation of workers.

Such arguments fail to notice that the sweatshop workers in developing countries have usually arrived there by choice, leaving behind backbreaking lives of rural poverty. Their wages may be a pittance, but they represent the beginnings of a way out; their conditions look bad, but are little different to those endured by our grandparents or great-grandparents when their countries were industrializing. Rand includes an essay by her colleague Robert Hessen, "The Effects of the Industrial Revolution on Women and Children," which notes the factory system in nineteenth century England allowed thousands of children who would otherwise have starved to have an income, allowing them to grow into adulthood. Income earned by women allowed a household to move away from the poor hygiene and squalor that was a fact of life in pre-Industrial times, a change which led to a sharp decrease in infant mortality. Child labor ended with the rising incomes of parents, paid for by the increasing prosperity of manufacturers and the financiers wanting to invest in them. Marxist scholars ignore such facts, preferring to evoke a romantic, but false, picture of life prior to industrialization.

The usual accusation leveled at Rand and her followers is of extremism. A more intelligent view is that she was a supreme rationalist who valued personal freedom to the highest degree. Capitalism for her was not just a system for people to get richer, but was the only system in which people were free to act according to their best interests—not according to some imposed idea of the "common good". Today, the comfortable lives most of us lead are taken for granted, and as a result we take capitalism for granted.

Ayn Rand

Ayn Rand was born Alisa Rosenbaum in 1905 in St. Petersburg. Her father had owned a business that was taken over by the state after the Bolshevik Revolution. She graduated from the University of Petrograd (Leningrad) in 1924, before beginning a screenwriting course. The following year, she traveled to Chicago, and after six months moved to Hollywood to become a screenwriter, changing her name to Ayn Rand. "Ayn" was the first name of a Finnish writer, "Rand" the model of her Remington typewriter. On her second day in Los Angeles she met Cecil B. de Mille, who offered her work as an extra on a film where her future husband, Frank O'Connor, was on the set.

Rand never broke into screenwriting, but in 1935 her play Woman On Trial *was performed on Broadway as* Night of January 16th. *Her first novel* We the Living *(1936), and* Anthem *(1938) were well-received critically but not best-sellers. Rand's fortunes changed with the success of* The Fountainhead *(1943), a 700-page story of a modernist architect who battles to realize his vision. In 1958 Rand and Nathaniel Branden (who was her lover for several years) opened the institute in New York which would spread Objectivist philosophy.*

Having railed against government anti-smoking campaigns, Rand suffered from lung cancer, and died in 1982. A floral dollar sign was placed over her coffin.

1817

Principles of Political Economy and Taxation

"Under a system of perfectly free commerce, each country naturally devotes its capital and labour to such employments as are most beneficial to each. This pursuit of individual advantage is admirably connected with the universal good of the whole. By stimulating industry, by rewarding ingenuity, and by using most efficaciously the peculiar powers bestowed by nature, it distributes labour most effectively and most economically: while, by increasing the general mass of productions, it diffuses general benefit, and binds together by one common tie of interest and intercourse, the universal society of nations throughout the civilized world. It is this principle which determines that wine shall be made in France and Portugal, that corn shall be grown in America and Poland, and that hardware and other goods shall be manufactured in England."

In a nutshell

Trade is the great facilitator of world prosperity, because it allows participating countries to make the most of their resources, people and skills.

In a similar vein

Thomas Malthus *Essay on the Principle of Population*
Dani Rodrik *The Globalization Paradox*
Adam Smith *The Wealth of Nations*

CHAPTER 36

David Ricardo

Operating out of the London Stock Exchange, David Ricardo was one of the great names in finance of his day, a George Soros or Warren Buffett of the early nineteenth century. Cut off from his Dutch-Jewish family's wealth thanks to his marriage to a Quaker woman, he had to start from scratch. But his judgement, such as a bet that Wellington would defeat Napoleon at Waterloo (and thereby see his British government bonds jump in value), saw this fortune steadily grow, and at the time of his early death he had retired in some splendor to the English countryside.

Yet he took his talent for finance for granted, and developed a new love. From the age of 27, when he chanced upon a copy of Adam Smith's *The Wealth of Nations* while on holiday in Bath, he became entranced by the emerging discipline of political economy, reading some of its early thinkers including Turgot, Jean-Baptiste Say, and Sismondi. His insightful articles brought him to the attention of James Mill (economist father of John Stuart Mill), as well as Jeremy Bentham and Thomas Malthus. With Malthus in particular he became great friends.

The *Principles of Political Economy and Taxation*, cajoled into being by his mentor James Mill, is Ricardo's great work. It is not a great pleasure to read. In attempting to make economics more scientific, Ricardo wrote in a dry style that totally lacks the flourish and colorful examples of Adam Smith, and much of the book is devoted to contemporary economic debates. Yet Ricardo went to some lengths to make his arguments clear, and as a result they can be easily followed by a reader of today.

Building on Smith's foundations by providing a comprehensive theory of how the economy worked, the book made Ricardo's name as a political economist, which in turn allowed for his entry into parliament. His labor theory of value dominated his time and was taken up by Marx, and his theory of comparative advantage provided the foundation of international trade economics.

What are you worth? Ricardo's theory of value

Ricardo observed that capitalists are often able to make big profits for a time in a particular economy or industry, and for as long as these profits last they enjoy a high "market" price. But the product they deal in soon reverts to its "natural" price, which reflects the capital, including labor and machinery, that goes into producing the product or commodity. The market prices for things may deviate from the natural price for a time, but as soon as people see big profits being made in some industry, capital piles in, competition increases, and prices go back to their natural level, reflecting the cost of production.

Labor, Ricardo said, is like any commodity: it has its natural and market price. For a time, perhaps because of a labor shortage, workers can command higher wages, and in this position, "the condition of the laborer is flourishing and happy . . . he has it in his power to command a greater proportion of the necessaries and enjoyments of life, and therefore to rear a healthy and numerous family." But this prosperity has an effect. As workers have more children, this creates a larger work force and increased supply of labor, which drives the price of labor down to its "natural" price. As with any commodity, Ricardo argues, the price of labor is continually reverting to its real "cost of production", which in the case of a human being is the cost of feeding, clothing and sheltering him or her. Thus, wages will always be based on this "subsistence" cost of living of workers, which meant that capitalists would have a keen interest in keeping the price of food and household items low, so that their labor costs could be kept down.

Ricardo did admit that with the increasing wealth of a nation, the average worker would be able to buy more conveniences with his pay. "Many of the conveniences now enjoyed in an English cottage," he writes, "would have been thought luxuries at an early period of our history." Yet this did not mean that labor's share of national income would rise in relation to the share of capitalist profits, or rents on land. Workers could appear to be a lot better off, yet without land or capital they would be condemned to working week-to-week to pay for their basic needs. With this pessimistic view of the place of labor in the economy, it is easy to see why Marx took up Ricardo's theory of labor value without question, for Ricardo's vision is of a stratified society in which the haves and have-nots are divided by the possession of land and capital.

In a growing economy, who wins? Ricardo's theory of income distribution

Ricardo wished to make a forensic analysis of how wealth and resources were divided in society, between landowners, capitalists, and laborers. What was the distribution between rent, profit, and wages, and did it change over time?

The question of food sufficiency was the big issue of his day, expressed in the raging arguments over the Corn Laws (i.e. whether Britain should allow imports of cheaper grain, or protect landowners by artificially keeping prices high). Ricardo shared Malthus' basic insight that while land, and the capacity to grow food, was limited, there was no limit to human population. Therefore, the owners of land were in a very good place as economies grew. The level of rent on agricultural land, Ricardo said, depends on its fertility. When all the good bits of land have been taken, people start to cultivate less good areas of land, and as the population grows, a premium is placed on the best quality fields, where rent rises. This was his differential theory of rent.

For Ricardo, profit was simply what the business owner was left with after paying out wages to workers and rents to landowners. His profit theory held that the rate of profit would remain surprisingly stable across an economy, because as soon as one sector or industry was seen to be enjoying high profits, capital would enter that industry. This would have the effect of more goods being produced, so depressing prices and thus profits. At the same time, industries with comparatively low profits would see capital flee. With fewer goods now being made, those enterprises still left in the industry could charge a decent price and see profits creep up again.

This was a rational exposition of how economies worked in a time when economics was in its infancy. But Ricardo fell into the same trap of other economic thinkers of his day in taking as given the Malthusian theory of overpopulation and scarcity. It seemed obvious to Ricardo that as a country's need for food grew along with increasing population, it would put pressure on the stock of agricultural land. Farm rents would grow, causing a spike in the price of food, which in turn (given the subsistence theory of wages) would mean industrialists having to pay more for their workers. With their profits falling (and rents on land rising) the incentive to invest would evaporate, causing economic depression.

Ricardo's solution was repeal of the Corn Laws, which would allow more grain imports, thus lowering the price of grain and therefore wages. This would mean higher profits to keep the economy humming, and more investment in land and machinery. It was not surprising that Ricardo favored a repeal of the Corn Laws, since he was not an aristocratic landowner who depended upon rents on land. The battle between landowners and capitalists raged on, with Ricardo believing that the landed aristocratic class would be triumphant. In the end, Napoleon's defeat meant the price of grain went down, and the Corn Laws were eventually repealed. The grip of the landowning class on Britain's economy had been broken.

Ricardo, like Malthus, turned out to be wrong about population outstripping food supply, and wrong about landowners lording it over the industrialists. In fact the opposite happened. Agriculture would become more and more productive (thanks to agricultural machinery and plant science) and countries would provide for a greater amount of their food needs through imports (thanks to liberal international trade). Which brings us to the contribution Ricardo is perhaps best known for.

International trade and comparative advantage

Absolute advantage, as Adam Smith pointed out, is simply one country's ability to make something (and sell it on the international market) cheaper than another country, thanks to its cost of labor, climate, terrain, or other factors. Ricardo's example is that it is easier for Portugal to make wine, given its climate, than Britain, while Britain may be well suited to growing wool and turning it into clothing. If both countries trade their surplus of wool and wine with each other, each will be better off.

But what if Britain was better at both wine *and* wool production? Surely the reason for trading with Portugal would no longer exist? Ricardo's counter-intuitive answer was that, even if Britain was better at both in an absolute sense, it still made more sense for it to specialize in either wool or wine. Specializing in wool would make it even more efficient in that production, while Portugal, even though it was not as good as Britain in producing wine, by specializing in it could increase its efficiency and its *comparative* advantage.

The outcome, as Ricardo says, is that specialization based on a country's comparative advantages increases efficiency globally. This is why international trade works. After all, if Portugal stayed in wool production, there would be an opportunity cost of it not putting resources into wine production, which it is better at. By putting half its national resources into wool production, it would be foregoing what it could invest in winemaking.

Ricardo's theory also explains why a country that has no absolute advantage in anything can still trade profitably in the world economy, because although there may be a dozen countries that are better than it at producing wheat, wool, cars, or clothing, there is a cost to those other countries in not engaging in what they are *really* good at, such as IT services, or commercial aviation, or biotechnology.

Ricardo's theory works well in a free-trade world in which domestic and international politics are not a factor, yet it is a fact that countries hang on to production in things in which they no longer have any real advantage (agriculture is the obvious area) for political and social reasons, and their protection of these industries warps the international economy. But it is not just rich countries that do this: most developing countries are only able to grow, it can be argued, by creating import-replacing industries under high tariff walls which allows them to create jobs and industries. Ricardo's theory also assumes that capital will flow to the industry or country that has a comparative advantage in something. But he admitted that capital was only mobile in theory; people preferred to invest at home rather than abroad.

Another problem with the theory of comparative advantage is that when a country specializes in only one or two commodities which experience big fluctuations in price, it can be disastrous. For instance, the union of Ireland with Britain in 1800 led to the exposure of Ireland's protected textile industry. Unable to compete with England's textile production, and in the absence of success in grain production, its people defaulted to local potato crops. When potato blight hit, a million people died. The Ricardian answer is that free trade allows countries to diversify and develop manufacturing or service industries which, by being more specialized, have a higher chance of price stability—but obviously, such a process of adjustment only takes place over many years or decades, and in the meantime there can be big social costs.

Ricardo's trade theory made a break with the mercantilist view that countries grow rich and strong at the expense of others. Rather, countries trading with each other all feel they are "getting a bargain," and so all can grow at the same time. The Ricardian theory of trade also remains a crucial counterpoint to arguments in favor of economic nationalism and protectionism. The recognition that his model still works in its essence is what drives the array of international free trade agreements, which seek to reduce tariffs and protectionism. Because countries can see that open trade regimes bring rising living standards, and achieve quite a good allocation of resources, Ricardo's theory remains one of the great achievements of economics.

Final comments

In the decades after his death, the two things Ricardo advocated—lower protectionism and increased international trade resting on the theory of comparative advantage—would form the foundation of nineteenth-century Britain's power and wealth, and create the template for international economics. Today, the face of Ricardo is reflected in every new trade agreement that makes the world more economically linked, but which still preserves the power of the nation state. The key criticism of Ricardo is that he failed to see how land would become increasingly less important as the source of wealth, and how the landowning aristocratic elite would give way to the new industrial classes and the growing power of finance.

The *Principles* is a long and detailed work, with many chapters on taxation and money. Taxation was a crucial issue in his time, because Britain was having to find ways to fund the wars against Napoleon, and then was left with a mountain of debt after fighting ended. To pay its bills, the state could either raise taxes or issue more public debt, neither of which Ricardo was keen on. The more a country is taxed, he believed, the more likely it is that people with capital will take their money elsewhere, overcoming the natural human wish to invest capital at home. Yet the issue of bonds to raise money had negative effects too. A $20 million war loan would mean $20 million "withdrawn from the productive capital of the nation." In terms of social equality, Ricardo felt that taxation was marginally fairer, particularly the taxing of luxury goods. A minister could tax heavily the "horses, carriages, wine, servants, and all the other enjoyments of the rich," he said, without damaging the stock of national capital used for productive purposes. Through the sheer logic of the financier, not social conscience, he was led to this fairer position.

David Ricardo

Ricardo was born in 1772 in east London, twelve years after his Dutch Sephardic Jewish parents had emigrated from Amsterdam. At 14 he began working in his father's brokerage business, and his skill in currency arbitrage helped make it successful.

When at 21 Ricardo decided to marry Priscilla Ann Wilkinson, a Quaker, and renounce the Jewish faith, his father cut him off from any family money. He started his own brokerage business using borrowed capital, and by his mid-twenties had made his own fortune. Ricardo retired at 42, and divided his time between a house in London and Gatcombe Park, a large estate in Gloucestershire, where he raised his sons as country gentlemen, two of whom would become MPs. Gatcombe Park would remain in the Ricardo family until 1940, and now belongs to Princess Anne.

In a practice common to his day, in 1819 Ricardo bought a seat in parliament (Portarlington in Ireland, which he never visited). As an MP he was an important contributor to the economic and financial issues of his day, championing minimal government, low taxation, religious tolerance, and freedom of speech.

Ricardo died 1823 and left an estate of around £700,000 which, relative to other incomes and wealth of his time, would be the equivalent of around £1 billion today.

2011

The Globalization Paradox

"Give too much power to governments, and you have protectionism and autarky. Give markets too much freedom, and you have an unstable world economy with little social and political support from those it is supposed to help."

"We cannot have hyperglobalization, democracy, and national self-determination all at once. We can have at most two out of three. If we want hyperglobalization and democracy, we need to give up the nation-state. If we must keep the nation state and want hyperglobalization too, then we must forget about democracy. And if we want to combine democracy with the nation state, then it is bye-bye deep globalization."

In a nutshell

Globalization involves a deep contradiction between the national focus of governments and the global nature of trade and finance.

In a similar vein

Liaquat Ahamed *Lords of Finance*
Ha-Joon Chang *23 Things They Don't Tell You About Capitalism*
Naomi Klein *The Shock Doctrine*
Michael E. Porter *The Competitive Advantage of Nations*
David Ricardo *Principles of Political Economy and Taxation*

CHAPTER 37

Dani Rodrik

When anti-globalization protesters disrupted the Seattle meeting of the World Trade Organization in 1999, they seemed very much on the fringe. There were valid labor and environmental issues with trade liberalization, but most countries' governments believed that the only real route to prosperity was through eliminating trade barriers and national transaction costs. If the world could become more like one big market, the consensus said, everyone would win.

Then something changed. The British public's vote to leave the European Union, France's Marine Le Pen talking of "globalists" as being an insidious species, and Donald Trump's standing on an anti-globalization platform for the US presidency, calling for a return to high tariff walls to protect American jobs, the repeal of the NAFTA free trade agreement with Canada and Mexico, and withdrawal from negotiations for the TTIP and Trans-Pacific Partnership trade agreements—each phenomenon has become indicative of what Harvard's Dani Rodrik calls "the deep tension between national sovereignty and globalization."

Though *The Globalization Paradox* was published before Brexit, Trump, and Le Pen, it remains a brilliant guide to confusing times. Rodrik's idea that trade policy and efforts to globalize capital markets can't be insulated from domestic politics yielded the famous "trilemma" (discussed below), which continues to throw light on current events. In short, his argument is that globalization should never be an end in itself, but a means for countries to achieve prosperity and freedom. Nations have a right to protect their own institutions, values, and legal systems if that is what people vote for. At the same time, politicians have a responsibility to highlight the benefits of trade and openness.

Globalization that works: The Bretton Woods system

The two architects of the post-war world financial order, America's Harry Dexter White and Britain's John Maynard Keynes, wanted to create an open system that encouraged trade—but they also knew that ignoring domestic politics would only lead to more political and economic instability. The Bretton Woods system they helped engineer (named after the resort town in New Hampshire where parties met in July 1944) gave priority to full employment, national economic growth, social insurance, and the welfare state over a fully free-trade system. But the biggest innovation was "multilateralism," the facilitation of international economic policy through dedicated institutions including the World Bank, the International Monetary Fund (IMF), and the General Agreement on Tariffs and Trade (GATT); these would take the place of naked hegemonic state power or imperial rule.

Though this rules-based system was supported and guaranteed by the new might of the US, it was non-discriminatory and aimed to represent and help all nations. The GATT, for one, was a big success. By eliminating many tariffs over successive rounds of negotiations, it helped world trade grow by an average of 7 percent a year between 1947 and 1990. This, despite the fact that the GATT did not touch on agricultural tariffs, services, or textiles and clothing (they were subject to another agreement), and had plenty of loopholes around anti-dumping practices.

The freedom that nations had to move in the Bretton Woods regime led to "varieties of capitalism" (for example, the French planning state, the Swedish welfare state, the German social market economy, and the Japanese exporting state with a highly protected traditional economy) in which every nation had the space to fashion their own tax regimes, welfare provision, and labor market laws. For Rodrik, the Bretton Woods system was a sort of "globalization lite," allowing full national sovereignty yet lifting some of the worst kinds of protectionism between countries. The result was a success, with three decades of rising prosperity around the world.

Hyperglobalization: the WTO era

The monetary problems which emerged in the Bretton Woods order by the 1970s saw a new drive towards globalization and integration of markets. By 1995, when the GATT was replaced by the World Trade Organization (WTO) after the Uruguay round of negotiations, the emphasis shifted from national priorities to "hyperglobalization"—a more ideological economic and financial globalization for its own sake. If the GATT had succeeded in increasing world prosperity, the reasoning went, wouldn't a lot more prosperity come from liberalizing economies further, eliminating restrictions on trade, and removing transaction costs from global finance?

The collapse of communism only seemed to confirm that government was an evil best kept to a bare minimum. As part of this intellectual victory, big corporations pushed for lower taxes, the curtailment of union power, and deregulation. All obstacles to free trade were seen as "an abomination to be removed." Agriculture and services were duly included in the new WTO agreements.

Yet as time went on, governments felt put out by WTO rulings which did not take full account of national values. By the time of the infamous 1990 Seattle WTO meeting, the organization was portrayed by anti-globalization protesters as a vehicle for the dismantling of labor and environmental standards and part of a neoliberal agenda to shaft developing countries and protect big business.

There was also a worry that globalization was a prime cause of widening income inequality in the United States. Since the 1990s, America's imports from developing countries had doubled, measured against the size of the American economy, and those countries had much lower wages than US workers. China's rise as a manufacturer meant the evaporation of many American jobs. The famous Stolper-Samuelson theorem of 1941 (named after the two American economists Wolfgang and Paul, respectively) had predicted as much, pointing out that trade with low-wage countries inevitably hurts workers in high-wage ones. The policy implication was that it was quite reasonable to give countries some protection from global market forces, but the free-market fundamentalism driving trade agreements seemed to forbid such things.

Asia and globalization: the inconvenient truth

The "Washington Consensus" of monetary stability coupled with market and financial liberalization, became a sort of religion followed by developing country policy makers in the 1980s and 1990s. But in place of the mixed, pragmatic strategies embraced by the Asian tigers and China, followers embraced openness to the global economy. Anyone pushing a role for state intervention, or even the traditional mode of development known as "import substitution industrialization" was seen as a protectionist crank. Globalization had become a sacred cow.

The evidence tells another story. The World Bank's own 1993 report, *The East Asian Miracle: Economic Growth and Public Policy*, largely funded by Japan, tried to explain how South Korea, Hong Kong, Singapore, Malaysia, Thailand, and Indonesia had succeeded economically by substituting imports with locally made products, and becoming exporters in a global economy. Yet apart from Hong Kong they were not actually free-market economies.

China and India have done spectacularly well in the last 20 years, Rodrik notes, only because they played by Bretton Woods rules rather than the rules of New Globalization. They did not fully open themselves up to international trade and finance, but maintained a level of protectionism that suited their own interests, including the cosseting of state-run enterprises and a good degree of state intervention in the economy. China could only afford to join the WTO in 2001 because by this time it had built a solid industrial base that could compete evenly with the rest of the world. Industrial policies were phased out and tariffs brought down to single digits. In the same period, countries in Latin America and Africa that had embraced globalization fully experienced much more modest growth, or stagnated.

Financial globalization: a bit more volatility than we bargained for

In 1997, the IMF was pushing for the liberalization of the capital accounts of developing countries, which had many restrictions to prevent sudden outflows of funds (they liked foreign direct investment but naturally didn't want "hot" money to destabilize their economies). Free global capital flows would result in the most efficient allocation of savings capital worldwide, the IMF argued, and so raise economic growth.

Amazingly, this argument was made even as the Asian Financial Crisis unfolded. In 1996, Indonesia, Malaysia, the Philippines, South Korea, and Thailand had attracted private capital inflows amounting to $12 billion. The following year, they saw a collective outflow of $12 billion. Only a few months before, the IMF had talked up the "sound fundamentals" of these countries, so it was clear that markets had totally overreacted. Yet the IMF and the US Treasury over the ensuing years kept pushing for developing countries to remove capital controls, even making it a condition of trade agreements.

Rather than a safety valve, floating currencies had become a source of instability because their movements were magnified by currency traders and speculators who stood to gain by movement in the pound, ringgit or baht. By 2007 there was $3.2 trillion of foreign currency transaction a day, dwarfing the global trade in real goods and services and making it hard for national economies to chart a course of stability in terms of jobs output and inflation.

Rodrik admits that the world has grown hugely in the period of much greater financial liberalization and capital mobility which has taken place since the 1980s, but it still doesn't match the rate of growth in the Bretton Woods era after World War Two, when countries were allowed to keep capital controls, restrain foreign finance and speculation, and insist on controlling the domestic economy. It is said that a world without capital controls imposes discipline upon countries, because they will be punished by markets and speculators. But is what countries want, and what the markets want, the same thing?

Rodrik traces the precipitous drop in American public support for economic globalization dating back to 2007–2008. The huge savings of Asian countries and Middle East "petrostates" had gone looking for higher returns, which they partly found in US real estate securities. These in turn drove irresponsible lending and the housing bubble and bust. The event was not contained within America, however, because of financial globalization and the sharing of balance sheets across borders. Yet economists had by and large been cheerleaders for financial globalization, ignoring the hazards and risks it brought.

Globalization's political trilemma

Rodrik concludes that the pursuit of democracy, national self-determination, and economic globalization are not compatible. This is the "fundamental political trilemma of the world economy," he says. If we move closer towards globalization, it has to come at a price—less national sovereignty over domestic policies including labor laws, environmental standards, and social provision. If democracy is the main goal, there is a choice to be made between the nation state and global economic integration.

Rodrik doesn't believe that "hyperglobalization" should trump national self-determination and social arrangements. But rather than see countries turning in on themselves, or creating some kind of global government, this path of "re-empowering national democracies" is the sensible way to go. "A thin layer of international rule that leaves substantial room for maneuver by national governments is a *better* globalization," he writes. "It can address globalization's ills while preserving its substantial economic benefits. We need smart globalization, not maximum globalization".

Rodrik addresses the notion that nation states are not fit to be the primary modes of power in the global economy, because they are all fighting for their own interests and so won't do anything to preserve the "global commons." National policies on greenhouse emissions, and their effects on climate change, are the classic example. This is where international co-operation *is* important. But there is no such thing as a global economic commons, Rodrik argues. Each country should follow its own priorities. This is not "parochialism," he says, but respecting the fact of democracy, which transnational institutions do not generally possess.

Final comments

In the pro-globalization bestseller, *The Lexus and the Olive Tree*, Thomas Friedman argued that international capital created a "golden straitjacket" which forced countries to submit to free trade, free capital markets, and small government. When the straitjacket is donned, Friedman said, "your economy grows, and your politics shrink." In fact, Rodrik contends, "when globalization collides with domestic politics, the smart money bets on politics."

Those not in favor of total globalization are often painted as ignorant and small-minded, compared to the educated and broad-minded globalists. There was no better illustration of this dynamic than the British public's vote to leave the European Union. The "experts", mostly urban, educated, and well-off, gave 1001 good reasons why Britain should not revert to economic nationhood. In many less democratic nations, the experts and elite would have won the day, but something got in the way of the hyperglobalizers' dream: democracy.

International trade and openness bring manifold benefits, and politicians should make the case for them, Rodrik says. Yet globalization must be of a type that focuses on what works, guided by history, and shorn of ideology. The world is not simply a big market, but an intricate tapestry of political beliefs, customs, laws, and values. Markets do not exist in a vacuum but must be run, maintained, and enforced by national governments. The uncomfortable truth for ideologues is that bigger markets require government to expand too, not just to set the rules but to protect citizens from the risks and insecurities the open markets invariably bring.

Dani Rodrik

Rodrik was born in Istanbul in 1957. His father was a pen manufacturer whose business was protected by high tariffs, and could afford to send his son to be educated at Harvard. Rodrik went on to do a Masters in Public Affairs (1981) and a PhD in economics (1985) at Princeton University. He has spent his entire career at Harvard, with the exception of four years at Columbia University and two years at the Institute for Advanced Study (Princeton). He is currently Ford Foundation Professor of Political Economy at Harvard's John F. Kennedy School of Government.

Rodrik's books include Has Globalization Gone Too Far? *(1997),* One Economics, Many Recipes *(2007), and* Economics Rules: The Rights and Wrongs of the Dismal Science *(2015). Rodrik is married to Pinar Doğan, a Harvard lecturer in public policy whose father is the retired Turkish general Çetin Doğan. Doğan was imprisoned in 2010 as a suspect in an alleged coup attempt and released without charge in 2014. The couple had campaigned for his release.*

1948

Economics

"The tools of economics are indispensable to help societies find the golden mean between an efficient market mechanism and publicly decided regulation and redistribution . . . But those who would reduce government to the constable plus a few lighthouses are living in a dream world. An efficient and humane society requires both halves of the mixed system—market and government. Operating a modern economy without both is like trying to clap with one hand."

"International trade has replaced empire-building and military conquest as the surest road to national wealth and influence."

In a nutshell

Markets don't always deliver prosperity, and government interventions are often flawed. To be really useful, economics must be built on common sense, not ideology.

In a similar vein

John Maynard Keynes *The General Theory of Employment, Interest, and Money*
Paul Krugman *The Conscience of a Liberal*
Alfred Marshall *Principles of Economics*

CHAPTER 38

Paul Samuelson & William Nordhaus

"I don't care who writes a nation's laws or crafts its advanced treatises," Paul Samuelson said, "if I can write its economics textbooks."

When, in his early thirties, he published the first edition of *Economics*, he was already a wunderkind of ten years' standing, known for bringing a new mathematical rigor to his field. Academics always hope their textbook will become the standard text for their discipline, but Samuelson could not have imagined that, sixty years later, in his 90s, he would be writing a preface for the nineteenth edition. What accounts for its popularity?

Initially, a big part of the book's success was bringing the ideas of Keynes to the American public. The work was emblematic of the academic divide between older professors hanging on to classical economic ideas, and Young Turks fired up by Keynes (in a biographical sketch, Samuelson used the phrase "many-sided genius" to describe the Englishman). *Economics* was not the first Keynesian textbook, but it was the first really influential one in America. The weight that Samuelson gave to the possibilities for managing the economy, as opposed to simply leaving it up to market forces, meant that the book was attacked by conservatives who thought it left-wing or socialist. Yet in elevating macroeconomics, Samuelson was just expressing the post-war zeitgeist. If the war years had seen such a shaping role of government in the economy, and the war had followed hot on the heels of the Great Depression and an increased role for government in Roosevelt's New Deal, it seemed clear to Samuelson that a minimal "market state" was a fantasy.

Samuelson later wrote that he had been "born an economist" on January 2, 1932, when he attended his first economics lecture (on Thomas Malthus) at the University of Chicago, but was turned on to Keynesian theory after having to spend four summers lazing on the beach at Lake Michigan because of the Great Depression, when he had been unable to find a job.

Economics has been popular with students (with 4 million copies sold) for good reason: In contrast to most textbooks, it has an informal, even self-deprecating style, with not too much math (but in no way dumbed down either) that became the template for the genre. There are wry quotes (Part 1 begins with Edmund Burke's line, "The Age of Chivalry is gone; that of sophisters, economists, and calculators has succeeded"), and the electronic edition even has a link to an economics jokes website. Later editions of *Economics* are co-authored by William Nordhaus of Yale, an environmental economist who has given it a more contemporary feel, with sections on pollution, climate change, and emissions trading schemes.

Beyond ideology

Samuelson wrote a frontispiece to the nineteenth edition of *Economics*, entitled "A Centrist Proclamation." In his mind centrism celebrates "an economy that combines the tough discipline of the market with fair-minded governmental oversight."

It was obvious to Samuelson and Nordhaus that, in the wake of the 2008 meltdown in the financial and housing markets, lax regulation of both, inspired by a "lazy but misguided libertarianism," had brought the world close to economic disaster. The centrist approach is not ideological but looks at the evidence, and events of the previous 20 years had clearly shown that neither unregulated capitalism, nor a centrally planned economy, were viable routes to prosperity. If economies had been run along Hayek-Friedman lines, there would have been no welfare system, no minimum wage, no national parks, nor any regulation of pollution and global warming—yet citizens had voted for such things "in large majorities" around the world. What people want, the authors say, is the rule of law to achieve certain social objectives, combined with a sufficient amount of freedom to compete in markets. The market system gives feedback to producers in the form of profits or losses. By seeking profits, a company naturally produces more of what people want or need, so society's resources are allocated efficiently. But the invisible hand of efficiency only works when the market itself is open and functions well. If there are market failures, you can still get negative externalities such as pollution, or monopolies. Perfect competition rarely, if ever, exists.

Samuelson's economics: the "neoclassical synthesis"

In the fourth edition (1958), Samuelson first used the term "neoclassical synthesis" to describe his approach, arguing that economics could no longer be divided into Keynesian or anti-Keynesian camps; Keynes' thinking had become part of mainstream economics. There was no mechanism in a laissez-faire economy that naturally balanced investment and employment, as classical economics held, and if that did happen it was pure luck. It was necessary for government to spend when the private sector was not, and for central banks to keep inflation down through manipulating and setting interest rates, and acting as lender of last resort.

Later editions of the book were more cautious about the state's role in the economy. Deficit spending is fine in times of recession, Samuelson and Nordhaus noted, but it has serious consequences for investment and growth in normal times. When a government runs a deficit in any given year, the amount it has to borrow to fund the military, education, welfare, and health is added to the long-term government debt mountain, which of course must be repaid by future generations. For the first 200 years after independence, the American government usually presented balanced budgets, but during the Cold War, the US government ramped up social and military spending to new heights, and the tax cuts during the administrations of Ronald Reagan and George W. Bush led to further government deficits. By 2009, Samuelson and Nordhaus note, the American government was running a $2 billion deficit, "the largest percentage of GDP since World War II."

Fiscal policy in the form of higher government spending or lower taxes certainly stimulates spending and investment in the short run, increasing use of society's idle resources, but this is often balanced out by the need for central banks to raise interest rates to head off inflation caused by the spending, and by financial markets which put pressure on exchange rates. So government intervention is often self-sabotaging.

The macroeconomic stance you take is a matter of whether you trust government to run the economy. The "neoclassical synthesis" allows for the failure of markets to regenerate (at least in the short run) that sometimes plagues capitalist economies, while giving due recognition to the brilliance of markets in optimal utilization of resources, improving productivity and increasing wealth. Samuelson's conclusion is that most of the time, monetary policy is the "front line of defense" in fine tuning the business cycle to ensure stability in the economy. And yet, it was clear that in the wake of 2008, simply having low interest rates would not jumpstart the American economy. The stimulus package Congress voted for was a recognition of this, as was the bailout of banks in order to prevent a liquidity crisis. In the palace of modern capitalism, it seemed, most of the time Keynes could be relegated to a back room and forgotten. But every so often he must be put into a butler's suit and asked to get the house in order.

Growth and government

The goal of macroeconomics is not just stability, Samuelson and Nordhaus stress, but the creation of rising living standards through growing output per worker.

But how does growth happen? The authors cite the "four wheels" of growth: human capital, natural resources, capital, and technological capacity and innovation. Neoclassical growth models say that if you just build more factories like the first, or expand the number of farms farming the same way, without using new technologies, then you enter a "long-run steady state." The economy may get larger, but standards of living will not rise. You need both capital deepening and technological change for rising productivity and wages. So what puts one country at the frontier of creating and adopting new technologies, while others lag? The key, Samuelson says, is competition. If there is vigorous competition, companies need to keep ahead of the curve to survive and thrive, and this usually means developing or adopting new technologies to increase productivity.

Growth is not just about "getting out of the way of business," as conservatives and libertarians believe, but seeing what role there may be for the state given the reality of market failures. "New growth theory" (exponents include Paul Romer) points out that technology doesn't just happen, but requires a combination of private market forces, institutions and public policies for it to really benefit the wider economy. Companies can reap big profits from inventions, but many innovations and research would not be carried out were it not for government providing money for research, which is not economic for companies to do, and through fostering innovation through the establishment of intellectual property rights, including patents and copyright. What Keynes called the "spirit of enterprise" is probably universal, but sustained growth and productivity invariably need the soil of good government to take root.

Final comments

In "The Perseverance of Paul Samuelson's *Economics*" (*Journal of Economic Perspectives*, Spring 1997), Mark Skousen noted that successive editions of the textbook became less overtly Keynesian and gave recognition to competing schools of economics, including the Chicago and Austrian schools. Yet these were portrayed as outside "mainstream economics," that is, the synthesis of neoclassical market economics and the Keynesian welfare state which has dominated political economy the last sixty years. As a result, Skousen noted, *Economics* provides plenty of examples of market failure, but many fewer corresponding examples of government failure. Conservatives also complained that Samuelson was taken in by the liberal view that communism was a durable form of economic and political organization that could exist alongside market liberalism.

"Economics is above all a living and evolving organism," Samuelson said, and the success of *Economics*, in its many changes and iterations over the decades, owes much to this admission. Even with its frequent updating, though, the work is strangely light on one of the discipline's revolutions of the last 20 years: behavioral economics. Indeed, Deirdre McCloskey invented the term "Samuelsonian" to denote an approach to the discipline that assumed human beings were much more rational than they actually are. This flaw notwithstanding, in a discipline of competing ideologies the book stands out for its moderation. Samuelson died in 2009, but his realism about the role of markets and government lived on in many of his students, who included George Akerlof, Joseph Stiglitz and Paul Krugman.

Paul Samuelson

Samuelson was born in 1915 in Gary, Indiana, to Polish Jewish immigrants. They moved to Chicago, and at 16 Samuelson enrolled at the University of Chicago, where his contemporaries included Milton Friedman and George Stigler.

He earned a Masters degree in 1936, then a doctorate from Harvard in 1941, where he studied under Joseph Schumpeter and Alvin Hansen, a proponent of Keynes. His dissertation became the prize-winning Foundations of Economic Analysis, *published in 1947. Samuelson became an assistant professor at the Massachusetts Institute of Technology, and would stay at MIT until his death. He was an adviser to the US Treasury, the Federal Reserve Board and American presidents, and famously tutored John F. Kennedy on the beach at Hyannis Port after the 1960 election. Like his friend and intellectual sparring partner Milton Friedman, he had a strong desire to engage with the public, and wrote a column for* Newsweek *from 1966 to 1981. He admitted that* Economics *was written partly for money, after his wife Marion had just given birth to triplets, in addition to their first three children.*

The Collected Scientific Papers of Paul A. Samuelson *runs to five volumes and spans a 50-year period. Among his many contributions is the Samuelson-Stolper theory, which argued that free trade could result in a reduction of wages in rich countries, as jobs are "exported" to low-wage countries.*

1973

Small Is Beautiful

"Scientific or technological 'solutions' which poison the environment or degrade the social structure and man himself are of no benefit, no matter how brilliantly conceived or how great their superficial attraction. Ever bigger machines, entailing ever bigger concentrations of economic power and exerting ever greater violence against the environment, do not represent progress: they are a denial of wisdom. Wisdom demands a new orientation of science and technology towards the organic. the gentle, the non-violent, the elegant and beautiful."

"Man is small, and, therefore, small is beautiful. To go for gigantism is to go for self-destruction."

In a nutshell

Mass production and consumption is not the only way of organizing the world economy.

In a similar vein

Diane Coyle *GDP: A Brief but Affectionate History*
Elinor Ostrom *Governing the Commons*
Karl Polanyi *The Great Transformation*
Thorstein Veblen *The Theory of the Leisure Class*

CHAPTER 39

E. F. Schumacher

Between Henry Ford's perfection of the assembly line technique in the early part of the twentieth century, and 1970, industry had become so advanced that it was said that the "problem of production" (creating enough heat, fuel, food, light, and transport for all) had been solved. Virtually everything could be mass produced, and at reasonable cost, to satisfy a growing world population. Yet this apparent success was built on an assumption, E. F. Schumacher observed: that humans were outside nature, and that use of natural resources had no cost.

Just as we thought we had solved the "production problem," new, unintended consequences of pollution and environmental degradation became apparent. The new problems stemmed from a faulty assumption that natural resources were "income" when in fact they were rapidly dwindling *capital.* We were doing this, Schumacher pointed out, because we are "inclined to treat as valueless everything that we have not made ourselves." If we didn't make it, it's free. This faulty reasoning threatened our future, he wrote in *Small Is Beautiful: Economics as if People Mattered*, and a quiet revolution was needed in agriculture, industry, and society.

As a young German economist, Schumacher accepted what he had been taught about economic growth, and played a role in Britain's and Germany's post-war reconstruction efforts. But by his forties, he had become a radical whose mission was to expose the idea that "If only there were more and more wealth, everything else . . . would fall into place." At the time he was writing, the United States had only 6 percent of the world's population, but was using 40 percent of the world's primary resources. When does the drive for "growth," he wondered, become nonsensical?

Sales of *Small Is Beautiful*, a collection of Schumacher's previously published essays, were initially slow, but it "went viral" in the emerging middle-class movements concerned with world poverty, ecology, alternative energy use, and grow-your-own sustainability, and became an icon of the embryonic environmental movement, selling millions of copies.

A more permanent prosperity

While Keynes famously imagined that a time would come when people would have enough, and so could focus on the non-material aspects of life, Schumacher reasoned that the human quest for enrichment meant that there is no limit to production and consumption.

The defining features of modern capitalism, Schumacher asserts, are greed and envy. Unable to fulfill their needs just from increased consumption, people resort to selfish and even unsocial ends. This is why you get a battery of social problems amidst plenty, and why rising Gross Domestic Product tells us little about the true state of a society. Indeed, it may simply be an indicator of oppression, inequality, and natural resource exploitation, along with technological advance. The better alternative is what Schumacher calls "permanence," a form of society and economy which is more durable and resilient because it evolves in full recognition of the earth's resources and human needs. It is summed up by Gandhi's remark, "Earth provides enough to satisfy every man's need, but not for every man's greed."

Towards a new economics

Economics has become so central to our civilization, Schumacher says, that it threatens to overshadow all other things. Anything labeled "uneconomic" is framed as the activity of fools; the only thing that seems to matter is whether something is turning a profit. But for Schumacher, this obscures the fact that profits may not benefit society as a whole, in fact may *damage* it. What is good for General Motors, to corrupt a famous line, is *not* necessarily what is good for the United States.

Judgements about what is "economic" are strongly biased towards the short-term, and assume that many of the inputs needed for production, such as clean air and water, and good soil, are "free". Activity can be seen as economic even if it is terrible for the environment, while another activity that goes to some length to protect and conserve the same environment, can be cast as "uneconomic."

The other failing of economics is how it reduces all goods and services to a market transaction between buyers and sellers. The buyer is not concerned how a product is made, only that it is the right price. Schumacher's insight is that the market is merely "the surface of society," and does not account for "the natural or social facts" that lie like icebergs beneath. "The market is the institutionalisation of individualism and non-responsibility," he writes. Schumacher coins a new term, "meta-economics," meaning the study of economics in terms of the qualitative impact of goods and services within the context of nature. Economists talk of "goods", without making the distinction as to whether they are human-made goods or goods provided by nature, and whether the goods are easily replaced (or "sustainable," to use today's language).

Buddhist economics

Buddhist countries believe they can combine their spiritual heritage with modern economics, but wouldn't it make more sense, Schumacher asks, for them to have their own kind of economics?

The modern economist sees "labor" as a unit separate from the human beings that provide it. For many people, work is a necessary evil, and for employers, labor is just an input of production. As such, everything that can reduce the human workload is seen as good, including breaking down tasks to their simplest in order to get the gains from specialization. Yet in Buddhism, work has three purposes: development of one's faculties, overcoming ego-centeredness by joining others in a common task, and creating goods and services that will improve people's existence. If one follows these precepts, it no longer becomes right that people do boring, nerve-wracking or meaningless work in the service of creating products to sell, because this would mean that the products were more important than the person who made them. The idea of working just to get some leisure time is also alien to Buddhist thinking, since life is seen as a whole and not broken into compartments. The Buddhist, Schumacher notes, "sees the essence of civilization not in a multiplication of wants but in the purification of human character." If character is created by doing meaningful work that uses and develops the skills and potential of the worker, using a machine to do all the work doesn't make sense. Unemployment is a disaster for a person not only because it reduces their income, but because they suddenly have no disciplining factor in their lives which is crucial for their development. Work provides order and meaning.

Buddhist economics is defined as "maximum well-being with the minimum of consumption." Whatever is produced should in some way contribute to enlightenment. This strikes Schumacher as very rational. In contrast, the measurement of a national economy in terms of consumption, where the one who consumes the most is the richest, is utterly irrational.

The hallmarks of Buddhist economics are "simplicity and non-violence." People living in self-sufficient communities are less likely to start or get involved in big conflicts, because their existence doesn't depend on international trade. Producing things from local resources for local needs does make sense, while production that involves dependence on foreign imports is not ingenious but a failure. The Buddhist view makes one see oneself as one of billions of sentient beings existing within an ecosystem on which all depend. It is therefore madness to expropriate pieces of this ecosystem for personal gain.

We are not faced with a choice, Schumacher says, between modern industrial growth and rural stagnation. There is a middle way between "materialist heedlessness and traditionalist immobility," and we should use our minds to find this "right livelihood."

Appropriate technology

In the chapter on "Technology with a human face," Schumacher writes that capital-intensive "technology transfer" may have worked in many developing countries to the extent that it increased GDP, but that it also created a two-tier society of the urban elite who benefited from the jobs and investment related to the new industries, and the rural poor whose situation went backwards. He proposes replacing the mania for high-capital technology with "intermediate technology" that releases people's potential rather than crushing it. Such "Self-help technology" or "People's technology", as opposed to gigantic industrial production, could be deployed locally, uses limited amounts of power or fuel, is sparing on natural resources, requires little or no debt, fits in with social and cultural norms, and obviates the need for large plants and infrastructure. Schumacher's intermediate technology became better known as "appropriate technology," but now usually falls under the "sustainable development" umbrella.

Schumacher's ideas are an echo of Gandhi's vision for a nation of cottage industries, which was a far cry from the industrial power that Hindu nationalists wanted India to become. With the relentless march of industrial capitalism around the world, the Schumacher/Gandhi vision now seems quaint, yet Schumacher had a point when he noted that economic and military power go hand-in-hand. If one is not lusting after the former, the causes of war are eliminated, because a country is no longer in a fight for resources with others, or ruining the natural sources of its own prosperity. For Schumacher, slower development was a price very much worth paying to get higher levels of societal well-being, and peace.

Final comments

Schumacher's thinking presaged the organic, low-food-miles, craftsmanship outlook that has become an alternative to mass consumption, high-energy-use lifestyles. He was ahead of his time in some areas, but in others *Small Is Beautiful* now seems utopian. While he sought to help the poor with his "appropriate technologies", developing countries saw them as an euphemism for inferior technology for poor people. Most nations wish to replicate the industrial scale and technologies that had made the rich world rich. Nor did he appreciate that technology could mean better use of existing resources, or that increasing wealth means smaller families. (After increasing to around 9–10 billion this century, Earth's population will stabilize or even begin to fall). He did not see that international migration, and migration to cities, provides opportunities that people would never had had if they stayed in rural backwaters.

Schumacher's real legacy is in the explosion of awareness of environmental issues since the book was published. *Small Is Beautiful* foreshadowed the rise of ethical consumers who loudly protest when cheap clothing is the result of sweatshop conditions in Bangladesh, or when the low price of smartphones is only achieved through paying subsistence wages to Chinese workers. His ideas that human justice and environmental health go hand-in-hand, and that simplicity in economics means a less violent world, remain powerful.

E. F. Schumacher

Ernst Friedrich "Fritz" Schumacher was born in Bonn in 1911. His father was a political economy professor. After studies in Bonn and Berlin, in 1930 he won a Rhodes Scholarship to Oxford, and then took a further degree in economics at Columbia University in New York.

Schumacher returned to Germany and married but, horrified by the rise of Nazism, moved to England. As a German national he was interred at Prees Heath camp on the England–Wales border, but after a few months was allowed to return to his farm in rural Northamptonshire. A 1943 paper he had written for Economica *on international clearing mechanisms brought him to the attention of John Maynard Keynes, and he also found a mentor in Lord Beveridge, architect of Britain's welfare state. In 1945 he became a British citizen and for four years worked for Britain's Control Commission charged with reconstructing post-war Germany. In 1950 he began a twenty-year career with Britain's Coal Board. In the mid-1950s he spent several months in Burma, where he developed his concept of Buddhist economics. He also worked as a development adviser in India and Zambia.*

Schumacher died in 1977. His other key book is A Guide for the Perplexed *(1977) a philosophical critique of materialism.*

1942

Capitalism, Socialism, and Democracy

"The opening up of new markets, foreign or domestic, and the organizational development from the craft shop and factory to such concerns as US Steel illustrate the same process of industrial mutation—if I may use that biological term—that incessantly revolutionizes the economic structure from within, incessantly destroying the old one, incessantly creating a new one. This process of Creative Destruction is the essential fact about capitalism."

"Since capitalist enterprise, by its very achievements, tends to automatize progress, we conclude that it tends to make itself superfluous—to break to pieces under the pressure of its own success."

In a nutshell

Capitalism only works because it is in a state of constant flux. Instability is the price we pay for wealth-generating renewal and reinvention.

In a similar vein

William J. Baumol *The Microtheory of Innovative Entrepreneurship*
Peter Drucker *Innovation and Entrepreneurship*
Karl Marx *Capital*
Ludwig von Mises *Human Action*
Ayn Rand *Capitalism: The Unknown Ideal*

CHAPTER 40

Joseph Schumpeter

While many of his contemporaries in economics are now forgotten, since his death in 1950 the star of Joseph Schumpeter has only continued to rise.

He drew attention to what now seems very obvious: the essentially *dynamic* nature of capitalism. It was not a mere machine of inputs and outputs based on the price mechanism, but a constantly moving and changing process totally shaped by the *minds* (in particular, the entrepreneurs) engaged in it. Schumpeter showed how capitalism, unlike a planned economy, has a nonlinear aspect to it, and therefore is unpredictable. We never really know what the next big industry will be, or the next hit product, or when the next economic bust will come, because capitalism is the sum of billions of people thinking and acting independently. In a planned economy, the unexpected success becomes an anomaly to be ironed out of the system. In capitalism, entrepreneurs seize on small successes to make them the center of a new business or industry. This focus on the new, and the willingness to write off old technologies and processes despite high investment, is what makes capitalism so successful and dynamic.

Yet there are real ironies in Schumpeter's work. The term he is famous for, "creative destruction," was derived from capitalism's arch-enemy, Karl Marx, and his chapter on creative destruction runs to only five pages in a 431-page work. Though considered one of capitalism's great saints, Schumpeter spends a large part of *Capitalism, Socialism, and Democracy* predicting the system's demise, to be replaced by technocratic socialism. He saw entrepreneurs being replaced by reams of bureaucratic managers, who offered more stability but lessened economic dynamism.

What capitalism really is: creative destruction and the desire for monopoly

One of Schumpeter's observations is that as an "organic process," capitalism is not uniform in its movement. Not only does it progress in fits and starts, but its very unevenness and imperfect utilization of resources becomes a spur for entrepreneurs to solve perceived problems and gaps in the market. This is a long way from the equilibrium and perfect system of the classical economists.

If you take a look at what the average worker could afford to buy, say 50 years ago, on the wages he earned, you would be astonished how relative prices have come down for just about everything. Yet rather than competition on its own having achieved this marvel (as the classical economists believed), Schumpeter argues that it has been big business and its desire to carve out monopolies that has improved our standard of living. This is not only because new companies can quickly grow huge on the back of a product or service that suddenly fills an unmet and often unrecognized demand, but because companies must continually reshape themselves to take account of the "perennial gale of creative destruction" that blows through capitalist societies. The essential point about capitalism, Schumpeter says, is not the way it runs existing structures and enterprises, but "how it creates and destroys them."

The classical economists, followed by Marshall and Wicksell, presumed we lived in a world of perfect competition in which monopoly was the exception. In fact, Schumpeter says, every enterprise or entrepreneur tries to carve out a little monopoly either through pricing or product differentiation, and achieving it is the reward for their efforts. In capitalism, monopoly is not an anomaly, it is the goal. According to the classical view, restrictive or monopolistic practices are always bad, and result in the diminution of a nation's possible output. This is wishful thinking, Schumpeter says. The reality is that such practices, including patents and intellectual property protections, allow companies and industries to grow to their full potential. Naturally, to claw back their investment companies often feel they have to thwart or buy up the competition, in the knowledge that a point will certainly come when another firm emerges with a new technology that can upend the industry. Schumpeter does not say that all forms of restrictive or monopolistic practice are good. Indeed, a cartel that dominates an industry or an economy for a long time could really damage it. His point is rather that monopolies, where they appear organically and as the result of a better product that becomes available to many, can be a plus for an economy, and more so than a system of perfect competition might be.

Monopoly theory says that monopoly prices are always higher and monopoly output is smaller, compared to a situation of perfect competition. But this is often not the case, simply because the monopolistic firm, thanks to its size and profits, develops superior methods of production and has greater bargaining power with suppliers compared to possible competitors. These advantages allow it to provide more of its product at a lower price, compared to what might have been achieved in a competitive market. The main value of having a monopoly position, Schumpeter says, is that it protects against market upheaval for the foreseeable future, and that it enables long-range planning.

At any rate, Schumpeter observes that real monopolies (where there is a single seller of a product or commodity) are actually pretty rare in capitalism, usually not existing for long enough to negatively affect total output in the economy. Therefore, he says, "there is no general case for indiscriminate 'trust-busting' or for the prosecution of everything that qualifies as a restraint of trade." Moreover, "especially in manufacturing industry, a monopoly position is in general no cushion to sleep on. As it can be gained, so it can be retained only by alertness and energy."

Capitalist civilization

Following his analysis of the power of capitalism, Schumpeter takes a surprising turn and spends the rest of the book pointing out its failings, which he judges terminal.

Though earlier in the book he demonstrates that it had benefited the average worker greatly in terms of increasing standards of living, the deeper problem with capitalism was that it was hard to like. After all, it was a rational, utilitarian system which had usurped centuries of feudal and tribal forms of society which, whatever their economic shortcomings, provided a real sense of meaning and place for the individual. Capitalism's relentless logic made it seem anti-human; its ceaseless change creates insecurity, which breeds social unrest, and the atomization and individualization of society leads to an undermining of the institution of marriage and the bourgeois family.

Surprisingly, it is not the workers who articulate a hatred for capitalism, as Marx hoped, but the middle-class intellectuals who come to consider it morally noxious. This is partly an effect of the universalization of education, which produces far too many educated people for the amount of challenging mental work to be done. Failing to see their potential realized, they turn against the system.

The future of capitalism

In the chapter, "Crumbling Walls", Schumpeter sketches out a time when most people's basic material wants have been satisfied. Like generals in an era of perpetual peace, entrepreneurs have nothing left to do. The smart people, he thinks, would turn from business to other pursuits. Where once advances were down to an individual's flash of genius, now it is teams of people in labs that create new futures. Innovation becomes routinized, and economic progress, Schumpeter argues, becomes "depersonalized and automatized." The committee and the lab takes the place of individual action, while big business absorbs the individualist entrepreneurs and their small enterprises.

With this automation of progress, Schumpeter foresees that economic growth cannot continue at the rate it had done in the age of red-blooded capitalism. He doesn't suggest that the Great Depression and the pro-government period which followed it were the death knell of capitalism, only that it experienced a "permanent loss of vitality." Given the natural human wish to decrease uncertainty and risk, along with the meddling of politicians, it was inevitable that the capitalist state would become bureaucratized and its benefits more evenly spread.

Schumpeter was not comfortable with the rise of the stock-owning society, in which possession of a tiny slice of an enterprise by millions of people was replacing direct ownership and control of assets. This shift to the diffusion and non-physicality of ownership meant that no longer are there owners personally fighting tooth and nail to protect and grow their factory or mill; instead they are run by impersonal institutions and their managers, working in league with government to ensure that broader societal benefits are achieved. Instead of revolution, capitalist countries would undergo a process of increasing bureaucratization and nationalization. Inequalities and the insecurities of constant boom and bust business cycles would lead to bigger welfare states and social protection. In this new mollified world, the entrepreneur, the lifeblood of capitalism, would shrink into the background, his work now done by large companies.

Final comments

Was Schumpeter right about the demise of capitalism and its driving force, the entrepreneur?

Although it could be argued that the post-war era has been dominated by big business, as Marx and he foresaw, at the same time capitalism continues to destroy and create new industries at some pace. Consider the online businesses such as Amazon, Facebook, and Google which have emerged in our time. They did not come out of the labs of existing corporations, but from the minds of individuals. Capitalism still allows for disruption, and the huge fortunes in the offing guarantee that people will be motivated to create products and services that create whole new markets. It is doubtful this would ever happen if the motivation was only "service to the nation" as technocratic socialism requires.

Schumpeter believed the life would go out of capitalism if companies were no longer owned by individual capitalists, but instead by large institutions or millions of shareholders. This hasn't happened. There are plenty of activist investors who demand that companies raise their game or be broken up. And the large stakes of institutions like pension funds ensure that big companies have long timeframes and can invest for the future. More people have an interest in their doing well, and the bureaucratization of enterprise prevents the irrational moves and mistakes of single owner-entrepreneurs.

Schumpeter seems to offer us a choice of either unregulated, red-blooded capitalism that brings massive wealth and social inequality at the same time, or a bowdlerized version that promises social utopia but kills off the engine of growth, the entrepreneur. Experience tells us that capitalism is a fine balancing act between not killing the golden goose (individual entrepreneurship and innovation), and ameliorating the effects of creative destruction. Yet the citizens of rich countries have to accept that all industries have a life span, and no job is guaranteed. Insecurity is a price of prosperity.

Joseph Schumpeter

Schumpeter was born in 1883 in Triesch, then part of the Austro-Hungarian Empire and now Trest in the Czech Republic. His father, who owned a textile factory, died when Schumpeter was only four. He attended an elite school, and studied law and economics at the University of Vienna, where his great influence was the economist Eugen von Böhm-Bawerk. He gained his doctorate in 1906, and in the next few years published several books including the Theory of Economic Development *(1911), and was given a professorship at the University of Graz.*

As Schumpeter had been a supporter of the Empire, after its fall at the end of World War One he was surprised to be offered the post of Finance Minister in the new Social Democratic government. He had to resign after six months, and a subsequent post as a banker also ended in failure when, after amassing a small fortune via private speculation, he lost it all and the position along with it. In 1925 he was rescued by an academic post at the University of Bonn.

In the late 1920s Schumpeter was invited to give lectures at Harvard. He became a US citizen and stayed in America until the end of his life. He was a vehement critic of Roosevelt's New Deal, and his warnings about Stalin as being a worse danger than Hitler led to him being investigated (no charge was laid) by the FBI for pro-Nazi sympathies. At the time of his death in 1950, Schumpeter was completing a History of Economic Analysis, *assisted by his third wife, the economic historian Elizabeth Boody Schumpeter.*

1978

Micromotives and Macrobehavior

"A good part of social organization–of what we call society–consists of institutional arrangements to overcome these divergences between perceived individual interest and some larger collective bargain."

"What we are dealing with is the frequent divergence between what people are individually motivated to do and what they might like to accomplish together."

"With people, we can get carried away with our image of goal-seeking and problem-solving. We can forget that people pursue misguided goals or don't know their goals, and that they enjoy or suffer subconscious processes that deceive them about their goals."

In a nutshell

Individuals can make decisions that are rational for them, but which lead to negative outcomes for society.

In a similar vein

Friedrich Hayek *The Use of Knowledge in Society*
Steven Levitt & Stephen Dubner *Freakonomics*
Elinor Ostrom *Governing the Commons*
Richard Thaler *The Making of Behavioral Economics*

CHAPTER 41

Thomas C. Schelling

Long before contemporary authors such as Malcom Gladwell, Stephen Levitt or Tim Harford created a new genre of "popular economics," picking up on the strange and interesting in the discipline for the fascination of the average reader, there was Thomas Schelling.

Schelling won a Nobel for Economics in 2005 (shared with Israeli–American mathematician Robert Aumann) "for having enhanced our understanding of conflict and co-operation through game-theoretic analysis." In books such as *The Strategy of Conflict* (1960) and *Arms and Influence* (1966) he delved into the calculus of influence and deterrence that was part of the Cold War nuclear era. Conversations Schelling had with director Stanley Kubrick and the novelist Peter George led to the film *Dr Strangelove or: How I Learned to Stop Worrying and Love the Bomb* (1964).

Micromotives and Macrobehavior was Schelling's application of game theory principles to everyday life. He defines game theory, pioneered by the mathematician John Nash, as "the study of how rational individuals make choices when the better choice among two possibilities, or the best choice among several possibilities, depends on the choices that others will make or are making." In other words, the fact that decisions are made in the light of the decisions of other people, who in turn make decisions in the light of what others do. His phrase "micromotives and macrobehavior" was simply the relationship between how individuals act and how "people" behave as an aggregate.

In the perfectly competitive markets theorized by economists, millions of individuals acting on their own have a good collective outcome, an equilibrium. If too many people drive polluting cars and they become too expensive, for instance, there is a shift to bus transport which benefits society at large. But in the real world, Schelling noted, the decisions one person makes may be good for them, but not so good for the community. Fishermen keep on fishing even as stocks are depleted, parents throw wet wipes down the toilet, bankers keep lending even in a house price bubble. In each case, an "equilibrium" may result (fish-free seas, clogged sewers, overpriced housing), but it is not one that is beneficial for the mass.

Where shall I sit?

The book starts with a famous analysis of seating patterns, provoked by an experience Schelling had as a visiting speaker. As he was about to go on stage to deliver his talk, he was perplexed by the fact that, although the auditorium seemed mostly packed, the first dozen rows were empty. They were not reserved, so why wasn't anyone sitting in them?

Schelling looked into the many possible reasons for the empty rows at the front, including the desire to avoid embarrassment or exposure by having to sit in the very front row, wanting to sit near others, or simply a preference to be nearer the back to make a quick exit. It seemed that people like to sit near others, but not *too* near them (leaving at least one empty chair between them and the next stranger). What was clear to Schelling is that our seating preferences are not only to do with rational things like comfort or having a good view of the stage, but are formed by the psychology of the situation. No one sat in the first couple of rows out of fear of being isolated if the rows behind them did not fill up. Seating decisions, then, were based on *where people thought other people* would sit.

Schelling's point is that the goals or choices people make in their own interests do not necessarily lead to a positive outcome for the group, crowd or community. In the case of the auditorium, individual choices led to a poor distribution of seating: empty seats despite the crowd. "How well each does for himself in adapting to his social environment," Schelling writes, "is not the same thing as how satisfactory a social environment they collectively create for themselves."

Economists believe that phenomena, particularly markets, are self-balancing and lead to optimal results. But in Schelling's mind this equilibrium is simply the state of things when the dust has settled. "The body of a hanged man is in equilibrium when it finally stops swinging," he writes, "but nobody is going to insist that the man is all right." Economists' approval of equilibrium in national economies has often led to tragic outcomes, for that equilibrium could be a state of constant high inflation, or high unemployment, or sluggish growth. In the auditorium example, an economist would call it equilibrium if the people were so distributed that no one can be bothered to move seats. But that doesn't mean it is close to an ideal distribution. In an economy, my decision to stop spending may be very rational, given my circumstances, but if millions of others take the same course, a depression may result. No one ever *wants* unemployment or a stock market crash or a bank failure, and yet they frequently happen.

Critical mass

A model fits the criterion of simplicity, Schelling says, if it not only shows how mechanical and physical systems work, but seems to describe social and human phenomena too. In nuclear energy production, there is a point when the process "goes critical," that is when the fission of the nuclear material becomes self-sustaining. This idea of achieving a "critical mass" is seen in the rise of social and political movements, the spread of clothing fashions and diseases, the naming of children and the adoption of new words. What matters is if something is perceived as "a thing" that has a momentum of its own, and that *other* people are enthused about.

Schelling saw examples of critical mass every day, from the traffic intersection where pedestrians were willing to go against the lights only if a whole crowd was doing so, to the exit of a professor on the last day of class: sometimes, a few claps leads to a round of applause; other times, the early claps peter out and there is embarrassed silence. In short, people do something when they see that it is "what everybody else is doing." Schelling's paradoxical observation is that we cannot presume that an outcome is preferred, even if it is universally chosen. Daylight saving, imperial measurement, the QWERTY keyboard—these are examples of things we go along with because others go along with it, not necessarily because they are the "best."

Segregation despite laws

Schelling became famous for his analysis of segregation, specifically his wish to find out what *individual* choices and incentives led to *collective* segregation.

He observed the phenomenon of "tipping," a subcategory of the critical mass phenomenon, in neighborhoods and public schools in terms of race. One or two minority families move into an area, which compels some members of the formerly homogenous (let's say white) population to leave. Their departure creates room for more minority families to move in, prompting more "majority" families to depart. The process snowballs until it is no longer a "white neighborhood." Schelling's point is not that all those who left were racist, but that people begin to leave simply because they fear that others' leaving will mean the value of their home will drop. People do not wait until some actual point of toleration is breached, but act in the expectation or fear that it will in the future. In the 1960s, the principle (later popularized by Malcolm Gladwell in *The Tipping Point*) was seen to operate in public schools, college fraternities, country clubs, and even beaches and parks. Informal segregation, Schelling noted, often continues long after legal segregation is outlawed, and indeed happens even if people are not consciously racist. There may be no policy of segregation, but it happens anyway as people tend to prefer living in sub-worlds that give them a feeling of familiarity.

People who can afford to live in the best area of a city generally do so, and if it is a society in which whites are generally richer than blacks, it will mean that the said area becomes mostly white without anyone designing it to be so. Yet Schelling also notes that people generally wish to avoid having minority status, so even if they have the money to live in the best area, members of a minority will not live there. In this way, without anyone really intending it, the segregation of a suburb can be compounded to the point where there is complete segregation. Alarmingly, such complete segregation becomes a "stable equilibrium" that proves resistant to change.

Schelling's point is that phenomena like racial segregation often just come about even though it serves no positive purpose. Indeed, segregation restricts choices and opportunities, and blights whole cities. It may seem to benefit some people, but does nothing to advance society as a whole, brings no "social efficiency."

Final comments

Markets, Schelling notes, are generally good at taking individual people's self-serving decisions and integrating them into a greater whole that results in a pretty good allocation of resources, but thanks to human psychology and imperfect or asymmetric information (others have more information than we do, and use it to their advantage), there are plenty of market failures too.

Schelling discusses George Akerlof's well-known 1970 article, "The Market for 'Lemons,'" which said that because used car buyers don't know which cars on the market are good ones and which are "lemons," the information deficit brings down the price of used cars generally. It is only warranties from dealers, and other certification, that keeps the used car market from dwindling to nothing. There are plenty of other markets where there is unequal information. Because a lot of people may try to hide health issues to get life insurance, insurance companies have to charge higher premiums to cover the human equivalent of "lemons." As a result, healthier people who have long-life genes won't bother buying a policy, and so the life insurance market becomes increasingly useless for people who want to insure against unexpected death, which is its purpose in the first place.

When economists say people are "rational" and "self-seeking," they tend to mean it in a good way, yet it stands to reason that in any market or society in which there is plenty of dishonesty, suspicion, and willful obscuration, the decisions that individuals make can lead to a poor collective result. Thankfully, it also works the other way: societies are not simply big markets but rather structures for upholding moral values; if everyone strives to be a little bit better than they rationally need to be, society as a whole benefits.

Thomas C. Schelling

Schelling was born in 1921 and grew up in San Diego, California. He first studied economics at the University of California, Berkeley, and took his PhD from Harvard University in 1951. He worked on the Marshall Plan after World War Two, then as an adviser in the Truman administration. In 1958 he became a professor of economics at Harvard, and for two decades from 1969 taught at Harvard's Kennedy School of Government. He was subsequently professor emeritus at the School of Public Policy, University of Maryland. Schelling died in 2016.

1981

Poverty and Famines

"Starvation is the characteristic of some people not having enough food to eat. It is not the characteristic of there being not enough food to eat."

"The mesmerizing simplicity of focusing on the ratio of food to population has persistently played an obscuring role over centuries, and continues to plague policy discussions today much as it has deranged anti-famine policies in the past."

"There is also need for . . . public institutions guaranteeing food entitlement. The last category includes not merely distribution of food when the problem becomes acute, but also more permanent arrangements for entitlement through social security and employment protection. What is needed is not ensuring food availability, but guaranteeing food entitlement."

In a nutshell

Even more important than the production of enough food to feed the world's population, is ensuring that people are entitled to food despite changing conditions.

In a similar vein

Thomas Malthus *An Essay on the Principle of Population*
Dambisa Moyo *Dead Aid*
Julian Simon *The Ultimate Resource 2*

CHAPTER 42

Amartya Sen

Most economists work in areas that impact lives and livelihoods. Amartya Sen's work involved the economics of life and death itself: hunger, starvation, and food supply. Growing up in Dhaka, where his father was a chemistry professor, he witnessed the Great Bengal Famine of 1943 first hand, and it left a mark.

Though he later wrote welfare economics bestsellers such as *Development as Freedom* (1999) his early research on famine changed the way it was seen. Even into the 1970s, people believed that famine followed the Malthusian logic of there being simply too many people for the amount of food available. There were alarmist predictions about world food supply failing to keep pace with rising population. Sen was suspicious of these forecasts, mainly because their methodologies varied so widely. He came to the view that food access is about relationships between income, politics, and food supply, and famine is more likely to happen if these relationships are disrupted, than there simply being not enough food.

Starvation and food supply

In the 1970s and early 1980s, Sen notes, there was much angst about the possibility of world food supply falling behind rising population. This did not happen, but neither did it mean that starvation was eliminated. Indeed, some horrific famines occurred without any decline in food supply. The focus on the ratio of food to population has been a mistake in thinking through the ages, Sen says, because how much food *exists* is rarely as crucial as the *command* of food supply. When we talk about the supply of food, we are talking about commodities, whereas when we talk about starvation, it is about the *relationship* of a person or group to the commodities, specifically, their ownership of food.

Sen's concept of "entitlement relations" means the accepted right of a person to own, exchange or use some resource, based on society's social or legal rules. There may be plenty of food in a society, but any number of reasons why a person is unable to procure it. If his wages suddenly drop, for instance, and the price of basic foodstuffs spike, he may be exposed to starvation even if there is plenty of food on the market. In a time of distress (a drought, a flood), an agricultural laborer may find there is no work available, whereas a peasant or a share-cropper (who gets to keep the produce he is farming, even if he doesn't own the land) will at least be unlikely to go hungry. In contrast, someone selling haircuts may see a drastic reduction in demand for her service, so that her income plummets even if there is no reduction in the food available to buy. She may starve amid plenty. A craftsman selling sandals may also be vulnerable to starvation if demand suddenly falls, or the supply of leather dries up. Seen this way, starvation is rarely a case of there not being enough food, rather that there has been some catastrophic failure in entitlement relations.

The Great Bengal Famine of 1943

In the 1940s, Bengal (basically, today's Bangladesh plus Kolkata) was part of British India. The famine that overcame parts of it in 1943 led to a government enquiry, which reported a death toll of around 1.5 million. Many believed the real figure was double that. The official report gave the causes of the famine as cyclone, flooding, and fungus diseases, which produced smaller than normal rice harvests. In addition, the Japanese occupation of Burma cut off rice supplies that would normally have been imported to make up the shortfall.

Kolkata (then known as Calcutta) was Bengal's capital, and fared differently to the hinterland because it was considered strategically important to the war effort. Its chamber of commerce, in co-operation with the government, started a scheme to ensure that all industrial workers received a sufficient amount of food to keep production humming. Those working for the government, and in railways and ports, would receive similar food supply protection. There was also a basic system of charitable food provision in place, which attracted thousands of people walking in from the countryside. Despite this, bodies of "destitutes" were a common sight on the streets. Good rice harvests eventually ended the famine, but by this point hundreds of thousands had died in the city, if not by starvation alone, then by famine-induced epidemics of malaria, smallpox, and cholera.

Sen rejects the official reason given that, in 1943, there was just not enough food to feed everyone in Bengal. In fact, he finds that the 1943 supply (taking into account local stores and imports of wheat and rice) was 13 percent *higher* than in 1941, when no famine had occurred. So what happened? He supplies a table showing the comparative indexes of wages, on one hand, and food prices on the other, between 1939 and 1943. The index of average wage levels shows a modest rise between 1939 and 1943, from 100 to 130. During the same time, the food grain price index went from 100 to 385—virtually a fourfold increase. Thus, in 1943, amid what was later shown to be the largest grain harvest in history, thousands of agricultural laborers were dying from lack of food. The subsidization of food for one group (government and industrial workers) kept the price high, too high for the rest of the population. The destitution in the countryside became self-fulfilling, as the producers of things such as milk, fish, and haircuts saw catastrophic falls in demand, because no one could afford them. They in turn joined the ranks of the agricultural laborers in being unable to afford basic foodstuffs. People who, in normal times, had prosperous mini-businesses, were now starving.

Sen chillingly describes the 1943 famine as "a 'boom famine' related to powerful inflationary pressures initiated by public expenditure expansion." The injustice of it, he writes, became a focus for nationalist criticism of British imperial policy in India. The British government, against the best advice of its own Indian Viceroy, had been unwilling to allow more food imports into India by changing shipping patterns as an emergency measure. "One can argue," Sen concludes, "that the Raj was, in fact, fairly right in its estimation of overall food availability, but disastrously wrong in its theory of famines."

The Bangladesh famine of 1974

Three decades after the 1943 Bengal famine, floods saw the Brahmaputra extend beyond its banks by up to 300 metres, when normally it flooded 30–60 metres. The price of rice immediately skyrocketed, and private and government food stations, *langarkhanas*, were set up in their thousands, providing relief to over four million people, or six percent of the total population of Bangladesh. As the waters subsided and the price of rice came down, the *langarkhanas* were shut down.

The official death toll due to starvation was put at 26,000, but it was probably much higher. Despite the relief the Bangladesh government was able to give to the starving, many lives could have been saved if it had had access to greater stores of grain. As it happened, the government was in a compromised position regarding food security, because the food aid Bangladesh was receiving from the United States had been stopped, because Bangladesh had insisted on trading with Cuba. In addition, the Bangladesh state had had to cancel two big grain orders from American grain companies for lack of funds. Bangladesh did eventually give in and stop trade with Cuba, and its food aid resumed, but by then the famine had already blazed a path of death.

Echoing Bengal, Sen notes that there was actually more food availability in Bangladesh in 1974, the year of the famine, than in previous years. So it was not, to use the jargon of development economics, a food availability decline (FAD) famine. Rather, it was the connection between wages and what you could buy with those wages that mattered. Even before the floods, rice prices had been rising sharply due to macroeconomic factors such as demand and the money supply. For agricultural laborers, "The entitlement ratio fell by 58 percent in Rangpur and Sylhet and by 70 percent in Mymensingh, and with that kind of decline in the entitlement to rice, laborers would be pushed firmly towards starvation and death."

As with other famines, the key issue was vulnerability of certain groups to starvation if demand for labor, or the price of labor, suddenly fell. One also needs to be very careful with poverty statistics, Sen notes. "The poor" cannot be seen as a monolithic group. For example, between the late 1960s and mid-1970s, although there was a fall in the total number living below a poverty line in Bangladesh, the number living in "extreme poverty" (i.e. those with income not enough to meet 80 percent of the recommended calorie intake) spiked sharply. Thus, the apparent rosiness of the official statistics hid a *greater* vulnerability to famine than before.

The role of markets and democracy in famine prevention

There have been many instances through history, including Ethiopia in 1973 (which Sen also discusses) and Bangladesh in 1974, when vital food was *exported* from famine-hit areas. We shouldn't be too surprised, Sen says, because "Market demands are not reflections of biological needs or psychological desires, but choices based on exchange entitlement relations." If the people of one region are not starving, but have money to spend, why wouldn't the market want to sell food to them over a region that is in trouble? Under the logic of the market, this makes perfect sense.

Though it now seems perverse, for much of the nineteenth century, particularly within the British Empire, it was an article of faith that famines were ended by leaving things up to the market. Officials were even scolded for taking direct action to provide relief. In the Orissa famine of 1865–66, administrators were surprised that private trade did not adequately step in to supply food at reasonable prices to end the famine. Yet if traders believe there is no money to be made (because they think people have no money to buy their stuff), they will not even bother trying to supply a market.

What clearly matters more than income or purchasing power, Sen says, is the deeper question of entitlement. The fact that a type of worker, or a region, can suddenly see purchasing power dry up due to any number of reasons, suggests that the chances of famine are greater than normally thought. As Sen would suggest in *Development As Freedom*, a democracy provides considerable protection against famine, because apart from the obvious risk of losing an election because a famine has occurred, over time people will demand social insurance programs that guarantee a certain minimum level of income for the basics of life. In contrast, an authoritarian state will always have ideological or administrative priorities which take precedence over the mere fact that people don't have enough to eat.

This was true in the case of the British Raj, for which hunger in Bengal was not as important as strategic imperatives that made it unwilling to change its shipping patterns to import more rice. Yet since its component states achieved independence in 1947 and became democracies, the subcontinent has not seen a famine. Democracy has another protection against famine, Sen notes: a free press. The absence of one means it will be hard to sound the alarm as to what's happening, or the government will try to cover up a famine because it is embarrassing. Indeed, in today's North Korea, just saying the word "famine" can put you in jail.

The truth is, you can't leave food security up to the market *or* the state. Only in a democracy do you get the societal pressure to make sure governments put people and their welfare above military or strategic objectives. This does not mean that democracies can't have famines (Ethiopia has been struck by famine after becoming democratic), but Sen is right that it makes it less likely.

Final comments

Critics such as Stephen Deveraux have argued that Sen's approach went too far in discounting sheer lack of food as the source of famine. Sometimes, this is exactly what a drought or a flood brings. On other occasions, political crisis or war is the trigger, and indeed since Sen was writing conflict has become more common as a cause of famine. Climate change is also displacing people from traditional lands and increasing the number of refugees. In terms of ending famine, some have pointed to land reform (see De Soto) as the most fundamental way to ending famine and poverty, and others insist that free markets, free trade, and access to capital are crucial.

Whatever the criticisms, Sen's monograph made the study of famines a proper area of study, and much development economics can be traced back to it. Sen's emphasis on food security, rather than simply the absolute amount of food, is now applied to the challenges of undernourishment. According to the World Hunger Education Service, between 1990 and 2014 there was a 42 percent drop in the number of undernourished people, and farmers in Africa and Asia are becoming more productive thanks to mechanization and the science of increasing crop yield. Increasing the sheer amount of food is very welcome, but is only one half of the equation; the other is whether poor government or changes in income prevent people from being able to access food and afford it. After all, drought is never a life-and-death matter in countries where food security is given primacy, and which are politically stable.

Amartya Sen

Sen was born in 1933 in Manikganj in Bengal, British India. At Presidency College in Kolkata he studied philosophy and economics, and took further economics degrees from the University of Cambridge, studying under Piero Sraffa and Joan Robinson. In 1956 he returned to India to start a new economics department at Jadavpur University in Kolkata. In the early 1960s Sen taught economics at American universities, then took up at post at the Delhi School of Economics (1963–71). Subsequent professorships included the London School of Economics, Oxford University, and Harvard University.

He received the Nobel prize in economics in 1998, India's Bharat Ratna award in 1999, and became a commander of France's Legion of Honour in 2013. He is married to Emma Georgina Rothschild, a Harvard history professor. Other books include The Idea of Justice *(2010) and* Collective Choice and Social Welfare *(1970).*

2000

Irrational Exuberance

"The valuation of the stock market is an important national—indeed international—issue. All of our plans for the future, as individuals and as a society, hinge on our perceived wealth, and plans can be thrown into disarray if much of that wealth evaporates tomorrow."

"The ancient term 'animal spirits' . . . refers to the fluctuations in the basic driving force in human actions . . . Both fluctuations in irrational exuberance and animal spirits are still very much a part of our lives. We must summon the whole arsenal of the social sciences to understand them."

In a nutshell

Market levels are in theory based on fundamental asset values, but their unexpected surges, swings and falls suggest human psychology is the driver.

In a similar vein

John C. Bogle *The Little Book of Common Sense Investing*
J. K. Galbraith *The Great Crash*
Michael Lewis *The Big Short*
Richard Thaler *Misbehaving: The Making of Behavioral Economics*

CHAPTER 43

Robert J. Shiller

In the year 2000, America's Standard and Poor's (S&P) 500 share Index had seen an astonishing rise in the previous five years: up 34 percent in 1995, 20 percent in 1996, 31 percent in 1997, 26 percent in 1998, and 20 percent in 1999. Early in 2000, Yale economist Robert Shiller began giving talks and doing radio interviews to accompany the release of a new book. Yet when he suggested that current prices were based on error and would not last, Shiller was struck by the blithe disbelief of both general and professional investors.

As it turned out, the timing of the publication of *Irrational Exuberance* could not have been better. March 2000, with stock prices averaging 44 times earnings, turned out to be the peak of the market. Technology stocks would drop precipitously later that year, and by March 2003 the market had dropped to around half of its previous value.

With such a plunge, Shiller notes, you would have thought most investors would be "burned" and get out of the market, causing a medium- to long-term decline in stock prices. In fact, by 2005 price-to-earnings ratios had climbed back into the mid-20s, way above the historical average of 16, and the housing market was becoming overheated.

What was happening? There were not any objective fundamentals (for example, fast rising earnings, a shortage of houses) that would justify such overenthusiasm. Rather, Shiller says, markets were kept high by hope and belief that, whatever the crash or correction, they always rise again. The media and investing professionals (who have their own interests at heart) encouraged the public not to be content any longer to preserve their savings to keep pace with inflation, but to see their nest eggs as capital chasing the highest returns.

The theme of Shiller's bestseller, now in its third (2015) edition, is the psychological dimension to economies and markets, which after all do not exist as objective realities but are the creation of millions of minds. To understand "irrational exuberance" or "animal spirits" in markets and their effects on economy and society, the responsible economist must look across the social sciences, particularly psychology. With Richard Thaler, Shiller was a pioneer of behavioral economics as applied to finance, and *Irrational Exuberance* is based on his own research over three decades.

Shiller took the book's title from a December 1996 remark by Alan Greenspan, the normally very cautious chairman of the US Federal Reserve Board. Greenspan's suggestion that stock market investors were behaving with "irrational exuberance" scared world markets into sudden drops of 2 to 4 percent. The conventional explanation was that markets dropped because Greenspan was signaling a tightening of monetary policy, but Shiller believed there was a deeper reason why the phrase had such an effect: people could see for themselves the strong psychological element in the rising market, aside from objective values.

Rare among those in his profession, Shiller has shown an uncanny ability to call the top of the market; anyone who fancies their abilities as a stock or real estate speculator should first read this book.

I'm a believer

Shiller uses the stock market boom of the late 1990s and 2000 to analyze market booms generally. Are there powerful fundamentals that push stocks higher in a boom, he asks, or is it just a case of "wishful thinking on the part of investors that blinds us to the truth of our situation?" He aimed to show beyond any doubt that the "efficient markets hypothesis" which says that current prices are an accurate expression of the sum of all available economic information, is wrong. This theory provides a totally misleading story of market efficiency, and never properly accounts for bubbles and booms.

It is understandable why people will buy stocks at high levels: if the price keeps going up, surely the experts have done their research and validated that these prices are in line with value. But this research is often of pretty low quality, "no more rigorous than the reading of tea leaves," Shiller argues, and moreover average investors are swept up by a cheerleading media which drowns out more cautious voices. There is also the view, popularized by brokers and mutual funds, that stocks are always the best performing asset class over the long run.

Between 1994 and 1999, the Dow Jones Industrial Average *tripled* from 3,600 to over 11,000, while in the same period, personal incomes and GDP only rose by 30 percent. Shiller calls it "the most dramatic bull market in US history," dwarfing previous stock rises including the fabled 1928–29 market and that of the early 1960s. When the market collapsed in 2000, the Millennium Boom was seen for what it was: a Millennium Bubble. Yet prices soon began rising again above historic averages because, Shiller argues, people still had a religious faith in the long-run supremacy of stocks as an asset class. But Shiller's crucial insight is that big falls in the stock market generate hangovers lasting much longer than is commonly thought. After the stock market peak of 1901, for instance, there was a 20-*year* decline, only for stocks to rise again with the bull market of the 1920s. Then, after the Great Crash of 1929, there was not only a Depression lasting virtually until World War Two, but the Standard & Poor's Composite Index did not return to its 1929 value until *1958*. Yes, there was a market boom from 1960 to 1966, but with the long bear market followed, the market did not return to its 1966 levels until 1992. If an average investor had stayed in the stock market for the 15-year period following 1966, she would have lost money, and even if she had hung in there for 20 years (until 1986) would have been ahead only 1.9 percent (adjusted for inflation).

Shiller includes a graph comparing price to earnings ratios and 10-year returns on stocks, showing that the higher the price compared to earnings, the lower the returns over the subsequent decade. (Writing in 2000, he suggested "a poor long-run outlook for the stock market" in the next 15 years, which was prescient). Conversely, the lower the price of a stock compared to its earnings at any given point, the better the returns over the following ten years. This "buy low, sell high" truth, unfortunately, is lost amid market frenzies, when it is believed that a "new era" has begun in which higher than normal prices are justified by new technology or demographic trends. At such a point, the stock market ceases to reflect fundamentals, but becomes an expression of all the minds invested in it, a self-fulfilling prophecy. A new height reached by an index should not therefore be seen as an "achievement," but as simply a mirror of current thinking.

This price isn't right

If markets are basically efficient, the theory goes, then "bubbles" can't really exist, since "financial assets area always priced correctly, given what is publicly known, at all times." Yet tech stocks during the internet boom, Shiller says, reflected "an exaggerated view of their potential" by the public. For example, companies like the internet retailer eToys had in 1999 a stock market value exceeding that of the established retailer Toys R Us, even though it was losing money while Toys R Us was in profit by $376 million, and had sales *400 times* larger than eToys. Given such crazy overvaluations in particular stocks, Shiller reasons, it makes sense that the *overall* market can be overpriced.

But who is to say that some stocks are overpriced in the long run? This was the argument of Jeremy Siegel, who showed that fashionable stocks like IBM and McDonalds, although apparently overpriced in 1970, would, if you had held onto them through the stock falls of 1973–74 and up to 1996, have done as well as the S&P 500 Index. Perhaps, but most people would not have held on that long, Shiller says, and would have sold at a loss.

The conventional, rational view of markets is that price growth will always correlate with earnings or dividend growth. Shiller not only finds no evidence for this, but rather says that, "stock prices clearly have a life of their own." They are way more volatile than might be suggested from the actual earnings data. There must be other factors at play.

The (un)wisdom of the crowd

Most human thinking, Shiller observes, "is not quantitative, but instead takes the form of *storytelling* and *justification*." In the context of markets, "information cascades" and feedback mechanisms mean that information feeds on itself and disseminates, whether or not it is correct. If the stock market is high, people tend to believe that all the other people investing in it cannot be wrong. They don't need to use their own research and judgements, but trust the crowd.

Shiller defines a bubble as a "sort of psychological epidemic," and a symptom of the disease is complacency. Though individuals worry about soaring prices, the dominant sentiment is "one of public inattention to the thought that prices could fall, rather than firm belief that they can never fall." Such errors of judgement "can infect even the smartest people," he observes. Overconfidence, lack of due diligence, and excessive trust in others' judgement leads to a situation of "the blind leading the blind," and disaster soon follows.

While the original edition of *Irrational Exuberance* was focused on stock bubbles, later versions include a chapter on the dramatic rise in house prices in the US between 1998 and 2006. As with stock bubbles, there was a popular belief among the general public that one could get rich through real estate. Yet viewed from the longer time span of history, home price growth has been *less* than real income growth, which has been around 2 percent a year from 1929 to 2013. The prices of most American homes have only increased by between 0.7 and 1 percent a year over a century. It *seems* like a big increase if your grandmother bought her house for $16,000 in 1948 and it sold for $190,000 in 2004, but not when adjusted for inflation. As with the idea of getting wealthy through stocks, the popular wisdom is wrong.

Shiller has lobbied insurance companies to offer "home equity insurance", allowing people to be less dependent on the current value of their homes, by receiving compensation if the property market drops. He also established a housing futures market on the Chicago Exchange which offers the opportunity to hedge against collapses in the property market.

Final comments

Why is it important to analyze stock and real estate booms, which after all seem to be a normal part of capitalism? Because, Shiller says, they vacuum up savings and resources which may otherwise have gone into building infrastructure, schools, universities, social insurance, and other kinds of social and human capital. People with savings, universities with endowments, charities with funds to invest for the future, all need to know whether current market prices are roughly in line with economic reality, or whether being involved in the market may damage what they have built up.

The fact that more people are depending on personal assets like real estate to secure their futures, rather than a traditional pension or savings, means more exposure to risk. There can be great and surprising gains made by the average person (owners of homes in London saw the value of their properties on average *double* between 2010 and 2016) but also great and unexpected falls in their paper wealth, with consequent effects on their standard of living. Indeed, one of pernicious effects of stock and real estate bubbles, Shiller notes, is that people think they do not need to save. In 2007, the US national savings rate had fallen to only 2.9 percent of income. Two years later, in the midst of the financial crisis, it had gone up to 8.1 percent, even though resources were more limited. The old idea of having a savings buffer came back to prove its worth. It is time for a return to more conservative investing strategies, Shiller says, which make provision for bad outcomes.

Robert J. Shiller

Born in 1946 in Detroit, Shiller was educated at Kalamazoo College, the University of Michigan, and the Massachusetts Institute of Technology (MIT), where he gained his PhD in economics in 1972. He began teaching at Yale in 1982, and is currently Yale's Sterling Professor of Economics and Professor of Finance at the Yale School of Management.

In the early 1990s Shiller developed, with economist Karl Case, an index of national house price changes, which became the widely used Case-Shiller Index. For his work on "empirical analysis of asset prices," along with Eugene Fama and Lars Peter Hansen, he was awarded the 2013 Nobel Prize for Economics. With Richard Thaler, Shiller has since 1991 been giving workshops in behavioral economics at the National Bureau of Economic Research.

Other books include Market Volatility *(1989),* The New Financial Order *(2003),* The Subprime Solution *(2008), and with George Akerlof,* Animal Spirits *(2009) and* Phishing For Fools *(2015).*

1996

The Ultimate Resource 2

"So we tell again the important story: humans have for tens of thousands of years created more than they have destroyed. That is, the composite of what they sought to produce and of the by-products has been on balance positive. This most fundamental of all facts about the progress of civilization is evidenced by a) the increasing standard of material living enjoyed by generation after generation, b) the decreased scarcity of all natural resources as measured by their prices throughout history, and c) the most extraordinary achievement of all, longer life and better health. The treasures of civilization that one generation bequeaths to the next, each century's inheritance greater than the previous one, prove the same point; we create more than we destroy."

In a nutshell

Standards of living keep rising even with a larger population. This suggests that arguments about "scarcity" lack foundation.

In a similar vein

Gary Becker *Human Capital*
Milton Friedman *Capitalism and Freedom*
Robert J. Gordon *The Rise and Fall of American Growth*
Friedrich Hayek *The Use of Knowledge in Society*
Thomas Malthus *Essay on the Principle of Population*
E. F. Schumacher *Small Is Beautiful*
Amartya Sen *Poverty and Famines*

CHAPTER 44

Julian Simon

Like most people, business school professor and economist Julian Simon fully accepted the Malthusian view that the world had to limit an "exploding population": production of goods and services would not keep up, and scarcity would produce ever rising prices and people going hungry, while the environment was trashed.

But when Simon delved deeper into the economics of population, he was shocked to find not only that this vision never seemed to become reality, but that standards of living had consistently risen alongside population growth. What about the negative effects on the environment and the using up of finite resources thanks to such "prosperity"? In fact, Simon noted in his early work on population economics, the quality of our environment is considerably better today that it was 150 years ago, when cities were enveloped in coal-burning smog, many houses even in rich countries were not connected to sewerage systems, and people routinely died of diseases which have been all but wiped out today. Simon also dismissed belief in finite resources (the world was running out of oil, or wheat, water, or whatever); if a country has relatively free markets, he said, price signals combined with human ingenuity will ensure sufficient supply of any good. It had always been like this, and he saw our era as no exception.

The Ultimate Resource was a popularization of his scholarly research. The 1996 "2" version included another 15 years of examples and data, and so is the one to read. It is a polemic, and Simon sometimes goes too far in his reasoning. He argued that species loss had been grossly overestimated, that there was even surprisingly little evidence of a link between deforestation and species loss. Overall, though, his arguments are hard to refute. In a letter to Simon, Friedrich Hayek said that the book provided an empirical basis for what Hayek had argued for years, calling it "a first-class book of great importance which ought to have great influence on policy."

Yet Simon was a lone voice in a new environmental paradigm which began to generate stars such as Paul Ehrlich, a forerunner to Al Gore who wrote *The Population Bomb* (1968), Dennis Meadows (co-author of the famous *Limits to Growth*, 1972) and Garret Hardin (who popularized the idea of the "tragedy of the commons"). Yet Simon was no crackpot (his many journal articles included a much-cited piece in *Science* ("Resources, Population, Environment: An Over-supply of False Bad News," June, 1980), and denied that he was a "cornucopian" economist, that is believing in unlimited natural abundance. His point was rather that humanity always has enough of the resources it needs to progress, and that these resources change over time to reflect new demands and technology. The important thing was that the human mind (his "ultimate resource") not be bridled in the name of "resource depletion" that never actually happened.

People: not the problem, the solution

In 1969, Simon was visiting the Washington offices of USAID to discuss a project aimed at lowering fertility in poor countries. Nearby, he spotted a sign to the Iwo Jima Memorial, and recalled the words of a Jewish chaplain on the Iwo Jima battlefield: "How many who would have been a Mozart or a Michelangelo or an Einstein have we buried here?"

Simon began to wonder what right he had to tell people to have fewer children. For even if a child didn't turn out to be an Einstein or a Mozart, they would still be a joy to their family and a contributor to their community, not to mention enjoying their own life. He was happy to admit that the addition of more people to any community causes problems, but it also brought an addition of brain power and knowledge to solve those problems.

While his environmentalist contemporaries were painting nightmare Malthusian scenarios of a smoking, parched Earth overrun by people, Simon began to ask: is "population growth, along with the lengthening of human life, a moral and material triumph"? The planet's population growth had occurred alongside its economic growth, which had provided the means to feed, clothe, and house billions of extra people, while giving them longer and healthier lives. Not even sporadic famines, wars, or depressions could hide this fact.

Resources: they do keep making them

Simon's argument that there is never any lack of natural resources was shocking when he made it, and still shocks people educated in the idea of scarcity. So too was his assertion that pollution was on the whole not increasing, but in most places decreasing. Simon considered the scarcity arguments one by one, and offered a rejoinder.

When he was writing, the press was full of handwringing stories about a coming shortage of agricultural land, as cities and urban sprawl took over the landscape. But Simon pointed out that it is not the quantity of land under cultivation that matters, but its increasing productivity. Even as its population had grown, the total area of American farmland had decreased, because much higher yields had been wrought from the same land. New forms of watering and irrigation meant that farms used less water to grow more food, and food production had become more intensive, allowing for a more efficient use of resources (for example fish farming and feedlots for beef). As the world's population increases, hydroponics, massive greenhouses, high-yield crops, genetically-modified crops, drought-resistant crops, and advances in farm machinery will ensure that food remains cheap and plentiful. This process will have a surprising outcome: more forests and wilderness areas left for recreation and the preservation of species. Simon also argues that as world population increases, there will actually be *less* population density across a country's land mass, because more people want to live in cities. There will never be a shortage of land, only more costly land in certain places.

In terms of natural resources, Simon argues that the Earth has no "carrying capacity." Granted, if you put rabbits in a pen they will soon eat all the grass and starve to death, but humans are different. For us, an apparent decline of one resource prompts us to look for an opportunity to find other resources, or use the existing ones much, much more efficiently.

History shows that virtually every natural resource has become less costly compared to average wages over time, because the presence of more people speeds up the development of new energy supplies. Once, people lit their homes using whale oil, but the expense and difficulty in procuring it prompted people to discover and use crude oil from the earth, which has powered the modern age. In the last 20 years, uncertainty over the security and price of crude was the major factor in the technological development of the "fracking" process to access shale gas, which now promises a cheap and inexhaustible supply of energy.

If there is any kind of shortage in manufactured goods, economists assume that it won't last, that companies will quickly step in to provide for the demand. But we somehow think that commodities like copper, aluminium, and oil are different, that if prices shoot up for any of these things we are in an "impending age of scarcity." Yet statements of "known reserves," which also give forecasts of when a commodity will be "exhausted" are nonsensical. We can measure known reserves to a limited extent, but technology allows for new reserves to be discovered all the time. The US Geological Survey once pronounced that there was no oil in Texas or California.

The fact is, reserves of anything rise in line with consumption. There is no point when a material "runs out," because human ingenuity always finds ways of creating more of it. Copper, for instance, was once only mined; now a considerable portion comes from recycling. As an old man, reflecting on the news stories about scarcity, once commented to Simon, "we've been just about to run out of oil ever since I've been a boy." The quantity of any known reserve always remains, as if by magic, one step ahead of demand.

The Simon–Ehrlich Wager

Simon's book is great for giving a sense of the dominant thinking on resource and environmental questions in the late 1960s and early 1970s. Paul Ehrlich's *The Population Bomb* began with "The battle to feed all of humanity is over. In the 1970's the world will undergo famines—hundreds of millions of people are going to starve to death," and went on to write, "I have yet to meet anyone familiar with the situation who thinks India will be self-sufficient in food by 1971, if ever."

Against this backdrop of alarmism, Simon had an idea. In September, 1980 through the pages of *Social Science Quarterly*, he invited the doomster's poster boy, Ehrlich, to a bet that any bundle of commodities (including foodstuffs) would fall in price over a period of several years. Ehrlich leapt at the chance, and to ensure he would win, chose four metals that seemed very likely to rise steeply in value (chromium, nickel, tin, and tungsten), and bought $200 of each. What happened? Despite the world's population growing by 800 million over the next decade, by September 1990 the price of all the metals had fallen, some significantly. Ehrlich mailed Simon a check.

Even if Simon had been lucky, his point was that over any long period, a glance at any official statistics on human well-being would always show he was more right than lucky. Ehrlich would also be proved wrong on food prices, which have taken up an ever smaller proportion of wages over the last century.

Political views

If Simon had a political agenda, it was for open societies (he heartily approved of immigration) and economic freedom. While all forms of collectivization and government control of agriculture had failed, he noted, "Any country that gives to farmers a free market in food and labor, secure property rights in the land, and a political system that ensures these freedoms in the future will soon be flush with food, with an ever-diminishing proportion of its workforce required to produce the food." When he was writing in the 1990s, 3 percent of the US population was directly employed in agriculture, down from 50 percent in the 1890s. Today, even after an increase in national population by 50 million people since 1996, the figure has fallen to under 2 percent.

Final comments

Interviewed for a *Wired* article ("The Doomslayer," February 1997, Ed Regis) the year before he died, Simon said, "Resources come out of people's minds more than out of the ground or air. Minds matter economically as much as, or more than, hands or mouths." Because the human mind was unlimited, so were resources. This was an inconvenient fact for those who made a living out of dark scenarios. "It's the difference," Simon said, "between a speculative analysis of what *must* happen versus my empirical analysis of what *has* happened over the long sweep of history." He forecast that material conditions and standards of living would continue to rise, and that "Within a century or two, all nations and most of humanity will be at or above today's Western living standards." However, he speculated "that many people will continue to *think and say* that the conditions of life are getting *worse*."

Julian Simon

Simon was born in Newark, New Jersey, in 1932. He attended Harvard as an undergraduate, majoring in experimental psychology, before spending three years in the US Navy. He took an MBA (1959) and PhD (1961) in business economics at the University of Chicago, and from 1963 to 1969 taught marketing and advertising at the University of Illinois, Urbana, before being appointed a professor of economics and business administration. He wrote widely on population economics, immigration policy, and aviation economics, and became known for proposing the practice of offering money or air miles to passengers who are willing to not take a flight due to airline overbooking, which became common practice. From 1983 until his death in 1998, Simon was a professor of business administration at the University of Maryland. He was also a senior fellow at the free-market Cato Institute.

Other books include The Resourceful Earth *(1984),* Theory of Population and Economic Growth *(1986),* Population and Development in Poor Countries *(1992),* The State of Humanity *(1995) and* Life Against The Grain: The Autobiography of an Unconventional Economist *(2001).*

1776

The Wealth of Nations

"It is not from the benevolence of the butcher, the brewer, or the baker that we expect our dinner, but from their regard to their own interest. We address ourselves, not to their humanity, but to their self-love, and never talk to them of our own necessities, but of their advantages. Nobody but a beggar chooses to depend chiefly upon the benevolence of his fellow-citizens."

"To prohibit a great people . . . from making all that they can of every part of their own produce, or from employing their stock and industry in the way that they judge most advantageous to themselves, is a manifest violation of the most sacred rights of mankind."

In a nutshell

The wealth of a nation is that of its people, not its government, and that wealth is achieved through the division of their labor and the ever-greater specialization of their skills. The foundation of all future prosperity is current savings.

In a similar vein

Milton Friedman *Capitalism and Freedom*
Ayn Rand *Capitalism: The Unknown Ideal*
David Ricardo *Principles of Political Economy and Taxation*
Max Weber *The Protestant Ethic and the Spirit of Capitalism*

CHAPTER 45

Adam Smith

In the eighteenth century, the words "capitalism" and "economics" had not yet been invented. Economic matters were seen as part of their political and social contexts, hence the term then used, "political economy".

Adam Smith was not the first political economist by any means (he was inspired, for instance, by the French "physiocrats," early thinkers on economic matters including Turgot, Condorcet, and Quesnay), but by identifying economics as a field of study in its own right, separate to politics, philosophy, law, and ethics, *The Wealth of Nations* established a new discipline. It was the first book on economics to really catch the public's attention, and is as much as anything else a great work of literature. Smith's informal style, and his fearlessness in criticizing the folly of rulers and the corrupting effects of vested interests, made him into a popular figure.

Not published until Smith was in his 50s, *The Wealth of Nations* took fully ten years to write, fills two volumes and weighs in at 380,000 words. Smith expounds at great length on details which are of only academic interest now, such as the production of wheat, ale, and barley in thirteenth-century England, the types of rents levied by lords and kings on agricultural land, how the price of silver dropped after the Spanish conquest of South America, and how a government might fairly tax salt, leather, soap, and candles.

Go beyond the historical details, though, and the book is surprisingly engrossing and relevant.

The effect of self-interest

Being a handbook of the new industrial capitalism that was emerging in his time, *The Wealth of Nations* led to a perception that Smith was an apostle of greed and self-interest. Yet seventeen years earlier, he had published a rather different work, *The Theory of Moral Sentiments* (1759), which argued that societies are bound by moral forces such as conscience and sympathy for others, along with self-interest.

In *The Wealth of Nations*, Smith argued that it did not actually matter whether people were mainly driven by self-interest, since the overall effect was good. The "invisible hand" of the free market made sure that individuals acting to their own highest benefit ended up elevating the whole. This was not an excuse to act greedily or unjustly. It simply meant that a person's honest labors to progress in life for the sake of himself or his family would lead to a good use of resources. A society allowed to act this way would inevitably make the most of what it had, and over time grow prosperous. His famous remark about the butcher, brewer, and baker (see quote above) was not just an insight into human nature, it underlined his philosophy of self-reliance: that we are more likely to help others, and be in a position to help them, when we have our own needs covered.

Wealth through specialization

It was no accident that Smith began his book with the subject of labor. He believed that how wealthy a country becomes depends more than anything on the "skill, dexterity, and judgment with which its labour is generally applied." It also rested on the proportion of the population engaged in useful work.

He noted that in rich countries, even though many people do not work, society as a whole abundantly supplies most people's needs. This is because rich countries characteristically have a much greater "division of labor" than poor ones. There is great efficiency in dividing up tasks according to the ability of people best able to do them, and time is saved in not changing from one task to another.

But it was not just in physical production that the principle of the division of labor applied. In advanced societies, he wrote, philosophy or the creation of new ideas becomes the "trade" of a whole group of people, co-existing beside the more mundane jobs. With such specialization, "Each individual becomes more expert in his own peculiar branch, more work is done upon the whole, and the quantity of science is considerably increased by it." In a well-governed society, the division of labor leads to "universal opulence", allowing even the lowliest workers to cover their needs.

Smith mentions the Scottish highlanders of his time, who, thanks to their remoteness from towns, had to be their own "butcher, baker, and brewer." In contrast, in advanced communities every person effectively becomes a merchant, since their work specialty allows them no time to make all the things that they need. Instead, they must sell the excess of what they produce (a shoemaker may need only six pairs of shoes a year for his family, but makes hundreds more) and with this money buy what they need and want. The bigger the city, the more specialized the workforce, and the greater the trade in goods and services. Big cities are wealthy precisely because of their increased division of mental and physical labor.

What determines value

According to Smith, it is the amount of labor that has gone into a thing's creation, which saves the buyer having to go through the same labor, that sets the value of something. People become rich by providing something of extremely high utility that saves other people the labor of having to make it themselves. The level of hardship and ingenuity involved in the creation of something becomes an important element in deciding its worth.

Yet Smith notes, "In this state of things, the whole produce of labour does not always belong to the labourer. He must in most cases share it with the owner of the stock which employs him." And this was, of course, Marx's problem with capitalism, that a person who does not put in the labor, who often does not even provide significant direction in the creation of a product, gets the bulk of the produce of the labor. But in Smith's mind this is fair, since without the stock or capital provided in the first place, the wages of the laborer could not be paid.

How nations grow rich

Smith provided a simple recipe for how countries could become wealthy, which begins with its citizens being good savers. "Parsimony, and not industry," he writes, "is the immediate cause of the increase of capital." Prodigal people are a "public enemy," while every frugal person in society becomes a "public benefactor." Secondly, these savings are invested towards productive ends, which naturally increases the amount of people usefully employed.

This wealth formula of savings-investment-employment may seem obvious to us today, but in Smith's time it was not at all the prevailing view of how nations could grow rich. Rather, the mercantilist view held that the economic object of a nation was to build up its store of gold, silver, and other precious metals, either through trade or war. Smith's recipe, in contrast, seemed rather middle-class and modest. It rested on the Protestant ethic of frugality, industry, and minding one's own business.

Smith said that what today we call a country's "gross domestic product", or the annual value of everything it produces, was made up of three things: rent obtained from land, wages from labor, and the profits of stock (things used in production). In a complex economy, the level of gain from any of these affected the other. That is, if wages increased, so would rent from land, or if profits went down, so might wages and rents.

Trading your way to prosperity

The other avenue by which countries could grow rich was trade. Smith observed that the most successful cultures of the past were all traders, usually maritime. Countries who trade will always be richer than those who do not, since the trading country is able to buy raw materials which it does not have itself, and turn them into manufactured goods. These are much more valuable than raw commodities, and can be sold at great profit to other countries.

Smith's insight, in part borrowed from the French physiocrats, was that trade always benefits both parties to the transaction. The mercantilist view was that trade was a form of war in which you sought to gain at the other's expense. The essential point about national wealth was that it grows when goods and money are circulated and exchanged. This was understood by the medieval European cities such as Florence, which amassed huge riches not by simply doing business with the countryside surrounding them, but with "the most remote corners of the globe." Cities and countries that myopically stayed within their own borders, in contrast, were destined to founder.

What not to do: Looting, wars, and luxuries

If a person spends their money on luxuries instead of building up capital, the day of financial reckoning will come. Likewise, Smith wrote, a sovereign that spent huge sums on palaces, the pageantry of court, and unnecessary wars was looking for trouble.

Equally bad was the nation that believed it could get rich, not by developing its land or industry, but by looting other countries. He notes that it was "the sacred thirst for gold" that brought the Spaniards to the New World, yet its end result was hardly beneficial to the long-term prosperity of Spain. Instead of plundering in search of fantastic gains, a country was better off slowly developing its own resources, and using trade to sell its surpluses and bring it what it needed to make high-value products.

Smith was skeptical of the monopoly trading companies (such as the East India Company) that used government mandates to make fortunes for its members, and he was not keen on imperialism and colonization. *The Wealth of Nations* was written at a time when America was still for the most part a collection of British colonies, and Smith advocates Britain withdrawing itself. Britain's rulers, he wrote, had always imagined America to be a gold mine, but it had, in fact, only ever been "the project of a gold mine." It had cost the British taxpayer more than it was worth; it was time for Britain to assume more modest ambitions.

In writing about imperialism generally, Smith is very sympathetic to the plight of the colonized, hoping that in the future the balance will be redressed, such that colonized peoples grow in power and wealth as the result of their connections with the rich countries.

Natural liberty

Along with self-interest, Smith's other great idea in relation to political economy was "natural liberty". He noted that rulers can either hinder or help the progress of their citizens. Most of the time, they help them by getting out of the way, and putting in place basic security and order so as to let people and their enterprises flourish.

Smith was writing when frustration with government red tape was at its zenith. Legions of officials ensured that every possible penny could be extracted by the state through taxes, customs, excises, and arbitrary rules. His book was a great success because it assumed people should be free to follow their economic interests with a minimum of government interference. He insisted there were only three areas in which government should have a role:

- Protecting a society from "the violence and invasion of other independent societies".
- Protecting citizens "from the injustice or oppression of every other member of it," and establishing a corresponding judicial system.
- Building and maintaining public works and institutions which are too expensive for a single individual to undertake, but which would benefit greatly society as a whole.

All these things should be paid for through taxes. However, when something benefits only a section of society rather than the whole, this should be paid for either privately, or by a tax on the users, for example tolls on roads. Though Smith advocated the creation of a basic schooling system to ensure everyone could read, write, and do basic arithmetic, he suggested that those who benefited the most from education should also be willing to pay for it.

Final comments

The Wealth of Nations was published at a time when Europe was entering a new industrial era, and great social change was afoot. People were fed up and wanted to be free to pursue their economic destinies. At first glance, rulers no doubt thought that the title of the book referred to the wealth of states, when in fact Smith used the term "nation" to mean the *people* of those countries. The smartest governments did not put faith in themselves to create prosperity, he believed, but rather in the ingenuity of their citizens.

The simplicity and common sense of Smith's delineation of government's limited role has largely stood the test of time. Today, governments inevitably grow large and bloated, moving into areas that are not really their business, and in time this inevitably makes the public poorer. Though they often believe in their ability to "pick winners" in terms of subsidizing particular industries to create jobs, Smith warned that such investment tended to corrupt the natural tendency of a society to allocate resources in the best way. Over 200 years on, his book still provides a solid recipe for national prosperity.

Adam Smith

Smith's father was the comptroller of customs in Kirkcaldy, Scotland, but died six months before Smith was born in 1723. At 15, Smith went to Glasgow University to study moral philosophy, and then on to Oxford University. In 1748 he began giving public lectures in Edinburgh, and in 1751 was appointed to a chair of logic (later moral philosophy) at Glasgow University.

He resigned his post in 1763 to become the private tutor of a young Scottish nobleman, the Duke of Buccleuch. The pair traveled around Europe and met intellectuals including Turgot, Helvetius, and Quesnay. On returning to Scotland, Smith spent most of the following decade writing The Wealth of Nations. *Following in his father's footsteps, in 1778 he was appointed commissioner of customs in Edinburgh.*

On his death in 1790, he left most of his considerable estate to charity. He never married.

2000

The Mystery of Capital

"Capital is the force that raises the productivity of labour and creates the wealth of nations. It is the lifeblood of the capitalist system, the foundation of progress, and the one thing that the poor countries of the world cannot seem to produce for themselves, no matter how eagerly their peoples engage in all the other activities that characterize a capitalist economy."

"Opening up capitalism to the poor will not be as simple as running a bulldozer through garbage. It is more like rearranging the thousands of branches and twigs of a huge eagle's nest—without irritating the eagle."

"If capitalism had a mind, it would be located in the legal property system."

In a nutshell

Assets do not become capital until their value can be fixed and made transparent to a wide market. To really advance and fulfill their potential, nations need integrated property systems.

In a similar vein

Milton Friedman *Capitalism and Freedom*
Thomas Piketty *Capital in the Twenty-First Century*

CHAPTER 46

Hernando de Soto

A decade after the fall of the Berlin Wall, and in the wake of the transition of many ex-communist countries to capitalism, development economist Hernando de Soto gave voice to the perplexity of the time: capitalism had "triumphed," the American stock market was reaching giddy heights, showing the power of the capitalist model to generate wealth, yet many poorer countries had found it a bitter pill. Free trade, globalization, and privatization had not delivered the stability and prosperity that had been promised.

Commentators in the rich world hinted that cultural factors, such as lack of an entrepreneurial spirit, or the psychological weight of being a former colony, were to blame. Yet de Soto, who had grown up amid Peru's bustling markets, knew that people in poorer countries are more entrepreneurial than those in the rich world. The problem was not insufficiency of entrepreneurship or markets, which abound everywhere, but something more fundamental to capitalism: capital itself. Poor countries could copy all the features of a capitalist system, and every technology "from the paper clip to the nuclear reactor," de Soto wrote, yet if they are unable to generate capital, labor cannot be made productive and wealth cannot be created. The "mystery" of capital is that it is not mere savings or money, but an outcome of law and institutions.

A capital idea

Most of the world's poor, de Soto says, "already possess the assets they need to make a success of capitalism." Even in the poorest countries, people save. In fact, private savings in the developing world dwarf all foreign aid and foreign investment. Haiti's people, for instance, possess assets 150 times the value of all foreign investment made in the country since it became independent from France two centuries ago.

But there is a problem with these assets. The ownership of many houses lacks the formal title taken for granted in wealthy states. Farms have crops but no deeds, businesses are not incorporated, and industries lack access to finance. Instead, assets are only traded in small circles of trust, and often cannot be used as collateral for loans.

When properly documented, assets "lead an invisible, parallel life alongside their material existence," de Soto says. For instance, in America the biggest source of finance for entrepreneurs is a mortgage on their own home. Well-documented assets like houses demonstrate a credit history, and link individuals to the wider economy. Having a mortgage or possessing a formal interest in a company makes people part of a *system* with all its rights. When ownership cannot be clearly demonstrated, in contrast, an asset is "dead capital," because it can't generate more capital through being securitized or collateralized. The history of capitalism, from the joint-stock company to junk bonds to mortgage securities, has been finding new ways to represent the value, and therefore unlock the potential, of assets. It is this ability "to transform the invisible to the visible," that separates the richer nations from the poorer, de Soto says. Adam Smith and David Ricardo pointed out that savings are the basis of the wealth of nations, but this is true only if the savings can become formal assets that can be easily traded and whose value is transparent to all.

Where the money is: the extra-legal economy

When de Soto and his team began researching formal property ownership systems in South America, they were told it was relatively easy to register a property title or set up a business. What they actually found shocked them. To formalise ownership of a home in Peru, it took de Soto's team six years and seven months, and involved 728 steps involving permissions from scores of government departments. They had a similar experience getting the go-ahead to build a house on former agricultural land. Was it any wonder, they concluded, that people put up homes illegally instead?

In developing countries, millions of people work in unregistered food stalls, shops, offices and factories, or operate extra-legal buses and taxis. In fact, extra-legality is the norm and legality the exception. In Haiti, 68 percent of people in cities and 97 percent of people in the countryside live in housing with no clear title. In Egypt the numbers are 92 percent and 83 percent. "The result," de Soto writes, "is that most people's resources are commercially and financially invisible." Yet added up, the value of all the shanties and extra-legal houses dwarfs the value of the legal housing stock. We are not talking about a peripheral economy, but the *main* economy.

De Soto's team estimated that in developing and ex-communist countries, 85 percent of urban land, and around half of rural land, is "dead capital". Yet combined, it was worth an amount equal to all the companies listed on the main stock exchanges of the richest countries, and twenty times all Third World foreign direct investment. The images of poverty and hopelessness in developing countries seen in the media obscure the reality of just how much money is swashing around in them. Instead of giving, aiding, and loaning to the developing world, rich countries would be much more useful if they used their influence to facilitate formalization of already-existing assets.

The value of a system

For Adam Smith, capital was a quantity of labor, *fixed* in some asset that could be realized at a later date. Capital was not simply money, but the condensation of productivity. Marx also understood this immaterial nature of capital, noting that a table is a table, but once made it also becomes a commodity of value. Thus physical things have a double life: as the object they were designed to be; and as a *representation* of value. Yet Smith and Marx barely touched on the crucial, if mundane, fact that you can only have such value recognized if it is properly recorded, in a legal sense, for all to see.

Why have the rich countries not pointed out to other countries what is the most obvious basis of their wealth, a formal property system? The answer, de Soto says, is that the formalities of ownership seem so obvious to those who enjoy them that they are taken for granted, contained as they are within thousands of pieces of legislation and regulation. Yet it took a hundred years for the United States to create one formal and integrated national property system, recognized across all states. Germany had had property registries since the thirteenth century, but a truly national system did not happen until 1896. It took a huge effort, finally achieved around the turn of the twentieth century, to integrate Switzerland's various property registries in its cantons.

What formal, national property systems did was finish off the old closed, familial, and community property customs, and make a much bigger, standardized market in property that allowed for greater investment, because the potential returns were so much clearer. People's right to property was now protected by law, instead of being up to custom or local arrangements.

In the America of the early 1800s, squatting farmers fought for rights to the land they had taken up, and miners battled over claims, because the laws of ownership differed from town to town. Every nation passes a point, de Soto says, when "bandits", "hustlers" and "squatters" stop being demonized and become small entrepreneurs instead, with the same right to make property claims as the well-off. When this point is passed, wealth becomes distributed more evenly, because the majority, not just the elite, can generate capital from what they own.

There is a massive difference between a system in which only your neighbor can say for sure whether you own the land you are on, and one in which the land can be shown to be yours in some national register. It means that the fruits of your labor can be recognized, traded, sold, or used as collateral within a hugely bigger national network and market. More than technology or any other factor of production, de Soto writes, it was this that allowed for the growth of modern market and capitalist systems.

Crossing the bridge

The concept of ownership is at heart a social construct, de Soto says, built on a consensus between people about who owns what, and why. This informal social contract usually evolves independently of government, and often has more local legitimacy than regulations imposed from on high. Yet for ownership claims to become formal assets, you need a bridge that people can walk across from the existing sub-legal arrangements into formal ones. They will only cross if the other side preserves and enhances what is already socially recognized as theirs already.

Formalization of property rights creates an expanded market for builders, constructions firms, banks, and insurers, and allows utility companies to invest for the long term because they can supply power to officially registered addresses which are legally liable to pay bills. Governments can provide more targeted services to specific households, by creating databases to help decisions on healthcare and education provision, and collect taxes to pay for them. Overturning the myth that the extra-legal economy is about avoidance of tax and the government, de Soto found that most people actually want to become part of the system, because they know the benefits outweigh the costs. A wider distribution of formal property ownership makes people feel they are "co-sovereign" of the nation. Law and order increases, because formal ownership rights make you respect the rights of others more. It turns social instability into contented conservatism. This is a well-worn path that all rich countries have taken.

Final comments

De Soto's original question was why capitalism had not really worked in many developing and post-communist countries. His answer: people see capitalism as "a private club, a discriminatory system that benefits only the West and the elites who live inside the bell jars of poor countries." It is no use opening up your economy to foreign capital and multinationals if it creates a two-tier society in which the poor live in another world because they can't sell their assets beyond their immediate community.

De Soto's cause now has new impetus thanks to blockchain software, which promises to create infallible property rights inventories that can be run independent of government. It is also cheaper than obtaining government property deeds. Blockchain seems to confirm de Soto's point that property is a bottom-up construct that rests on social consensus, before it is subject to law or regulation.

Influenced by Milton Friedman and other free-market economists, de Soto's work has been charged with being ideologically driven, promoting the welfare of better-off extra-legal property owners at the expense of the genuinely poor, and disrupting often successful forms of collective and customary land use. De Soto's response, based on decades of fieldwork, is that people everywhere are much the same; they want to possess more formal capital, and see it as the key that unlocks a brighter future. In a 2016 *Fortune* article, de Soto noted that it is exactly such localized, customary arrangements that five billion of the world's people who don't hold proper legal title to what they own, are trying to transcend.

Hernando de Soto

De Soto was born in 1941 in Arequipa, Peru. His father was a diplomat, and following a military coup in 1948, moved his family to Europe. After attending the International School of Geneva, de Soto studied at its Graduate Institute of International Studies.

He was successful in the corporate world, but in 1979 returned to Peru. While managing a group of mining companies, de Soto set up the Institute for Liberty and Democracy. He advised Peru's president, Alberto Fujimori, on land reform, which led to the granting of land titles to cocoa farmers, starving the now defunct Shining Path terrorist movement of resources and support. He also advised Egypt's Hosni Mubarak, and has worked in Haiti, Mexico, El Salvador, and South Africa. In recent years he has argued that terrorism can be defeated by capitalism by instituting stronger property rights, and that the Arab Spring was fuelled by entrepreneurs frustrated by the inability to protect their capital. He has strongly criticized French economist Thomas Piketty, whose work on inequality he says has ignored the informal economy that powers most developing countries, and urged Pope Francis to put property rights at the center of his social justice agenda.

De Soto also wrote The Other Path: The Invisible Revolution in the Third World *(1986), now published as* The Other Path: The Economic Answer to Terrorism.

2016

The Euro

"It is hard for an economic federation to work if the different members of the federation have different views of the laws of economics—and there are fundamental differences in conceptions about how the economy works among the countries of the Eurozone that were present even at the time of the creation of the euro, but which were papered over."

"Many within Europe will be saddened by the death of the euro. This is not the end of the world: currencies come and go. The euro is just a 17-year-old experiment, poorly designed and engineered not to work. There is so much more to the European project, the vision of an integrated Europe, than a monetary arrangement . . . it is better to abandon the euro to save Europe and the European project."

In a nutshell

Currencies are meant to create independence and facilitate growth. For many European nations, the euro has achieved the opposite.

In a similar vein

Liaquat Ahamed *Lords of Finance*
Niall Ferguson *The Ascent of Money*
Thomas Piketty *Capital in the Twenty-First Century*
Michael E. Porter *The Competitive Advantage of Nations*
Dani Rodrik *The Globalization Paradox*

CHAPTER 47

Joseph Stiglitz

The project of "Europe" as a single political entity began modestly, out of the ashes of World War Two. In 1950, France's Minister of Foreign Affairs, Robert Schuman, who had been advised by French diplomat and political economist Jean Monnet, proposed that all French and German production of coal and steel come under a single authority. The European Coal and Steel Community, established two years later, was the first concrete step towards continental union, recognizing that peace and prosperity could not happen if the age-old military opponents, France and Germany, remained in opposition. Thus, right from the start, economic integration was used to advance the political agenda of a united Europe. In 1957, the Treaty of Rome established the European Economic Community involving France, Germany, Italy, Belgium, the Netherlands, and Luxembourg, declaring a determination "to lay the foundations of an ever closer union among the peoples of Europe." The United Kingdom would sign up only after a referendum in 1975, but the motivation was advantageous trading terms from joining the "Common Market" (the predecessor to today's Single Market), rather than enthusiasm for being part of a super-state in the making.

On paper, a single European currency seemed another sensible step towards "ever closer union," increasing economic performance and furthering political and social cohesion. The Maastricht Treaty of 1992 set out the path for the launch of a single currency, the "euro," but it was 2002 before actual euro notes and coins started circulating. In *The Euro: And its Threat to the Future of Europe*, Nobel Prize winning economist Joseph Stiglitz argues that, in contrast to the more cautious early days of the European Community, the move towards a single currency was a mistake: poorly thought out, hasty, and ideologically-driven.

Stiglitz is a well-known critic of laissez-faire globalization (*Globalization and its Discontents*, 2002) and wealth concentration (*The Great Divide*, 2015; *The Price of Inequality*, 2012), so it is fascinating that he would write a book that challenges the left-liberal consensus that the euro is a good thing. In his Introduction, Stiglitz likens himself to de Tocqueville, the Frenchman whose famous study of the United States was insightful precisely because he was an outsider.

Why should we care about the euro? With a population of 507 million,

Europe's economy is roughly the same size as that of the United States, so in a very globalized world its economic success matters—to everyone.

Flawed at birth

When the euro was launched, things seemed to go well. As expected, capital flowed from the richer, core members to the "peripheral" ones (including Spain, Greece, Portugal, and Ireland) and they grew rapidly because of plentiful loans at low interest rates. The vaunted equalizing effect was working. Unfortunately, it did not last. The same countries would later see equally quick withdrawals of capital and credit, and plunges into recession. Instead of the expected convergence came a transfer of capital and talented people to the rich, growing countries, who then had more resources to invest to increase their advantages. The periphery fell increasingly behind and into further debt. Rather than achieving political integration and prosperity, the euro has driven wedges through Europe: the rich North and the irresponsible South.

Why, then, did Europe voluntarily put on the straitjacket of the euro, a fixed currency which would inevitably make life tough for at least some of its members? The argument went that a united Europe would be more influential and powerful on the world stage, and to do this it should have a single currency, just as the United States does. But as Stiglitz notes, the American states may be very diverse in terms of wealth, population, and industry, but at least they have a common language and set of political institutions. Europe's linguistic and cultural barriers are much greater, and its political institutions much weaker and less "owned" by citizens. A person from South Dakota thinks of themselves as American first. Does a Frenchman think of himself as "European" first?

There was also an argument that closer economic integration, including a single currency, brings rising living standards, because producers are able to effect increasing economies of scale (it's cheaper to produce larger numbers of a product for a bigger market), and you get comparative advantage (countries focus on producing what they are relatively best at). But Europe already had free movement of goods, capital and labor through the European Union. Moreover, there is a fundamental mismatch between the EU's policy of "subsidiarity," which devolves powers and responsibilities to the member states as much as possible, and which means that the EU's budget is only 1 percent of the Eurozone's GDP (compared to the US central government's 20 percent of GDP)—and the push towards economic integration symbolized by the euro.

While the euro throws all states into the pot as if they are the same, there are yawning differences. For instance, the low-debt, low-deficit model that underpins the currency is a reflection of German attitudes to financial rectitude, particularly the horror of inflation, but it is perfectly legitimate for other countries to want to prioritize employment over inflation. Yet if you have a single currency and a central bank, how do you set interest rates: to prevent inflation at all costs, or to prevent unemployment at all costs? Different countries may also want varying exchange rates to control their balance of trade. A nation that imports more than it exports may want a lower-value currency in order to help its exporting industries prosper. Yet the centralization of monetary policy through the European Central Bank has meant that countries have to adhere to strict fiscal regimes (taxation and spending) and monetary policy, making it all but impossible to navigate their way out of recessions and financial crises.

The book is also an opportunity to for Stiglitz to lance the idea that markets, left to their own devices, are efficient. The experience of the Eurozone is the perfect case study of a situation in which markets, instead of moving towards equilibrium in the wake of economic dips and shocks, become more extreme. With financial liberalization and a single currency, its member countries have not converged economically through the power of markets; they have diverged. This is because free markets see money and resources flow to where the returns are greatest and safest, and unless proactive policies are adopted, there is little chance that poorer nations will be able to catch up. The euro was built on a belief in perfect markets, Stiglitz says, when it should have been based on market failures, imperfections, and the need for adjustments.

A dismal decade

The easiest way to consider the performance of the Eurozone, Stiglitz says, is to compare it to that of European countries that do not use the euro. In 2015, the non-Eurozone had grown by 8.1 percent since 2007, compared to growth of only *0.6 percent* in the Eurozone. And this excludes the growth of non-euro Poland (28 percent) and Romania (12 percent). In the same 2007–2015 period, the United States grew by 10 percent. The GDP of eleven Eurozone countries is still not back to 2007 levels, before the euro crisis hit, and in several countries, such as Greece, the crisis has been worse than the Great Depression.

Germany has been the "star" in the Eurozone, but even it has had growth of only 0.8 percent a year since 2007; hardly stellar compared to the rest of the world, and even that very modest growth has not been evenly shared. From 1992 to 2010 the proportion of income going to the top 1 percent in Germany increased by 24 percent, and incomes for large sections of the population has been stagnant in the last 10 years.

The euro has seen the weaker countries in the eurozone become weaker, and the stronger countries stronger. Inequality has also increased within countries. How? High unemployment hurts those most at the bottom of the economic pile by creating households with no wage-earner, and those who are earning see their income fall due to downward pressure on salaries. The euro's limitations on economic growth have also led to government austerity programs which hurt the existing poor and middle-income people the most. This wonderful single currency, designed to turbocharge European markets, and increase wealth and social mobility, achieved the opposite, helping to fuel the rise of far-right and xenophobic parties.

The need to preserve organizational, human, and social capital provides a compelling case for countercyclical economic policy which can keep an economy moving, keep people in jobs and companies afloat. What has actually happened in Greece is the destruction of such capital thanks to austerity measures, forced upon it by the "troika" of the International Monetary Fund, the European Central Bank and the European Commission. It became more important to stick to a certain debt or deficit level, in order to stay a member of the Eurozone, than it was to preserve jobs, companies, and communities. If such desperate choices must arise, Stiglitz asks, what really is the point of the euro? Such dilemmas are reminiscent of those faced by countries in the 1920s and 1930s deciding whether to reduce unemployment or to face the ignominy of coming off the Gold Standard.

Nothing conveys the terrible weakness of Europe's economy, Stiglitz says, as the way small improvements are trumpeted as the signs of recovery. When Spain's unemployment rate fell, in 2016, to 20 percent (from 26 percent in 2013), was it really cause for celebration, particularly given that so many young Spaniards have left the country looking for work elsewhere? Spain's GDP remains over 5 percent less than what it was in 2007, and if the euro stays unreformed there is little scope for the poorer nations to grow more quickly. Europe's lost decade could well turn into its lost quarter-century.

Fixing the euro . . . and the alternatives

The euro was a mistake, Stiglitz says, but "The European project is too important to be destroyed by the euro." He offers intriguing alternatives to the currency—either reform of the institutions that govern the Eurozone, or a move back to national sovereignty over monetary and fiscal powers. Either more Europe, or less, but not the failed halfway house of the present, in which countries have the appearance of being sovereign, but in the economic areas where it matters most, are not.

Stiglitz proposes a set of modest structural reforms, such as a full banking union, a bank deposit security scheme and the mutualization of debt, that could bring the convergence of economies that the euro promised on but did not deliver, and which would increase solidarity. But there is a catch: most of them would involve some diminution of national power and sovereignty, so could be politically difficult. The possible ways forward:

- Muddling through: "doing the minimum to keep the Eurozone together but not enough to restore it to prosperity."
- Divorce: not reversion to a patchwork of 19 different currencies, but a transition to two, three, or four currency blocks—for instance, a smaller Eurozone including countries that have a lot of economic and political similarity, or having two Eurozones, North and South.
- A "flexible euro," in which each country has its own form of euro that takes account of national differences and priorities.

Divorce is actually a sound option, Stiglitz says, that could be achieved without high costs and even have benefits, certainly with lower economic costs than muddling through. It would be much better for Greece, which has been poorly treated by European bodies and Germany, giving it back full democracy. Greece could issue a new electronic currency, the "Greek-euro," which would be lower in value than the euro, to correct trade imbalances and make its economy stronger. As well as making it more attractive to tourists, Greece could become the "Sunbelt of Europe," attracting retirees and businesses that are electronically based and could be located anywhere.

Another option is simply for Germany (and some other rich, Northern countries) to leave the euro. The resulting lower value of the euro would restore many countries' trade imbalances without them having to resort to recessions or the suppression of imports. Meanwhile, Germany's trade surplus would be pared back and it would have to use other measures to stimulate its economy, like increasing wages and government spending.

Final comments

The story of the euro provides a lesson for all time: seeking economic integration before there is real political integration is always a mistake. The single currency was driven into being on the assumption that just because you have freer movement of goods and services across borders, all the countries involved will automatically benefit. Yet as these countries were very unequal in the first place, the absence of some trade barriers and national protections actually made them more vulnerable than before.

One former EU Council president called British PM David Cameron's decision to have the Brexit vote as "the worse policy decision in decades." In Stiglitz's mind, such views only confirm the antipathy towards democracy amongst EU elites. At nearly every opportunity in the last 15 years, when they have had the chance, Europe's voters have rejected the euro, the European Union, and the European constitution. For Stiglitz, the Brexit vote was the outcome of an ideological agenda which had put financial interests and trade liberalization above the interests of citizens and workers. Inspired by Brexit, the Visegrád countries (the Czech Republic, Hungary, Poland, and Slovakia) may yet form a breakaway faction within the EU that rejects ever closer union and insists on the importance of national and cultural identity. Meantime, the elites of Germany, France, Italy, Sweden (and large sections of their electorates, it must be said) are committed to the idea of a liberal Europe. It would be a tragedy if, in the end, the only thing uniting EU member states was a currency.

Roger Bootle's *The Trouble With Europe* carries many of the same arguments as Stiglitz's book, but from a British perspective. Both are required reading if you still believe in the "European project," but question the very institutions that have created it.

Joseph E. Stiglitz

Stiglitz was born in 1943 in Gary, Indiana. He attended Amherst College, and obtained his PhD in economics at the Massachusetts Institute of Technology. After a four-year stint as a research fellow at the University of Cambridge, he began a teaching and research career that included periods at Yale, Princeton, Oxford, and Stanford universities. Since 2001 he has been a professor at Columbia University in New York, and is chief economist at a think tank, the Roosevelt Institute.

Stiglitz was on President Clinton's Council of Economic Advisers in the 1990s, before becoming Chief Economist at the World Bank. He was awarded the Nobel Prize in Economics in 2001 along with George Akerlof and Michael Spence for their work on markets with asymmetric information. He has been an adviser to several European centrist and center-left parties and governments.

Books include Globalization and Its Discontents *(2002),* Making Globalization Work *(2006),* The Three Trillion Dollar War *(2008, on Iraq),* The Price of Inequality *(2012), and* The Great Divide: Unequal Societies and What We Can Do About Them *(2015).*

2015

Misbehaving: The Making of Behavioral Economics

"There is, however, a problem: the premises on which economic theory rests are flawed. First, the optimization problems that ordinary people confront are often too hard for them to solve, or even come close to solving. Even a decent-sized grocery store offers a shopper millions of combinations of items that are within the family's budget. Does the family really choose the best one? And, of course, we face many much harder problems than a trip to the store, such as choosing a career, mortgage, or spouse. Given the failure rates we observe in all of these domains, it would be hard to defend the view that all such choices are optimal."

In a nutshell

"Homo economicus," or rational man, is quite a different species to *homo sapiens*, which often seems to make decisions that seem to go against its own interests.

In a similar vein

Steven Levitt & Stephen J. Dubner *Freakonomics*
Michael Lewis *The Big Short*
Thomas Schelling *Micromotives and Macrobehavior*
Robert Shiller *Irrational Exuberance*

CHAPTER 48

Richard Thaler

When Richard Thaler was a young economics professor, he would give exams in the usual way, marked out of 100. The average grade would be 72 percent, which was a bit lower than the students were used to, and they complained vigorously that the exams were too hard. Wanting to keep his job and stop the complaining, Thaler had a brainwave: he made subsequent exams not out of 100, but out of 137. Why this odd number? It meant that the average mark would now be in the 90s. The change had a dramatic effect: complaints not only stopped, but most people were delighted with their grades, even though, when converted into a percentage out of 100, their grades were exactly the same as before.

The fact that you could make smart people a lot happier by changing the total marking score, even if it didn't change their A, B, C, or D grades, went against everything that orthodox economics taught about human beings being rational. It was not that people were stupid, Thaler says, but simply *human*. The economics discipline, and its models, was based on a fictional creature—*homo economicus*, or what Thaler calls the "Econ." Whereas Econs always act rationally, Humans "misbehave," and this misbehavior, or departure from the models, has a major implication: economists' predictions would come out wrong. For instance, not only did hardly any economists foresee the 2007–08 financial crisis, but their models told them it *couldn't* happen. Unfortunately, in the making of public policy economists hold a very privileged position, their theories taken much more seriously than those of practitioners of other social sciences.

The economist Orley Ashenfelter called Thaler's research "wackonomics," because it seemed to be the economics of triviality. Yet just as the exposition of small anomalies can end up overturning whole paradigms of belief (see Thomas Kuhn in *50 Philosophy Classics*), Thaler's observations of human foible and irrationality exposed the rigid "theory blindness" of economics. *Misbehaving*, with its frequently amusing character vignettes of the key players in the making of behavioral economics, tells the story of that exposure. Thaler's Damascene moment was the discovery, in the 1970s, of an article by Daniel Kahneman and Amos Tversky, two Israeli psychologists investigating the limits of human rationality. At that time there wasn't much communication between the worlds of economics and psychology, but Thaler went to some lengths to befriend the pair and work with them.

While Kahneman went on to become "the greatest living psychologist" (see *50 Psychology Classics*; Tversky died in 1996) Thaler's research, building on some of their insights, made him a seminal figure in behavioral economics. He prefaces the book with a 1906 quote from Vilfredo Pareto, the Italian economist:

> *"The foundation of political economy and, in general, of every social science, is evidently psychology. A day may come when we shall be able to deduce the laws of social science from the principles of psychology."*

The world of academia being what it is, economics and psychology remain silos with their own preoccupations and outlooks, but economics has arguably gained the most from the cross-fertilization.

Just human

Early in his career, Thaler started a list of situations (drawn from his own life and people he knew) in which people's actions contradicted what rational choice theory would suggest, such as:

- A man likes a cashmere sweater in a store, but doesn't buy it because he can't justify the expense to himself. But when, at Christmas, his wife gifts him the same sweater, he is delighted. He and his wife pool all their finances, and neither have any separate sources of money.
- I am willing to drive an extra ten minutes down the road to save $10 buying a $45 clock radio, but when the chance comes to save $10 when buying a $495 television set, I don't bother going to the other store. Why, when $10 is $10?
- Thaler was having a dinner party for some young economists, and noticed that a bowl of cashew nuts he had put out at the start was quickly being gobbled up. Fearing that the food to follow would be left uneaten, he promptly removed the bowl of cashews. The guests thanked him.

Conventional economics has it that people like as many options as possible, so why were the guests pleased when Thaler removed the cashew bowl? Economists don't see that humans have a problem with willpower. Because we are weak, we will *purposely* restrict our options. Adam Smith foreshadowed the self-control problem in *The Theory of Moral Sentiments*: "The pleasure which we are to enjoy ten years hence, interests us so little in comparison with that which we may enjoy today."

The economist Franco Modigliani came up with the "life-cycle hypothesis," according to which people work out how much money they are likely to earn over a lifetime, and working back from that how much they should spend in each period of their life. When Thaler explained the theory to an audience of psychologists, they laughed. How many people would do that in real life? The models of economists like Modigliani assume that people are very smart, very self-disciplined, and look far into the future. Behavioral economists like Thaler assume people are myopic, that present enjoyment matters more than some delayed benefit, and that they don't think too much about decades ahead. Economics assumes there is one, unitary self, yet psychology has for a long time been open to there being many selves—or at least loci of control, from Freud's id and ego, to Kahneman's "fast" and "slow" thinking—within us, and that frequently these selves conflict each other.

Weird ways we value

Thaler's life changed, he says, after reading Kahneman and Tversky's 1974 *Science* paper, "Judgment Under Certainty: Heuristics and Biases." The paper's basic argument was that because people have only limited brainpower, they use simple rules of thumb—"heuristics"—to help them make judgments and come to decisions. For instance, if someone asked an American if Dhruv was a common name, they would likely say "No," because they don't know anyone called Dhruv. But Dhruv happens to be a common name in India, and given the large population of India there are likely to be many more Dhruvs in the world than Grahams or Barrys. Because of the way humans think, we make *predictable errors*. This was a big idea for Thaler, because the economics discipline assumed that the errors in thinking people made were unique to them, but that in the main behavior and markets were rational.

"Economists get in trouble," Thaler writes, "when they make a highly specific prediction that depends explicitly on everyone being economically sophisticated." For example, if scientists find that farmers would be better off using less fertilizer, economists assume that the best policy is to just make the information and research available, and farmers will—in their own interests—follow the advice. Yet this takes no account of the fact that many farmers will continue existing practices simply because that's the way they've always done things. Another example: if as a government you wanted to get people to invest more in their pension plans, all you should do is provide the information on how beneficial it is to them to save now to have a nest egg in the future. But this could in fact be an irresponsible approach, since people have a well-known bias in favor of the present over the future, and unless they are "nudged" (by, for instance, making sizeable pension contributions the default option when starting a new job) or pushed, they won't save enough for their future.

Thaler was struck by another of Kahneman and Tversky's findings that what mattered to people was not so much the absolute level of wealth, but its relative utility, or more specifically, *changes* in wealth. People are not rational in that they hate losses more than they like gains. This aversion to loss sometimes makes us make bad decisions, such as unwillingness to sell a stock that has never performed well, when rationality would suggest cutting our losses and buying something more promising. Thaler coined the term "endowment effect" to explain the fact that people value what they already have (their endowment) more than they value what might become theirs in the future.

Mental accounting

Thaler's research increasingly fell into an area he called "mental accounting," or the way we think about money and wealth that differs from what rationality would suggest.

When we have outstanding credit card bills, or loans, it makes sense for us to dip into our savings to pay off the loans, since the borrowings will be at a much higher interest rate than the rate we get for savings. But people have very rigid mental categories like "rent," "bills," and "savings," and don't seem to remember that money is fungible (meaning money is money, and can be put to any use). This irrationality is highlighted by our gambling habits. The money we lose at the blackjack table is "our" money, while the money we win is the "house's money," and so is less valued. We are desperate to break even in order to preserve our money, but happy to gamble away whatever wins we have made on the night. But doesn't money won at the casino buy the same things as money earned through work?

According to economists, money we have already put into something that can't be recovered is a "sunk cost." Whether we gain something or not from the payment or investment is irrelevant; it's now in the financial past. But this isn't how real people think. Thaler gives the example of "Vince," who had paid $1000 for a season's membership of an indoor tennis club. After a couple of months into the membership he developed tennis elbow, but kept playing for another three months *even though it was painful*, because he didn't want to "waste" his membership. What economists call the "sunk cost fallacy" has more serious effects. Some believe the United States continued the war in Vietnam because it had invested so much money and people in it that it would be terrible for it all to be "for nothing." Companies like Costco and Amazon exploit our vulnerability to the sunk cost fallacy by getting us to join up as a member. Paying $99 a year for "Prime" membership is likely to make us use Amazon even more, because we will feel like we "have to get our money's worth."

Thaler also discusses his research into consumer psychology. Supermarket strategies of "everyday low prices" tend to fail, he notes, because we love to feel we are getting bargains through sale prices or the use of coupons, rather than the more boring saving of a few pennies on every item we buy. This is "transaction utility" in its essence. We need to feel a reward when we buy something to make us feel smart or lucky. Even retailers who have an everyday low prices strategy make sure they provide lots of transaction utility in other ways, such as offering rebates, low interest options, or refunds of money when goods bought were found to have been cheaper elsewhere. There is a reason even rich people shop at Walmart and Costco: because every human being "gets a kick from transactional utility," even if on a rational basis the gains can be misleading.

Nudges towards optimality

Economics has been built on the idea that people, left free from government meddling, make the best choices about their lives and resources. But do people *choose* to be obese, for instance, or is obesity influenced by the environment around us, including fast food places on every street? Studies show a tendency for people to stick with the default option, from mobile phone settings to employer retirement plans. The power of inertia is great, but this has a flipside: policy makers can use inertia to bring about positive outcomes for both individual and society.

History is full of movements and governments that have wanted to exercise control over other people's choices "for their own good"—with awful consequences. Thaler is sensitive to such charges, and explains his thinking as "libertarian paternalism." Governments already offer incentives to people in order to achieve certain policy aims, but incentives do not always work. A combination of incentives and apparently irrelevant "nudges," such as presenting to new employees a favored option (bigger, rather than smaller pension contributions) as first on the list of choices, can lessen the negative effects of our natural cognitive biases, such as overvaluing pleasure today at the expense of happiness when we are older. Thaler is suggesting an approach which assumes that, if the same people had more information, they might choose otherwise.

Thaler's ideas caught the attention of policy wonks in Britain, where a

Behavioral Insights Team, which was immediately dubbed the "Nudge Unit," was set up under the government of David Cameron in 2010. The unit had to justify its existence by helping departments introduce measures that would save the government ten times the cost of setting up the unit. One of its first trials involved telling people owing tax money that the "great majority" of other people had paid their taxes on time, and that "you are one of the very small minority" who has not. It led to a five percent increase in people paying up within a certain period, amounting to £9 million. Not bad for one line in a letter. In other instances, text messages to people owing court fines led to a dramatic increase in payment, and a new default setting on driver licensing forms has led to an increase in the supply of organs for life-saving transplants.

Having demonstrated its success, Britain's nudge unit was privatized and now sells its services to UK public bodies. There is an equivalent nudge unit within the New South Wales government, and a Social and Behavioral Sciences Team in the White House. Over 130 countries now apply some form of behavioral science to public policy.

Final comments

Thaler devotes two chapters in the book to the impact of behavioral economics on finance (for more on this area, read the commentary on his colleague Robert Shiller's *Irrational Exuberance*), which is extensive. For several years he wrote a quarterly column, "Anomalies" in *The Journal of Economic Perspectives*, pointing out the research showing, for instance, the "calendar" effects in the stock market (stocks tend to go up on Fridays and down on Mondays, on the days before holidays, and in January). The column was read much more widely than most academic articles, and brought Thaler some renown. But after 14 columns it was discontinued, the new editor feeling that readers had had enough of anomalies.

As a keen reader of Thomas Kuhn's *Structure of Scientific Revolutions*, however, Thaler was inspired to keep pointing out anomalies. He didn't dream that bringing a psychological approach to economics could cause a Kuhnian revolution, but ultimately it has. Behavioral economics is no longer "wackonomics" but a serious sub-field of the discipline, forcing purely rational models onto the defensive. Yet when the time comes that all economists can incorporate behavioral aspects into their work, Thaler notes, "behavioral economics" as a field need no longer exist, since "all economics will be as behavioral as it needs to be."

Richard Thaler

Thaler was born in 1945. After a BA degree from Case Western Reserve University, in 1974 he obtained his economics PhD at the University of Rochester. He is currently Professor of Behavioral Science and Economics at the Booth School of Business, University of Chicago.

He is also the author of The Winner's Curse: Paradoxes and Anomalies of Everyday Life *(1992),* Advances in Behavioral Finance *(Vols 1 & 2, 1993 and 2005), and with Cass Sunstein,* Nudge: Improving Decisions About Health, Wealth, and Happiness *(2008).*

Thaler had a cameo role playing himself in the 2015 film The Big Short, *in which he demonstrates at a casino gambling table the "hot-hand fallacy" (the belief that winning streaks are possible, beyond what randomness would predict).*

1899

The Theory of the Leisure Class

"Abstention from labour is the conventional evidence of wealth and is therefore the conventional mark of social standing; and this insistence on the meritoriousness of wealth leads to a more strenuous insistence on leisure."

"The existence, function, and practice of religion in a socially-stratified society, is a form of abstract conspicuous consumption for and among the members of the person's community, of devotion to the value system that justifies the existence of his or her social class. As such, attending church services, participating in religious rites, and paying tithes, are a form of conspicuous leisure."

In a nutshell

Societies are wholly driven by emulation and the need for status. The more resources we have the means to consume, the greater our social esteem.

In a similar vein

Deirdre McCloskey *Bourgeois Equality*
Richard Thaler *Misbehaving: The Making of Behavioral Economics*
Max Weber *The Protestant Ethic and the Spirit of Capitalism*

CHAPTER 49

Thorstein Veblen

Why do we work longer hours, seek better jobs and build businesses? American economic sociologist Thorstein Veblen believed it was because of social aspirations that had little to do with mere survival. In contrast to his countrymen's belief that their culture represented the height of noble individualism, Veblen believed that modern American society was basically of the "barbarian type." Barbarian peoples, he wrote in *The Theory of the Leisure Class*, have "a well-developed predatory scheme of life and . . . a lively sense of status."

Veblen contrasted consumerist America with the prudent, frugal nature of his Norwegian farming background, and wondered where this drive for excess originated. He concluded that modern America was no different from past civilizations in the way the masses naturally sought to emulate the class that did not work. The instinct of this "leisure class" for winning, showing off, and worldly pursuits is always peculiar to the class at first, but its materialist, status-seeking outlook becomes characteristic of society at large. The consumer culture we know today arose from millions of people mimicking what they believed were the styles and habits of the rich. Veblen gave us the term "conspicuous consumption," which he describes as a "higher or spiritual need" as demanding as food and shelter.

Understandably, such reductionism offended American readers, but *The Theory of the Leisure Class* was a hit. Veblen saw his book as a work of economics which employed sociological observation, and his daring to see capitalism as very much driven by pride and envy contradicted the rationality underpinning classical economics.

The style of the book is long-winded and discursive, with a complete absence of figures and facts, but it is a fascinating read.

Look, I'm not working: conspicuous leisure

Since ancient times, Veblen notes, physical labor had been seen as antithetical to higher thought, while a life of leisure was "beautiful and ennobling in all civilized men's eyes." "Leisure" does not mean indolence, but simply "non-productive consumption of time." A person of leisure may be very busy, but his activities are not carried out with the purpose of subsistence or financial gain. His achievements are likely to be of the immaterial kind, such as knowledge of art, history, or music, or at the other extreme skill in hunting, war, or sports. The positions in human society that have always been most esteemed are those which give the possessor the ability to use overwhelming force or violence, to take life whether animal or human. In times past the higher classes engaged in war and took the spoils of war from their victories, and this form of gain was esteemed much more than the fruits of productive industry and work. The same applied to hunting, which demonstrates skills and prowess, as opposed to the hard work of animal husbandry which is about producing food for survival.

Manners, Veblen says, are so important to the leisured class because they show that years of training have gone into learning them, which lesser types would have had to spend on earning a living. "Good breeding requires time, application and expense," he writes, and "the abiding test of good breeding is the requirement of a substantial and patent waste of time."

I am what I can buy: conspicuous consumption

Veblen observes that the consumption of "the best" in terms of food, drink, clothing, shelter, transport and so on is a sign of wealth, and therefore an honorific. Knowledge of "the best" indicates that time has been spent cultivating good taste, when others were having to work. Costly present-giving and entertainments are another key aspect of "conspicuous consumption," showing that the giver can afford to lavish money and energy on such trifles. Entertaining is never a spontaneous act but part of one's obligations in being a member of a certain class, and a chance to demonstrate skills of etiquette which are shorthand for wealth. The number of people economically dependent on one is also a key signifier of wealth and standing. A key indicator of status is the possession of a wife who does not have to work. Indeed, a husband may work his socks off to achieve the distinction of having a wife who devotes her days to fashionable charities, involvement with arts bodies, and the children's private school. This ornamental wife becomes "the ceremonial consumer of goods which he produces," and her making of a beautiful home, its size and furnishings being well beyond what the family actually needs, will be evidence of what Veblen calls "the law of wasted effort": the greater the unnecessary use of resources, the higher the status.

In earlier stages of society, Veblen notes, conspicuous leisure is the best sign of the possession of wealth, while in later stages it is the conspicuous consumption of goods. This is because, in the modern economic age, an individual is exposed to many more people who do not know him or know of his family, so the simplest way to judge his reputation is by noting the extent of unnecessary goods and resources he displays. Through our clothes, cars, holidays, entertainments, and houses, we are communicating to others all the time without speaking. Veblen compares a city family to a farming family. While they may be of similar wealth, the city family has to spend more on clothes to indicate their social standing, and do so "on pain of losing caste." The country family's repute may rest on things such as their level of home comforts and savings in the bank, which, being in a smaller community, becomes easily known. In this community, savings give "more bang for your buck" in social terms, whereas in the city, no one knows your true financial situation, but they can see you are well-dressed and eat in nice restaurants.

People spend money less according to their needs than to manifest what they believe is their rightful station in life. We prefer to have fewer children so as to maintain a higher standard of living, than to have more and yet be unable to live according to the standards of the class we believe we are part of. One of Veblen's cutting observations is that the class of people involved in "scholarly pursuits" (academics, journalists, clergy and so on) consider themselves of a certain elevated status, yet they usually do not earn as much as others with whom they mix. As a result, they must spend a greater proportion of their income on conspicuous consumption (private school fees, overseas holidays) to show they are above other strata of society, even if this display is maintained with some difficulty.

The meaning of goods and fashion

Veblen observes that machine-made products are usually a better fit between form and function than hand-made goods—they have to be, to justify the making of millions of copies. Yet we revere anything hand-made, even if it is less efficient to use, and has visible imperfections, because we feel it marks us out from the rest. The "return to craftsmanship" that John Ruskin and William Morris celebrated was actually a return to those who could afford the inefficiency of hand-made goods, and who had the money to turn up their noses at things which were affordable to everyone. What is "wasteful," that is, indicating wealth, changes with time. In an age when even luxuries are mass-produced, and so cheaper, the genuinely rich must have things made bespoke by the best designers and craftspeople. It is not the utility of the object that matters, but its uniqueness.

"Our dress," Veblen writes, "in order to serve its purpose effectually, should not only be expensive, but it should also make plain to all observers that the wearer is not engaged in any kind of productive labor." Extravagant dresses, top hats, and highly polished shoes, all indicate the lack of any need to make or produce things for a living. For women, cumbersome long dresses that restrict movement demonstrate that the lady is unsuitable for any kind of work, as does unnecessarily long hair. The sociological purpose of fashion is to demonstrate that we can afford to throw away last year's look and buy a new look, even if the old clothes are still perfectly good. If you find it impossible to imagine a world without fashion, you begin to understand how consumption for status is a *need* that drives society.

Setting the standard: the economic sociology of education and religion

In a chapter on education, Veblen observes that traditional areas of learning are more prestigious than purely functional subjects. For instance, knowledge of the classics shows that one has had the means to study things that have no practical or pecuniary benefit. As no one speaks Latin or Ancient Greek now, the ability to quote Latin instantly shows you are of a higher order. Veblen observes that endowing chairs and universities remains a favorite way for the newly rich to gain esteem, because it links the donor to the best and finest in humanity. Even if there may be better options in terms of actual learning, we want our children to go to an Ivy League or Oxbridge university because of their leisure class connotations. Attending them, one does not just get an education, it is thought, but is given the key to a social world.

Veblen shocked readers by stating that religion was merely "a form of abstract conspicuous consumption," the style of one's religious practice serving to confirm one's class. Attendance at church and paying tithes were a form of conspicuous leisure. He further argued that the "consumption of ceremonial paraphernalia . . . in the way of shrines, temples, churches, vestments, sacrifices, sacraments, holiday attire, etc.," because it serves no material purpose, is a prime example of "conspicuous waste." The donor of funds to build a church could not only feel he was doing something for the community, but the largesse proved that his family was at the top of the social mountain.

Final comments

Though the leisure class was worth studying, in Veblen's mind, because it set the standard for the rest of society, he also admits that we may be less influenced by those several classes above us, or people well below us in the social strata, than those slightly above. This has been borne out by psychological studies in the last 30 years, which suggest that, in terms of happiness, it is not our absolute wealth that matters as much as how wealthy we are in relation to our friends, neighbors, or co-workers. If we are not just keeping up with the Joneses, but doing better than them, we feel good. This desire for status seems hardwired into us. Veblen, who grew up on a farm, noted how status on the land was measured differently than in the city. A large acreage could be defended on the grounds of efficiency and productivity, when in fact it conferred great social status because everyone knew that, at any time, the land could be sold and its owners could sell up and live in luxury.

In an age of environmental worries and care over resource use, flashy displays of wealth are sometimes frowned upon, yet the human desire for status is timeless, continuing to be the driver and shaper of economies.

Thorstein Veblen

Veblen was born in 1857, and grew up on a farm in Wisconsin, with eleven siblings and his Norwegian immigrant parents. The family prospered enough to send Veblen to Carleton College in Minnesota. After graduating in 1880 he studied philosophy under Charles Sanders Peirce at Johns Hopkins University, then did his PhD in philosophy at Yale University.

After Yale, Veblen was unable to find an academic post (he was a declared agnostic at a time when there were close links between churches and universities), and went back to living on the family farm for several years. In 1891 he took up graduate studies in economics at Cornell University, before becoming a teaching fellow at the University of Chicago. The success of The Theory of the Leisure Class *led to an assistant professorship at Stanford University, but his controversial views and affairs with women made him unpopular, and he had to resign. After a few years teaching economics at the University of Missouri, Veblen began working in Washington DC on post-World War One peace settlement plans.*

In 1919, Veblen worked with other academics to set up the progressive New School for Social Research, and was closely involved until 1926. He died in California in 1929. Other writings include The Theory of Business Enterprise *(1904),* The Instincts of Workmanship and the State of the Industrial Arts *(1914), and* Imperial Germany and the Industrial Revolution *(1915).*

1904

The Protestant Ethic and the Spirit of Capitalism

"Unlimited greed for gain is not in the least identical with capitalism, and is still less its spirit . . . But capitalism is identical with the pursuit of profit, and forever renewed profit, by means of continuous, rational, capitalistic enterprise."

"He avoids ostentation and unnecessary expenditure, as well as conscious enjoyment of his power, and is embarrassed by the outward signs of the social recognition which he receives . . . He gets nothing out of his wealth for himself, except the irrational sense of having done his job well."

In a nutshell

The spirit of capitalism is not greed and consumption, but the creation of order and the best use of resources. For those with a "calling", there is no problem in reconciling the spiritual and economic aspects of life.

In a similar vein

Peter Drucker *Innovation and Entrepreneurship*
Adam Smith *The Wealth of Nations*
Thorstein Veblen *The Theory of the Leisure Class*

CHAPTER 50

Max Weber

Sociologist Max Weber was fascinated by the influence of thoughts and beliefs in history, and particularly in why religion seemed to be a significant factor in determining levels of wealth.

Weber noticed that in the Germany of his time, the business leaders and owners of capital, not to mention the bulk of more highly-skilled workers and managers, were Protestant. Protestants also had higher levels of educational achievement than Catholics. The conventional explanation was that, in the sixteenth and seventeenth centuries, particular towns and regions in Germany had thrown off the rule of the Catholic church, and in the sudden freedom from a repressive regime controlling every aspect of their lives, they were able to pursue their economic interests and become prosperous.

In fact, Weber notes, it was the very laxness of the Church in terms of moral and societal rules that turned the bourgeois middle classes against it. These burghers actually *welcomed* a tyranny of Protestant control that would tightly regulate their attitudes and behavior. Weber's question was, *why* did the richer classes in Germany, the Netherlands, Geneva, and Scotland, and also the groups that became the American Puritans, want to move in this direction? Surely freedom and prosperity comes with less, not more, religious control?

The capitalist spirit

At the outset of this famous but short book, Weber admits that discussing the "spirit" of capitalism seems pretentious. Forms of capitalism had, after all, existed in China, India, Babylon, and the classical world, and they had had no special ethos driving them aside from trade and exchange.

It was only with the emergence of modern capitalism, he suggests, that a certain ethic grew linking moral righteousness with making money. It was not just that Protestants sought wealth more purposefully than Catholics, but that Protestants showed "a special tendency to develop economic rationalism," that is, a particular approach to creating wealth that was less focused on the gain of comfort than on *the pursuit of profit itself*. The particular satisfaction was not in the money extracted to buy things (which had always driven money-making in the past), but in "wealth creation" based on increased productivity and better use of resources. Long after all needs had been met, the capitalist did not rest, forever seeking greater profit for its own sake and as the symbol of more profound ends.

Weber had studied non-Christian religions and their relationship to economics. He observed that Hinduism's caste system, for instance, would always be a big obstacle to the development of capitalism because people were not free to be professionally or socially mobile. The Hindu spiritual ethic was to *transcend* the world, an outlook not dissimilar to Catholicism's creation of monasteries and convents to remove the holy people from the sins and temptations of the world outside. The Protestant ethic, in contrast, involved living with your eyes on God but fully *in* the world.

The expression of spiritual energies through work and business obviously gave its believers tremendous economic advantage. Instead of being told that business was an inferior quest compared to the holy life, one could be holy *through* one's work. Capitalistic enterprise was transformed from being simply a system of economic organization, to a domain of life infused with God.

The Protestant difference

Weber is careful not to say that there was anything intrinsically better about the theology of Protestantism. Rather, the general outlook on life and work that the early Protestant sects—Calvinists, Methodists, Pietists, Baptists, Quakers—drew from their beliefs made them singularly well adapted to modern capitalism. They brought to it:

- A spirit of progress.
- A love of hard work for its own sake.
- Orderliness, punctuality, and honesty.
- Hatred of time-wasting through socializing, idle talk, sleep, sex, or luxury (expressed in the sentiment, "every hour lost is lost to labor for the glory of God").
- The absolute control of self (emotions and body) and an aversion to spontaneous enjoyment.
- Attention to the most productive use of resources, represented by profit. ("You may labor to be rich for God, though not for the flesh and sin," said Calvinist Richard Baxter).
- Belief in calling, or "proving one's faith in worldly activity."

Many Calvinist writers had the same contempt for wealth that the Catholic ascetics did, but when you looked more closely at their writings, Weber noted, their contempt was for the enjoyment of wealth and the physical temptations that came with it. Constant activity could drive out such temptations, therefore work could be made holy. If it was where your spiritual energies could be expressed, then work could be your salvation.

Thus, the peculiar nature of the early Protestant capitalists emerged: famously focused on their business, and as a result highly successful—yet going to great lengths not to enjoy its fruit. Catholicism had always had a degree of guilt about business and money making, but unrestricted by a bad conscience the Puritan sects became known as reliable, trustworthy and eager to please in their business dealings. This combination of "intense piety with business acumen," as Weber describes it, became the cornerstone of many great fortunes.

Calling and capitalism

Weber argues that the idea of "calling" only came in with the Protestant Reformation. Martin Luther had discussed it, but it took the Puritan sects to make it central to their way of life. Calling was related to Protestant theologian Calvin's idea of "predestination"—that you did not know while you were alive whether you were one of God's "elect", that is, whether you would live in eternity or be eternally damned. Therefore, you had to *appear* to be one of the elect, and this meant leading a spotless, well-ordered life of extreme self-control. If you were successful in your work, it was a sign that you were one of the chosen.

This irrational, spiritual concept of calling ironically gave rise to a very rational brand of economic activity. Two of its notable effects were the self-limiting of consumption and the "ascetic compulsion to save." As Weber puts it: "Man is only a trustee of the goods which have come to him through God's grace. He must, like the servant in the parable, give an account of every penny entrusted to him, and it is at least hazardous to spend any of it for a purpose which does not serve the glory of God but only one's enjoyment." The outcome was that capital was freed up for systematic investment, making the rich even richer.

Final comments

Today we criticize ourselves for being a consumerist society, buying and using instead of saving and creating. Weber is worth reading to be reminded that capitalism is not actually about a mad rush to spend and consume, but about the creation of wealth through good use of resources.

Yet Weber also noted that the modern capitalistic system was losing its religious impulse. If you had a calling, it was a meaningful system which could release all your potential. If you did not, it could seem soulless and even oppressive. There is always a gulf between people who are little concerned with the nature of the work they do as long as it brings in the money and gives them some social standing, and those who must feel that their work is inherently meaningful. With a calling, Weber told us, there is no problem at all in squaring up the spiritual and economic aspects of life.

The Protestant Ethic showed how character traits, strongly shaped by religion, could play a massive role in the creation of wealth. Yet these traits, as outlined above, do not necessarily depend on a certain religion for their flowering, and can be witnessed the world over where economies have taken off. The Asian economies that have had such a spectacular economic rise over the last thirty years have only minor Protestant populations—but their industrious, conscientious citizens have much in common with the dutiful and self-denying burghers of seventeenth-century Germany.

Max Weber

Weber was born in 1864 in Erfurt (then Prussia), the oldest of seven children. His father was a liberal politician and bureaucrat whose family was wealthy from linen weaving. His mother was a devout Calvinist.

In 1882 he enrolled in the University of Heidelberg to study law, followed by a period of compulsory military service. He later transferred to the University of Berlin, obtaining a doctorate in law with a thesis on Roman agrarian history. His wide-ranging interests in history, economics and philosophy, plus a willingness to comment on German politics, turned him into a leading intellectual. However, in 1896 his father died and The Protestant Ethic and the Spirit of Capitalism *was one of his first writings to emerge from a long period of depression, initially published as an article in a social science journal. It was translated into English in 1930.*

After World War One, Weber helped draft Germany's new constitution and played a role in the founding of the German Democratic Party. He died in 1920, and in 1926 his wife Marianne Weber, a feminist and sociologist, published a celebrated biography of her husband. Weber's writings include The Theory of Social and Economic Organization, The Religion of China: Confucianism and Taoism, The Three Types of Legitimate Rule, On Charisma and Institution Building, Economy and Society, *and the essay* "Politics as a Vocation."

50 More Economics Classics

As with the main list of classics, the following array of notable works combines old and new, academic and popular, and can be a stepping stone to further reading.

1. **Kenneth Arrow *Social Choice and Individual Values* (1951)**
   In a seminal book in social choice theory, Arrow demonstrated that economics can explain individual choices, but not group outcomes or outcomes involving power. This 'impossibility theorem' poses many questions for government legitimacy, welfare economics and the place of the individual in society.
2. **Dan Ariely *Predictably Irrational* (2009)**
   MIT behavioral economist's fascinating exposition of our mostly irrational choices, flying in the face of rational choice orthodoxy.
3. **Walter Bagehot *Lombard Street: A Description of the Money Market* (1873)**
   Bagehot was one of the first popular writers on finance, banking and money, and his book was a response to the collapse of the Overend, Gurney bank. It provided a rationale for the existence of central banks (i.e. the Bank of England) arguing that they must be lenders of last resort in a credit crunch.
4. **Abhijit Bannerjee & Esther Duflo *Poor Economics* (2011)**
   Subtitled 'A Radical Rethinking of the Way to Fight Global Poverty', this book departed from the development economics paradigm in providing a micro-analysis of how the very poor live and what incentives are the most effective in lifting them out of poverty.
5. **Edward E. Baptiste *The Half Has Never Been Told: Slavery and the Making of American Capitalism* (2014)**
   Rather than being a pre-modern institution in decline (as often believed), slavery's expansion in the first eight decades after independence was thanks to its early adoption of managerial innovations. This 'dirty secret' of American business drove the modernization and

prosperity of the United States. A prize-winning work which draws on recent research across a range of disciplines.

6. **Ben Bernanke *Essays on the Great Depression* (2000)**
   This academic set of essays became the intellectual template for Bernanke when he became chairman of the Federal Reserve just before the 2008 financial crisis hit. He shows how the Depression, so clearly the result of bad policy, triggered a realization of the importance of macroeconomics.
7. **Peter L. Bernstein *Against The Gods: The Remarkable Story of Risk* (1996)**
   The history of finance amounts to the history of risk analysis and probability.
8. **Mark Blyth *Austerity: The History of a Dangerous Idea* (2013)**
   Brown University political economist traces the origins of the austerity principle, using Keynes and others to demonstrate that it has never worked and continues to hobble economies that might otherwise prosper.
9. **James Buchanan & Gordon Tullock *The Calculus of Consent* (1962)**
   Nobel Prize winner Buchanan was the founder of public choice theory, which attempts to view politics through an economic lens. This groundbreaking work argued that if all humans are rational and seek the best outcome for themselves, this must include politicians themselves. There is no 'greater good' being established in democratic politics, simply concessions being won by various groups. Because democracies can become corrupt and tyrannical, the political process must be balanced by private property rights, which bring prosperity and stability.
10. **Richard Cantillon *Essay on the Nature of Commerce* (1755)**
    Pre-Adam Smith, one of the first attempts to explain how economies work.
11. **Paul Collier *The Bottom Billion* (2008)**
    Oxford economist provides a reality check on the lowest earning people in the world and how they are being left behind.
12. **Tyler Cowen *The Great Stagnation* (2011)**
    Most of the 'low hanging fruit' in terms of technology have been picked in America, which accounts for the stalling of innovation and stagnating economy of the last 15 years.
13. **Barry Eichengreen *Hall of Mirrors: The Great Depression and the Great Recession* (2015)**
    Drawing parallels between the two major financial events of the last century.

14. **Thomas Friedman *The Lexus and the Olive Tree* (1999)**
Friedman's bestseller sought to explode the idea that globalization was about American hegemony or the Disneyfication of the world. The truth was more complex, involving new paradigms of international relations and the rise of individuals relative to the power of nations.
15. **David Graeber *Debt: The First 5,000 Years* (2011)**
Economic anthropologist argues that debt preceded both money and the barter system, and is essential to understanding human relations and power. Sheds light on the position of Greece and the role of debt in contemporary political economy.
16. **Henry Hazlitt *Economics In One Lesson* (1962)**
Key work of the libertarian view that provides a convincing argument against government intervention in the economy, which invariably has negative effects. Praised by Milton Friedman and Ayn Rand, and an important influence on presidential contender Ron Paul.
17. **John Hicks *Value and Capital* (1939)**
The British economist was one of the most influential of the 20th century. *Value and Capital* remains a key work in microeconomics, expounding this theory of equilibrium.
18. **Nikolai Kondratiev *The Major Economic Cycles* (1925)**
The Russian economist argued that economies move in 40-60 year cycles, driven by innovation and technology, which result in long waves of expansion, stagnation and recession.
19. **Charles Kindleberger *The World in Depression, 1929-39* (1973)**
Arguably the best book on the Depression, particularly because of its global and historical perspective, tracing the calamity back to World War One.
20. **Frank Knight *Risk, Uncertainty and Profit* (1921)**
Risks are quantifiable and so insurable. Uncertainty can't be quantified, yet "Profit arises from the inherent, absolute unpredictability of things." An early member of the Chicago School along with Friedman, Stigler and James Buchanan.
21. **Simon Kuznets *Modern Economic Growth: Rate, Structure, Spread* (1966)**
Kuznets's empirical approach helped create the first accurate measurements for national wealth or GDP, allowing governments to make better-informed decisions. His work on comparative economics found that growth in poor countries leads to widening income inequality, while growth in rich countries tends to reduce inequality. The 'Kuznets cycle' is a period of 20-30 years in which economies wax or

wane depending on demographic factors which increase or decrease demand.

22. **David Landes *The Wealth and Poverty of Nations* (1999)**
    Harvard professor's view that national prosperity comes down to cultural factors, which goes against the 'accident of geography' approach of Jared Diamond's *Guns, Germs and Steel.*
23. **Angus Maddison *The World Economy: A Millennial Perspective* (1999)**
    The esteemed economic historian looks at economic growth, income and population over the last 1,000 years, demonstrating the extent to which prosperity is a comparatively recent phenomenon.
24. **Bernard Mandeville *The Fable of the Bees* (1714)**
    Preindustrial 'economist' scandalized society with his suggestion that the 'private vices' of greed and luxury led to 'public benefits', as they involved more expenditure to keep the economy growing. Spending was better than saving.
25. **Carl Menger *Principles of Economics* (1871)**
    Adam Smith and Ricardo believed that the value of particular goods derived from the effort that went into making them. Menger had the insight that value is in the eye of the perceiver. The economic world is simply a world of many minds and their preferences, so both sides can feel they have benefited from a transaction. There is no such thing as objective value. Menger also made contributions to the theory of marginal utility.
26. **John Stuart Mill *Principles of Political Economy* (1848)**
    This book guided economic policy until the 1930s. Consistent with his purely political writings, Mill believed that that economic systems were a political construct and so had to serve the polity.
27. **Franco Modigliani *The Life-Cycle Hypothesis of Saving* (1966)**
    People are rational, saving more during their working years so that they will have a similar income when they are not earning.
28. **Enrico Moretti *The New Geography of Jobs* (2012)**
    UCLA economist's research into the changing face of American cities, which are thriving or dying depending on their ability to create hubs of innovation and creativity. Yet 'brain hubs' don't just benefit the young and educated, but create huge numbers of jobs to service the brain workers.
29. **Thomas Mun *A Discourse of Trade from England unto the East Indies* (1621)**
    Mun provided the intellectual foundation for mercantilism, or the belief that government economic policy must be focused on

improving the balance of trade. A nation grows rich and powerful through exporting things of greater value than what it imports.

30. **Gunnar Myrdal *The Political Element in the Development of Economic Theory* (1990)**
    The Swedish economist and Nobel Prize winner provided an intellectual foundation for the modern welfare state.
31. **John von Neumann *Theory of Games and Economic Behaviour* (1944)**
    Mathematician's founding work in game theory and some of its economic implications.
32. **Douglass C. North *Institutions, Institutional Change and Economic Performance* (1990)**
    Long before Acemoglu & Robinson's *Why Nations Fail* (see *50 Politics Classics*), North showed how political and economic institutions create the incentives that shape a nation's economy.
33. **Vilfredo Pareto *Manual of Political Economy* (1927)**
    Pareto was the first economist to properly study income and wealth distribution, and in the process discovered a pattern that seems to hold true in every country: a small percentage of the population can possess up to half the country's wealth, a self-reinforcing situation that resists change because the rich have a lot of political clout. He is also known for the concept of 'Pareto optimality', which says it is impossible to make one person better off without making another worse off.
34. **Bill Phillips *The Relationship Between Unemployment and the Rate of Change of Money Wages* (1958)**
    The New Zealand economist's "Phillips Curve" claimed that high inflation correlates with low unemployment and vice versa. The stagflation of the 1970s called the theory into doubt, showing it was possible to have high inflation and high unemployment at the same time.
35. **Arthur Cecil Pigou *The Economics of Welfare* (1920)**
    The Cambridge economist was the father of modern public finance, providing rationalizations for government involvement in the economy.
36. **Francois Quesnay *Tableaux Economique* (1758)**
    Key Physiocrat economist who argued that national wealth came from production, particularly agriculture, in contrast to the mercantilist view that national wealth derived from the ruler's wealth or the amassing of bullion through trade.

37. **Robert B. Reich *Saving Capitalism* (2015)**
The former Clinton Secretary for Labor argues that voter cynicism abounds in today's advanced economies because the connection between work and reward has fallen apart, and politics are rigged in favor of special interests. The big question is not more or less government, or free markets versus socialism, but whether government is able to stand up for all in society.
38. **Carmen Reinhard & Kenneth Rogoff *This Time Is Different: Eight Centuries of Financial Folly* (2009)**
This exhaustive historical survey of panics, crashes, defaults and financial crises put the 2008-2009 recession into perspective, and provides a great study in human nature; we have short memories, allowing for the same economic mistakes to be repeated each generation.
39. **Murray Rothbard *Man, Economy and State* (1962)**
Rothbard provided the intellectual backbone for today's libertarian movement and 'anarcho-capitalism'; this is his *magnum opus*.
40. **Joan Robinson *Accumulation of Capital* (1956)**
The Cambridge economist was a key figure in debates with American colleagues in the 1950s and 1960s over the definition of capital.
41. **Jean-Baptiste Say *A Treatise on Political Economy* (1803)**
A great proponent of free trade and liberal economics in a time when it was under threat, Say gave us the word 'entrepreneur'. 'Say's law' says that the production of goods creates their own demand.
42. **Andrei Schleifer *Inefficient Markets* (2000)**
The Harvard economist's introduction to behavioral finance, highlighting many flaws in the efficient markets hypothesis.
43. **Robert Sidelsky *Keynes: Return of the Master* (2009)**
Keynes scholar observes that the global economy performed better under the Keynesian Bretton Woods period of 1951 to 1973, than under the monetarist free market 'Washington Consensus' which replaced it.
44. **Robert M. Solow *Growth Theory: An Exposition* (1970)**
Solow was one of the first to provide a fully worked out theory of economic growth, emphasizing the role of technological progress.
45. **Andrew Ross Sorkin *Too Big To Fail* (2009)**
Blow-by-blow account of the events precipitated by the fall of Lehman Brothers, and the desperate measures of officials and bankers to stop the financial world disintegrating.

46. **Thomas Sowell *Economic Facts and Fallacies* (2007)**
The African-American free market economist's myth busting best-seller.
47. **George Stigler *Theory of Price* (1947)**
Perhaps the best explanation of how economies can progress through unrestricted pricing of goods and services.
48. **R. H. Tawney *Religion and the Rise of Capitalism* (1926)**
Economic historian's magisterial treatment of the subject, including valid criticisms of Weber's "Protestant ethic" thesis.
49. **Nicholas Wapshott *Keynes Hayek: The Clash That Defined Modern Economics* (2011)**
Bestselling foray into the men whose competing economic visions shaped the 20th century world. The global financial crisis reminded us of the choice each offers.
50. **Marilyn Waring *If Women Counted: A New Feminist Economics* (1990)**
With this book Waring, a former New Zealand politician, created the new field of feminist economics. She argues that women's housework, looking after children, the sick and the elderly are deliberately excluded from national accounts, thus diminishing the contribution of women to the economy. Moreover, natural resources are counted only if they are 'exploited'.

Chronological List of Titles

Adam Smith – ***The Wealth of Nations*** (1778)
Thomas Malthus – ***An Essay on the Principle of Population*** (1798)
David Ricardo – ***Principles of Political Economy and Taxation*** (1817)
Karl Marx – ***Capital*** (1867)
Henry George – ***Progress and Poverty*** (1879)
Alfred Marshall – ***Principles of Economics*** (1890)
Thorstein Veblen – ***The Theory of the Leisure Class*** **(1899)**
Max Weber – ***The Protestant Ethic and the Spirit of Capitalism*** (1904)
John Maynard Keynes – ***The General Theory of Employment, Interest and Money*** (1936)
Ludwig von Mises – ***Human Action*** (1940)
Joseph Schumpeter – ***Capitalism, Socialism and Democracy*** (1942)
Karl Polanyi – ***The Great Transformation*** (1944)
Friedrich Hayek – ***The Use of Knowledge in Society*** (1945)
Paul Samuelson – ***Economics*** (1948)
Benjamin Graham – ***The Intelligent Investor*** (1949)
J. K. Galbraith – ***The Great Crash 1929*** (1954)
Milton Friedman – ***Capitalism and Freedom*** (1962)
Gary Becker – ***Human Capital*** (1964)
Ayn Rand – ***Capitalism: The Unknown Ideal*** (1966)
Jane Jacobs – ***The Economy of Cities*** (1968)
Albert O. Hirschman – ***Exit, Voice and Loyalty*** (1970)
E. F. Schumacher – ***Small Is Beautiful*** (1973)
Thomas Schelling – ***Micromotives and Macrobehavior*** (1978)
Amartya Sen – ***Poverty and Famines*** (1981)
Peter Drucker – ***Innovation and Entrepreneurship*** (1985)
Hyman Minsky – ***Stabilizing an Unstable Economy*** (1986)
Elinor Ostrom – ***Governing the Commons*** (1990)
Michael E. Porter – ***The Competitive Advantage of Nations*** (1990)
Ronald Coase – ***The Firm, the Market and the Law*** (1990)
Julian Simon – ***The Ultimate Resource 2*** (1997)

Robert Shiller – ***Irrational Exuberance*** (2000)
Hernando de Soto – ***The Mystery of Capital*** (2003)
Steven Levitt & Stephen Dubner – ***Freakonomics*** (2006)
Paul Krugman – ***The Conscience of a Liberal*** (2007)
John Bogle – ***The Little Book of Common Sense Investing*** (2007)
Niall Ferguson – ***The Ascent of Money*** (2008)
Naomi Klein – ***The Shock Doctrine: The Rise of Disaster Capitalism*** **(2007)**
Liaquat Ahamed – ***Lords of Finance*** (2009)
Dambisa Moyo – ***Dead Aid*** (2010)
William Baumol – ***The Microtheory of Innovative Entrepreneurship*** (2010)
Michael Lewis – ***The Big Short*** (2011)
Dani Rodrik – ***The Globalization Paradox*** (2011)
Ha-Joon Chang – ***23 Things They Don't Tell You About Capitalism*** (2012)
Erik Brynjolfsson & Andrew McAfee – ***The Second Machine Age*** (2014)
Diane Coyle – ***GDP: A Brief But Affectionate History*** (2014)
Thomas Piketty – ***Capital in the Twenty-First Century*** (2014)
Richard Thaler – ***Misbehaving: The Making of Behavioral Economics*** (2015)
Robert J. Gordon – ***The Rise and Fall of American Growth*** (2016)
Deirdre McCloskey – ***Bourgeois Equality*** (2016)
Joseph Stiglitz – ***The Euro*** (2016)

Credits

The following editions were used in researching the book. Quite a few of the older economics classics are now in the public domain and freely available online.

Ahamed, L. (2009) *Lords of Finance*, London: Windmill Books.

Baumol, W.J. (2010) *The Microtheory of Innovative Entrepreneurship*, Princeton, New Jersey & Woodstock, Oxfordshire: Princeton University Press.

Becker, Gary S (1993) *Human Capital: A Theoretical and Empirical Analysis with Special Reference to Education*, Third Edition, Chicago: University of Chicago Press.

Bogle, J.C. (2007) *The Little Book of Common Sense Investing*, Hoboken, NJ: John Wiley & Sons.

Brynjolfsson, E. & McAfee, A. (2016) *The Second Machine Age: Work, Progress, and Prosperity in a Time of Brilliant Technologies*, New York: WW Norton. Paperback edition.

Chang, H. (2011) *23 Things They Don't Tell You About Capitalism*, London: Penguin.

Coase, R.H. (1988) *The Firm, the Market and the Law*, Chicago and London: University of Chicago Press.

Coyle, D (2015) *GDP: A Brief But Affectionate History*, Princeton, New Jersey and Woodstock, Oxfordshire: Princeton University Press.

Drucker, P.F. (1985) *Innovation and Entrepreneurship: Practice and Principles*, New York: Harper & Row.

Ferguson, N. (2008) *The Ascent of Money: A Financial History of the World*, London: Allen Lane/Penguin.

Friedman, M. (1962) *Capitalism and Freedom*, Chicago: The University of Chicago Press.

Galbraith, J.K. (2009) *The Great Crash 1929*, London: Penguin.

George, H. (2016) *Progress and Poverty: An Inquiry into the Cause of Industrial Depressions and of Increase of Want with Increase of Wealth: The Remedy*. 1920. Library of Economics and Liberty. http://www.econlib.org/library/YPDBooks/George/grgPPCover.html

Gordon, R.J. (2016) *The Rise and Fall of American Growth: The US Standard of Living Since the Civil War*, Princeton and Oxford: Princeton University Press.

Graham, B. (1965) *The Intelligent Investor: A Book of Practical Counsel*, Third Revised Edition, Harper & Row: New York.

Hayek, F. (2016) "The Use of Knowledge in Society." 1945. Library of Economics and Liberty. http://econlib.org/library/Essays/hykKnw1.html

Hirschman, A.O. (1970) *Exit, Voice, and Loyalty*, Cambridge, Massachusetts: Harvard University Press.

Jacobs, J. (1970) *The Economy of Cities*, London: Cape.

Keynes, J.M. (1964) *The General Theory of Employment, Interest, and Money*, London: Macmillan.

Klein, N. (2007) *The Shock Doctrine: The Rise of Disaster Capitalism*, London: Penguin.

Krugman, P. (2009) *The Conscience of a Liberal*, London: Penguin.

Levitt, S.D. and Dubner, S.J. (2005) *Freakonomics: A Rogue Economist Explores the Hidden Side of Everything*, London: Penguin.

Lewis, M. (2010) *The Big Short: Inside the Doomsday Machine*, London: Penguin.

McCloskey, D.N. (2016) *Bourgeois Equality: How Ideas, Not Capital or Institutions, Enriched the World*, Chicago and London: University of Chicago Press.

Malthus, T. (2016) *An Essay on the Principle of Population*. 1798. Library of Economics and Liberty. http://www.econlib.org/library/Malthus/malPop.html

Marshall, A. (2016) *Principles of Economics*. 1920. Library of Economics and Liberty. http://econlib.org/library/Marshall/marP.html

Marx, K. (2016) *Capital: A Critique of Political Economy*, Volume 1, First English edition, 1887. https://www.marxists.org/archive/marx/works/1867-c1/

Minsky, H.P. (1986) *Stabilizing an Unstable Economy*, New Haven: Yale University Press.

Mises, L. (1998) *Human Action: a treatise on economics*, Auburn, Alabama: Ludwig Von Mises Institute.

Moyo, D. (2010) *Dead Aid: Why Aid Makes Things Worse and How There is Another Way for Africa*, London: Penguin (Kindle edition).

Ostrom, E. (2015) *Governing the Commons: The Evolution of Institutions for Collective Action*, Cambridge: Cambridge University Press.

Piketty, T. (2014) *Capital in the Twenty-First Century*, Cambridge, Massachusetts and London: Belknap Press of Harvard University Press.

Polanyi, K. (2001) *The Great Transformation: The Political and Economic Origins of Our Time*, Boston: Beacon Press.

Porter, M.E. (1998) *The Competitive Advantage of Nations*, London: Macmillan.

Rand, A. (1967) *Capitalism: The Unknown Ideal*, London: Signet.

Ricardo, D. (2016) *On the Principles of Political Economy, and Taxation*, Project Gutenberg. http://www.gutenberg.org/cache/epub/33310/pg33310.txt

Rodrik, D. (2011) *The Globalization Paradox: Why Global Markets, States, and Democracy Can't Coexist*, Oxford: Oxford University Press.

Samuelson, P.A. and Nordhaus, W.D. (2010) *Economics*, 19th ed., Boston: McGraw-Hill.

Schelling, T. (2006) *Micromotives and Macrobehavior*, New York and London.

Schumacher, E.F. *Small Is Beautiful: A study of economics as if people mattered*, London: Blond & Briggs.

Schumpeter, J. (2003) *Capitalism, Socialism, and Democracy*, London and New York: Routledge.

Sen, A. (1981) *Poverty and Famines: An Essay on Entitlement and Deprivation*, Oxford: Clarendon Press.

Shiller, R. (2015) *Irrational Exuberance*, Third edition, Princeton; New Jersey: Princeton University Press.

Simon, J. (2016) *The Ultimate Resource 2: People, Materials, and Environment*, Princeton, New Jersey: Princeton University Press, 1996. http://www.juliansimon.com/writings/Ultimate_Resource/

Smith, A (1910) *An Inquiry Into the Nature and Causes of the Wealth of Nations*, Vol. I, London: JM Dent.

de Soto, H. (2001) *The Mystery of Capital: Why capitalism triumphs in the West and fails everywhere else*, London: Black Swan.

Stiglitz, J.E. (2016) *The Euro, and Its Threat to the Future of Europe*, London: Allen Lane/Penguin.

Thaler, R. (2015) *Misbehaving: How Economics Became Behavioural*, London: Allen Lane.

Veblen, T. (1899) *The Theory of the Leisure Class: An Economic Study of Institutions*, Project Gutenberg, 2008. http://www.gutenberg.org/cache/epub/833/pg833.txt

Weber, M. (1992) *The Protestant Ethic and the Spirit of Capitalism*, London: Routledge.

Acknowledgements

I am very lucky to do what I do, and never take for granted the privilege of reading and writing about the great people, ideas and books that have made an impact on the world. However, my writing would go nowhere without a great team who help with editorial direction, editing of the manuscript, sales, publicity and language rights.

50 Economics Classics was originally commissioned by Nicholas Brealey, and the broad concept of the book was the result of enjoyable discussions. Following the Hachette Group's acquisition of Nicholas Brealey Publishing under the banner of John Murray Press, Nick Davies was keen to continue the 50 Classics series, and to make *50 Economics Classics* a key element of its relaunch.

At Hachette London, I thank commissioning editor Holly Bennion and publishing director Iain Campbell, who from the start have been enthusiastic about the series, and keen to bring out new titles. Also: Ben Slight, Louise Richardson, and Nadia Manuelli, who champion the series in sales, marketing, editorial, and publicity; the rights team including Joanna Kaliszewska and Anna Alexander; and the Hodder designers, who came up with the great cover.

At Nicholas Brealey in Boston I'm grateful to Alison Hankey and Melissa Carl for continuing to promote the 50 Classics series in the United States and Canada and achieve a wide distribution, and also the Hachette team in Sydney for their efforts to promote my work in Australia.

I'm grateful to the people who offered feedback on the list and concept for *50 Economics Classics* in its early stages, not least economics students Kacanik Sokoli and Natan Misak, who gave me a sense of what is (and what isn't) being taught in universities today. Thanks go to Kacanik for his help with research as an intern and reading draft chapters. Also grateful to Steve Kates of RMIT University, who offered comments on an early draft of the list of classics. Needless to say, I take full responsibility for the final book.

I thank all the living authors who feature in *50 Economics Classics* for their contributions to political economy, and particularly those who agreed to review chapters on their work and answer queries. Finally, I'm very grateful to Oxford's Bodleian Library, whose huge collection of economic literature was a great help in researching the book.

50 POLITICS CLASSICS

Your shortcut to the most important ideas on freedom, equality, and power

Tom Butler-Bowdon

From Abraham Lincoln to Nelson Mandela, and from Aristotle to George Orwell, *50 Politics Classics* distills the essence of the books, pamphlets, and speeches of the major leaders and great thinkers that drive real-world change.

Spanning 2,500 years, left and right, thinkers and doers, Tom Butler-Bowdon covers activists, war strategists, visionary leaders, economists, philosophers of freedom, feminists, conservatives and environmentalists, right up to contemporary classics such as *The Spirit Level* and *No Logo.* Whether you consider yourself to be conservative, liberal, socialist, or Marxist, this book gives you greater understanding of the key ideas that matter in our politically charged times.

"A refreshing tour of political thought unmoored by traditional chronological organization."

Library Journal